The

EVERYTHING®
Great Marriage Book

Dear Reader:

Our life together through the years has been one of ups and downs, good choices and bad decisions, happy times and moments of deep heartache. Together, we've successfully raised and launched four great kids and buried three infants. We know the joy that can result from being able to communicate feelings, and we know the frustration from distancing ourselves from one another. What we've shared in this book are tools and techniques we've experienced and used in our own marriage. It is our hope that this book will help you on your marital journey. We wish for you to happily grow old together and to be able to reflect on your own memories with great joy and a sense of accomplishment.

Bob & Sheri Strauss

The EVERYTHING® Series

Editorial

Publishing Director	Gary M. Krebs
Managing Editor	Kate McBride
Copy Chief	Laura MacLaughlin
Acquisitions Editor	Eric M. Hall
Development Editor	Karen Johnson Jacot
Production Editor	Khrysti Nazzaro

Production

Production Director	Susan Beale
Production Manager	Michelle Roy Kelly
Series Designers	Daria Perreault
	Colleen Cunningham
Cover Design	Paul Beatrice
	Frank Rivera
Layout and Graphics	Colleen Cunningham
	Rachael Eiben
	Michelle Roy Kelly
	Daria Perreault
	Erin Ring
Cover Artist	Eulala Connor

Visit the entire Everything® Series at everything.com

THE

EVERYTHING ®

GREAT
MARRIAGE
BOOK

Practical advice to ensure an exciting
and fulfilling relationship

Bob & Sheri Stritof

Adams Media Corporation
Avon, Massachusetts

We dedicate this book to Ted, Ken, Larry, and Judy.

An Everything® Series Book.
Everything® and everything.com® are registered trademarks of Adams Media Corporation.

Published by Adams Media Corporation
57 Littlefield Street, Avon, MA 02322 U.S.A.
www.adamsmedia.com

ISBN: 1-58062-962-8
Printed in the United States of America.

J   I   H   G   F   E   D   C   B   A

Library of Congress Cataloging-in-Publication Data
Stritof, Bob.
The everything great marriage book / Bob & Sheri Stritof.
p.   cm.
ISBN 1-58062-962-8
1. Marriage. I. Stritof, Sheri. II. Title.

HQ734.S9736 2003
646.7'8–dc21

2003011087

This publication is designed to provide accurate and authoritative information with regard to the subject matter covered. It is sold with the understanding that the publisher is not engaged in rendering legal, accounting, or other professional advice. If legal advice or other expert assistance is required, the services of a competent professional person should be sought.

  —From a *Declaration of Principles* jointly adopted by a Committee of the American Bar Association and a Committee of Publishers and Associations

Many of the designations used by manufacturers and sellers to distinguish their products are claimed as trademarks. Where those designations appear in this book and Adams Media was aware of a trademark claim, the designations have been printed with initial capital letters.

This book is available at quantity discounts for bulk purchases.
For information, call 1-800-872-5627.

Contents

Acknowledgments

Thank you to all the couples and individuals who have crossed our paths and changed our lives by both ruffling our feathers and supporting us. You know who you are.

Top Ten Characteristics
of a Great Marriage

1. Couples respect, enjoy, support, and love one another.
2. Both partners have a solid commitment to their marriage.
3. They know how to communicate and can handle conflict in their relationship.
4. They trust one another.
5. They know how to reach compromise and how to solve problems.
6. They have realistic expectations of themselves, one another, and their marriage and share these with each other.
7. They know the importance of having a sense of humor and believe in having fun together.
8. Each partner is supportive of one another and they speak in positive terms about their marriage.
9. Qualities of tolerance, caring, and nurturing are major aspects of a couple's friendship with one another.
10. Spouses are intimate with one another both sexually and emotionally.

Introduction

▶ COUPLES TODAY marry out of love and friendship with the hope of a long lasting, fulfilling union. As family life is the cornerstone of society, strong, long-term marriages are the backbone of the family. Studies have shown that marriage contributes positively to the physical, emotional, and economic health of society. When a marriage fails, more than just the couple involved and the kids suffer. How a couple loves, supports, and cherishes one another has an immediate and profound impact not only on their children, but also on others who cross their path.

When the partners in a couple truly love one another and keep their commitment to one another alive, they enrich all of society. Our world today needs married couples to be role models of lasting love and joy in spite of difficult situations and times. A couple loving one another doesn't happen magically. Their love for one another happens when two people work at their relationship 24/7. *The Everything® Great Marriage Book* will help guide married couples as they strive to achieve loving, fulfilling, joyful, successful long-term marriages using tools of communication to overcome roadblocks and pitfalls along the way of life. It also examines prevalent myths of marriage and divorce. Information is provided on how to deal with family of origin issues, in-laws, gender differences, interfaith and intercultural relationships, unrealistic expectations, mixed priorities, parenting concerns, financial disagreements, and sexual problems.

This book doesn't focus on just good times in a marital relationship. Advice on how to cope with domestic violence, disillusionment, and knowing when to call it quits, along with the consequences of divorce, are also included. Tips and suggestions for dealing with difficult situations and experiences, along with ways to celebrate love and marriage are offered. When you start to use a tool, it is awkward and you will probably make a lot of mistakes. As you use the tool more and more often, over time you get comfortable using it. Eventually, the tool actually feels like an extension of your body. Using it becomes second nature and it feels natural in your hand. The tools in this book will need to be used over and over again, too, in order to feel natural.

We hope that what you learn, glean, discover, and use from the pages of this book will be helpful in the day-to-day, month-to-month, year-to-year, marital journey that you and your spouse are traveling together. The suggested tools, suggestions, hints, tips, and techniques that you read about in this book have proved successful in many long-term marriages. However, just reading a book won't solve or prevent problems or turn your marriage into a great one. Great marriages are achieved by working together to truly know one another. You need to integrate what you read and assimilate it into your own lives on a daily basis. The real proof of anything is the journey. May your journey together be one of great joy.

Chapter 1

After "I Do": Getting It Right the First Time

You've come through the wedding preparations, which culminated in exchanging your vows. Now, the real part of marriage begins. If you don't want to become just another statistic in studies about divorce, then the two of you need to look at why you married one another, sharpen your coping skills in dealing with stress, treat one another with respect, and make time for one another for both communication and fun. Lasting relationships just don't happen. These marriages require work and they require commitment and dedication.

Looking at Motives for Marriage

Have you questioned yourselves as to why you married? Having an understanding of your reasons for being together can help you both discover areas that the two of you may need to work on, both individually and as a couple. So often, while in the wonderful grip of a new romance, practical thoughts can fly out the window. The old adage that "love is blind" is often true. Couples marry and then discover that they didn't know as much about one another as they thought they did.

Wrong Reasons for Marriage

Some couples embark on the marital journey together for the wrong reasons and think love will be enough, or that love isn't all that important. Or they marry someone thinking that they can make them change for the "better" in the future.

If you married for sex or because you were lusting after your partner, what happens if a serious medical condition enters your relationship, or the sex becomes boring, or one of you develops a low sex drive? If you married for money, what will you do if the money runs out? If you married because you were lonely, you may find you are still lonely even though you are sitting in the same room with your spouse. If you married for freedom, you may find yourself just as imprisoned in your marriage as you were when you were single. And having a baby with someone doesn't necessarily mean you should marry that person. This is a mistake many young teens make. People can still be good parents and not be married to one another.

It's not that you shouldn't want happiness or great sex or financial security in your marriage. Wanting to be free from your parents or having a baby are not wrong either. However, marrying just because you want money or because the two of you are expecting a baby, or because you lust after one another, or because you feel loved will generally lead to major problems later on in your marriage. If you find that you did marry for the wrong reasons, or if you were too young, don't throw in the towel on your relationship. Talk about it with one another with honesty. Perhaps you will discover that some of the right reasons have entered your marriage since you said, "I do." Look at what the two of you can do now to make your relationship stronger and more fulfilling.

Right Reasons for Marriage

Your decision to get married is probably the right one if your reasons include having a deep love for one another along with sexual desire. This type of love incorporates caring, trusting, and a commitment to one another. Another reason to marry is that you desire to share your life with each other, and to not only share your interests with one another, but to respect your individual interests. Being a lifetime companion to someone requires having realistic expectations, and a willingness to want to try and meet one another's needs and desires. There will be times when you will be unable to fulfill those needs and desires. The key is a willingness to try.

Questions to Ask One Another

Take some time each week to focus on discovering new things about each other. Ask one another questions about childhood memories. Talk about your values, both short-term and long-term goals, sexual likes and dislikes, religious and political thoughts. Find out what the other thinks about mutual decision making, handling conflict, having time alone, hobbies, and spending habits. Discuss family of origin issues, traditions, holidays, chores, fears, hopes, dreams, parenting styles, vacation preferences, career plans, and expectations about any of these areas.

Couples often don't realize how easily small, seemingly trivial matters can mushroom into larger problems. It may not seem like a big deal in the beginning of your relationship, but down the road, issues such as borrowing money from your parents, having separate vacations, whether to open presents on Christmas Eve or Christmas morning, purchasing a pet, the softness or hardness of a mattress, owning a one- or two-story home, watching television in bed, telling gross jokes, setting up a joint checking account, or drinking too much at a party can create a hostile environment in your home.

QUESTION?

What makes a strong marriage?
You need to be dedicated and committed to one another and know how to fight with one another fairly.

Don't make this a onetime question and answer session. Continue asking questions and learning more about one another throughout your life together. If you develop the habit of talking to one another each day about something other than your jobs, the house, the weather, TV shows, your pets, the news, the neighbors, and your kids, you will ensure that your marriage will remain intimate and interesting.

Starting Out Together

Most couples starting out experience a honeymoon phase that lasts beyond the romantic trip away from work and everyday worries. Your first few months together may be busy with settling in, visiting with friends and in-laws, making both large and small decisions together, and having fun. You will be setting up a home for the two of you, deciding on color schemes and where to put furniture, and working out how you will be handling finances and chores around the house. You may be discovering how you want to spend your free time together. You can be sure your marriage is on the right track if you are enjoying spending time together and you've been able to cope with areas of conflict in a positive way. It is also a good sign if making plans together is something you both want to do, and you can question one another without the discussion turning into an argument.

After-the-Honeymoon Blues

Your wedding was a wonderful experience, and you two had a great time on your honeymoon. So why are you both a bit depressed? Don't worry. It's okay. It's very natural to experience feeling down after the intense preparation and anticipation of your wedding and honeymoon. You are back in the real world. You may find yourselves having to deal with catching up at work after having taken some time off. Your new home beckons to have things done. Wedding gifts sitting around call out to be put away. Thank you notes nag at you to be sent. Dinners need to be cooked. Clothes have to be washed. You don't have as much time to be together as you once did. Life goes on and it isn't as interesting or as exciting as the planning of your wedding. You may experience the feelings of loss that many people feel to some degree after a holiday season.

If you often find yourselves at a loss as to things you can do together, spend an evening brainstorming some ideas. Write these thoughts down on small slips of paper and toss them in a "fun jar." When you reach one of those times when you just can't decide, pull one of the ideas out of the jar.

Some couples believe that once they have tied the knot, it is their responsibility to make their spouse happy. This isn't true. Very few people are happy all the time. Although couples should be supportive of one another, provide ways to have fun together, and accept one another's feelings, they can't make one another feel happy. You are each responsible for your own happiness.

You can get past the newlyweds blues easier when you are prepared for them. Tackle together the tasks that are weighing you down. Work out a schedule so that you can better manage your time. Remember the importance of scheduling time to be together. If you both are willing to make time for one another, you can create a successful marriage relationship. Finding time here and there for one another isn't enough. You have to commit to making that time. Otherwise, there will always be something or someone to snatch time away from your relationship.

Start planning for the rest of your lives together, and begin making sure that you keep the romance and sense of adventure alive in your marriage. Make short-term plans that include doing fun things together. Whatever you do, don't make excuses for not having time together. If finances are tight, you can still have quality time together by watching an old movie you haven't seen for awhile, having a picnic in the park, taking a walk, visiting a local museum, or going window shopping.

First-Year Stresses

The first year of marriage has many "firsts" such as your first holiday season together, your first vacation as a married couple, your first home, your first argument, your first budget, your first crisis, your first winter, your first spring, and so on. In spite of the stresses that all these "firsts" can bring into your lives, it should and can be a marvelous year for the two of you—especially if you enjoy one another and celebrate being together.

ALERT!

Don't hide from things that should be priorities during your first year of marriage, such as dealing with conflict, deciding on how household chores will be done, coping with religious issues, and making time to be sexually intimate with one another.

Stressful Situations

When you are able to communicate with one another about tough issues and difficult topics, you can lessen the impact of these top newlywed stresses in your first year. It is important to realize that many of these stresses will probably continue throughout your married life:

- **Being concerned over finances.** How will you handle paying bills? Will you have a joint checking account? How do you feel about individual accounts? Is one of you a spender while the other one is a saver? Are you willing to each have some "mad money" of your own? Do you have long-term financial goals? What are your thoughts about debt and charge cards?
- **Changing your expectations**. Do you know what your expectations of marriage are? Do you think your expectations won't change? Have you discussed your expectations with one another?
- **Dealing with time pressures.** Do you agree or disagree on how you each spend your time? Do you think TV, hobbies, volunteer work, careers, family, computer, and educational pursuits interfere with your marriage? Do you schedule time for just the two of you?

- **Deciding where to live.** How would you feel about relocating due to a job transfer? Do you want to buy a home or rent? Do you like city life or a more rural setting? How big a house do you need or want? Have you discussed styles of homes and interior decorating preferences? Do you want to be near recreational opportunities? Are you drawn to locales with mountains or with water access? Do you hate snow but love the sun? Is mass transportation important to you? What about being close to or far away from your extended families?

- **Quality of life issues.** Do you think you can have the type of life you want in your locale? Is the cost of living creating difficult decisions for you regarding having children, being close to extended family, or affording a home?

- **Developing your relationship with your in-laws.** What will you call your partner's parents? Do you refer to your mother-in-law as "Mom" or are you more formal and use "Mrs." or do you use the more informal "hey"? Do you see your in-laws as interfering or supportive? How much time do you anticipate visiting with or being visited by your in-laws?

- **Caring for aging parents.** Have you talked with your parents concerning their wishes and thoughts about their care if they reach a point of not being able to live on their own? Do you think this responsibility will have a negative impact on your marriage or lifestyle? Have you discussed this situation with one another? What options do you think you have?

- **Deciding when to have children.** Do both of you want to have children? If you do, will you want to wait a few years before having any? How many children do you want? Have you discussed fertility and birth control issues? Are you both taking responsibility for decisions about birth control and family planning? Do you want one of you to remain home when your children are young?

FACT

When husbands and wives turn to each other for support during stressful times, their own self-worth and self-confidence is strengthened.

- **Coping with holiday plans.** Are you expected to spend the holidays at either one of your parents' homes? Have you set yourselves up to make it difficult to change the way you celebrate the holidays once you have children of your own? Have you talked with one another about creating your own holiday traditions? How do you want to spend the holidays?
- **Handling faith issues.** Are you accepting of your spouse's religious preference? How important is it to you to have faith and spirituality in your marriage? If you believe in the same religion, can you accept different levels of commitment in your faith? Have you agreed to disagree?

Handling Stress

The way the two of you handle stress and difficult situations in the first couple years of marriage can set you up for the way you will handle stress together in the future. The stresses and tough times will continue throughout your lives together. If you've set a pattern for dealing with stress that isn't working, you can change it. Fine-tuning your stress management skills now in your marriage will make the later stress-filled stages of parenting and having an empty nest easier to survive.

Why the First Two Years Are Critical

How a couple gets through the first two years of their marriage can either make or break their marriage. The newlywed years are predictors of long-term marital success. Couples who find themselves in disillusionment in the first few months of their marriage are at a greater risk for divorce than couples who experience more positive feelings toward one another.

Disillusionment

Disillusionment can often be the result of miscommunication, lack of awareness of one another's feelings, feeling neglected or used, inability to handle conflict, and unrealistic expectations. Disillusionment also occurs when couples don't talk with one another about the important issues in their lives. Disillusionment follows a lack of communication not only about what's going on in their heads, but also about what they feel in their hearts. Positive feelings result when couples are able to be intimate with one another through their daily conversations.

Red Flags

A red flag issue is one that signifies a potential problem in a marriage. If you find any red flag issues in your marriage, it is critical that you two discuss them and express your feelings. Some issues may be serious enough to warrant seeking professional help through a counselor or therapist. Thinking that the issue will go away by itself, or saying that it isn't really all that important will only make the situation worse. Some things just can't be swept under the carpet.

Red flags to watch out for include selfishness, sexual problems, dwindling romance, lack of fun, no respect, unrealistic expectations, reliance on parents, addictive behaviors, conflict avoidance, financial irresponsibility, and physical and/or emotional abuse.

FACT

It is estimated that approximately 25 percent of divorces occur in the first three years of marriage.

Make your first year of marriage a time to begin the lifelong quest to discover who both of you are. Learn as much as you can about one another. All the quirks, likes, dislikes, attitudes, dreams, fears, and opinions that you glean from one another are important information. This knowledge can help you build a strong foundation for a lasting marriage.

Keys for a Successful Long-Term Marriage

To ensure that your marriage lasts, you must be willing to continue working on your relationship throughout your years together. For some couples, the word "work" seems inappropriate when applied to the marital relationship. However, marriage does indeed take work. Much like a garden, a marriage relationship must be cared for and cannot be taken for granted. If a garden is left alone, weeds will overrun and ultimately destroy the plants and flowers. Along with a commitment to one another, a marriage needs nurturing, care, and attention.

The qualities necessary to make your marriage last are to be:

- Receptive and responsive
- Patient and realistic
- Humorous and respectful
- Romantic and fun-loving
- Sensitive and present
- Trusting and forgiving
- Appreciative and assertive
- Supportive and understanding
- Communicative and sharing

Although it is high on many people's lists of what a successful marriage takes, romance is just one of the vital elements of a lasting relationship. Aren't qualities like commitment, caring, sharing, a sense of humor, flexibility, personal growth, companionship, thoughtfulness, trust, fidelity, generosity, ambition, and openness equally important? The only way the two of you will have these essential qualities in your relationship is to talk about them. Together, decide to find ways to incorporate them into your marriage. Make a list as a couple of the top ten qualities that are important to you both. It is critical that you are both open to discussing these qualities, especially if either of you discern that any of the qualities you've deemed important are missing.

ALERT!

Talk with one another about what you each believe is important for your marriage to be a long-term success. Set a time to discuss this on a regular basis—every month or two—to help keep your focus on what's important in your relationship.

Giving 100 Percent

If you want a fulfilling, intimate, and nurturing relationship, you both need to be willing to give 100 percent to your relationship. This is equivalent to giving with no strings attached. Loving this way isn't always easy, but the concept that you each give 50 percent to your marriage will not get you through any future challenges and difficulties that may cross your paths. When a couple lives out a fifty-fifty type of marriage, they often play the game of measuring how much they perceive the other is giving or doing.

Tough times require a willingness from each of you to give 100 percent. When you are each giving freely to your marriage, your marriage will be strengthened and will be able to weather the times when one of you is unable to give fully due to illness or other stresses.

Friendship

Everyone needs a sense of belonging and friends in their lives. There's nothing wrong with you each having your own set of friends. However, you and your spouse should be friends, too. Hopefully, liking your spouse and enjoying being together comes naturally. Being friends with one another means you continue to support each other's individual interests. As friends, you also recognize the need for some personal space in your lives and you encourage personal growth. This doesn't mean you live separate lives. Without having some common interests and without sharing your personal discoveries, you will be like two ships passing in the night. You will be close to one another, but you won't truly feel each other's presence in your hearts. You need to be able to find the balance that works for the two of you.

The Bottom Line

Don't go through your marital journey together with blinders on. Sharing all of yourself with your spouse is true intimacy. Remember to talk about everything in your lives. That includes the good times, the bad times, the silly times, the sad times, the glad times, the embarrassing times, and the questioning times along with your memories, fears, dreams, desires, hopes, and heartaches. Listen to your spouse with an open heart and a nonjudgmental mind.

The bottom line for getting marriage right the first time is to communicate with each other throughout your lives. You set the stage in the first couple of years of marriage for how you will react and respond to stresses and to one another. However, if you set the stage wrong, it is never too late to make changes in how and what you communicate with each other. Marriage can be a wonderful and fulfilling experience that enables both partners to truly be themselves and to grow intellectually and spiritually. Growing old together will be a delight and not a burden when married partners love, respect, and support one another through the years.

Chapter 2

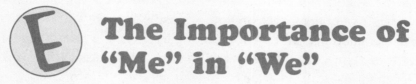

The Importance of "Me" in "We"

K nowing who you are as an individual is critical to having a successful marriage. Understanding the "baggage" you bring from your families of origin helps you in this quest for self-knowledge and allows you to fully give yourselves to one another: to truly love. The "Aha!" moments that you experience about yourselves need to be shared with your partner.

Finding Yourself

Before you can truly give of yourself to another in love, you must love yourself. To love yourself, you need to know who you are. You've probably heard this concept many times. Why? Because it's true.

As you grow and mature throughout your life, your masks and core behaviors generally won't change. Being aware of the impact of these aspects of your personality on your spouse can make you want to change some ingrained behaviors. For instance, let's say you have a tendency to want everything your own way and to not compromise. When you understand that this behavior hurts your spouse, you work on being more flexible in making decisions with your spouse. Learning about yourself can help you merge what is in your head with what you feel in your heart.

Masks and Core Behaviors

Everyone has a personality style. This style, or mask, is how you want other people to see you. It is a role you play. You probably have been wearing this mask or living out this personality style since you were a small child. Some examples of masks are being Superman, the Lone Ranger, Macho Man, the Good Provider, the Joker or Clown, the Know It All, Good Neighbor Sam, Mr. Nice Guy, the Peacemaker, the Savior, Goody Two Shoes, the China Doll, Superwoman, Mother Hen, the Rebel, Rock of Gibraltar, Nature Child, and the Perfectionist. Masks can reflect your core behaviors. Most folks usually have two main masks (also known as archetypes).

Discovering Your Masks

Where do you start? How can you know who you are? Look at the way you behave when you are with others. How do you like to be seen? List some behaviors that you have. Which ones did you have as a child? Which ones did you have as a teen? You should be able to see a pattern that will reflect your core behaviors. You can also ask your spouse to tell you how they perceive you.

Another approach is to determine if you are more focused on "doing" or in "being." Since society places a lot of importance of what people accomplish, many people judge their self-worth by their achievements and what they do. When was the last time someone asked you, "Who are you?" The usual question people ask when first meeting someone is, "What do you do?" Doers are people who don't like to waste time. They feel guilty if they aren't being productive all the time. They fill their daily lives with activity that makes them feel more valuable and builds up their self-esteem. Doers gauge their success by how many projects they finished, how much money they make, how many organizations they belong to, who they know, what they own, and so forth. They may end up with a long list of accomplishments, but they can also lose the ability to just "be."

The key isn't to give up being a doer, but to find a balance between doing and being. Both aspects of your personality are important. Husbands and wives need time to just be together and to learn how to enjoy that time together simply relaxing or whiling the day away.

When you understand your own personal motivations, patterns, and preferences, you will have more control over how you respond to your spouse and to life in general. Self- learning is a lifelong process and there are many ways to continue your personal growth and awareness. Taking personality tests can also help you have a greater understanding of your reactions to life situations and circumstances.

Personality Tests

The Myers-Briggs Type Indicator personality test measures your preferences on how you relate to the world by looking at noted psychologist Carl Jung's four psychological functions of thinking, feeling, sensing, and intuition. You can use the information you glean about yourself from this test to have a greater understanding, respect, and appreciation of not only yourself, but your spouse, too. The MBTI is not a tool to use to try to change your spouse, but it can give you insight into understanding *why* your husband needs to have his projects sitting in full view on the dining room table, or why your wife keeps a pile of magazines or books in every room. Taking this test may encourage you both to move out of your comfort zones and experience other aspects of your personality that you hide away.

FACT

Many personality and self-awareness tests are available now via the Internet. Some additional ones to check out are the Keirsey Temperament Sorter and the Rogers Indicator of Multiple Intelligences.

Enneagram

The Enneagram is a tool that is based on ancient wisdom and has been around perhaps as long as 10,000 years. Originated in the Near East, it describes nine different personality types:

1. Reformer
2. Helper
3. Motivator
4. Romantic
5. Thinker
6. Skeptic
7. Adventurer
8. Leader
9. Peacemaker

Again, this isn't a tool to manipulate or change your spouse. It will improve communication with one another by giving you insight to help you understand and view your spouse's perspective on life. In short, it's a way of walking in one another's shoes.

Importance of a Good Self-Image

Psychologist Abraham Maslow developed a theory of human needs based on a pyramid structure. Those needs at the lowest level must be satisfied before the higher levels can be achieved. He included five levels of human needs: physical needs, safety and security, love and acceptance, esteem, and self-actualization. The highest level, self-actualization, is knowing what is truly important to you and believing in your own potential. Your self-image has evolved since your birth and has been affected by your life experiences, those you've interacted with, and your perception of your physical body. It involves your personality traits, your beliefs, your talents, and your attitudes. Generally speaking, you have a good self-image if you have realistic perceptions and expectations, if you are flexible, and if you can live with failure along with your successes.

Doubting yourself will probably lead to doubting both your spouse and your marriage relationship. A poor self-image can mess up your sex life, too. For a marriage to be successful, it is vital that each partner can positively answer the question, "Do you value yourself?" It is important that you learn to not dwell on your past mistakes or failures, your real or perceived inadequacies, but to think more about what you've done right in your life.

ALERT!

When you have a healthy, positive self-image you are more able to treat your partner with respect and love.

Family of Origin Issues

Everyone comes with his or her proverbial "baggage." When you walk through an airport, you can't miss seeing all the people pulling suitcases with little wheels. With a little imagination you can picture you and your spouse each pulling one of those around packed full of family of origin issues. Some things you may be aware of and others you may have packed away and forgotten about. All the things you packed in that suitcase have a direct bearing on how you behave in your marital relationship. One of the tasks of marriage is to merge your two packed suitcases and to understand the contents.

What exactly are "family of origin issues"? Essentially, they are all of the stuff (behaviors, attitudes, actions, etc.) you were taught or that you picked up from your family when you were a kid. Your family of origin is your connection to your past. It is where the heart of your identity is located. Everyone has within him or her a legacy of family values and beliefs that have helped mold that person into who they are today.

Contributions of Your Family of Origin

Growing up in your particular family exposed you to unique ways of doing things. Through your family upbringing, you absorbed many things: your eating preferences, your ways of relating and being, and your sense of humor. You learned both directly and indirectly where and how to live, how to celebrate, how to handle conflict, how to spend or save money, how to parent, the type of vacations you enjoy, how to have fun, your values, your priorities, your goals, your sexual attitudes, and even your sleeping habits.

Even unstated beliefs and experiences from your family have a subtle impact on your current behaviors. In short, your family communicated many messages to you in a variety of ways. Impressions still play in your mind from dinner conversations, the way you were greeted when you came home from school, how you were disciplined or corrected, and what was said when you left on a trip. Consequently, your family of origin has a significant influence on all your adult relationships and especially on your marriage.

FACT

Many couples realize that the basic problems they have with one another are rooted in their own individual family of origin issues.

Consider, for example, a couple who decides to make Saturdays their "family day" to make sure the whole family has time together. Planning their first Saturday family outing turns into a disaster. They can't agree on how to spend the time together. He wants to take the kids to the park and do some playing and fishing. She wants the children and her husband to tackle some yard work and chores around the house. Neither can understand where the other is coming from in their preferences. As a child, she lived on a farm, and family togetherness was working side by side and the sense of joy that comes from accomplishing things together. He lived in an apartment, and his parents took the kids out to see and do things with one another and to have fun. Talking with each other about how their families spent time together when they were kids would have helped them see the bigger picture.

Family Systems

It is important to realize that everyone is part of a family system. It's not something you can avoid. Regardless of the type of family (traditional family, single parent, living with grandparents or other relatives, etc.) you grew up in, you had a role. Within that system, your role could have been the Scapegoat, Lost Child, Hero, Pacifier, Parent, Clown, and so forth. When you are able to not only leave your family of origin physically, but also to leave behind the unhealthy behaviors or roles you acted out in that family system, you've been able to cut the cord and reach emotional maturity. It is important to remember that you are not being disloyal to your family by putting your marriage relationship first; rather, this is a required step for being able to maintain a healthy marriage.

Codependent families may find ways of manipulating members back into their original roles if a member tries to change.

If your childhood home was abusive, addictive, or dysfunctional, you may need to have professional help through therapy in order to work through some of your family of origin issues. You may be aware of the core beliefs that are having a negative impact on your relationships, but in order to eradicate them, outside help may be necessary. On a positive note, your families of origin can enrich your lives and can be a wonderful reminder of the connectedness and closeness of family.

Some tips on dealing with family of origin issues:

- Respect your mate's family.
- Don't criticize one another's families.
- Look at your roots (both genetic and cultural) and see how they developed.
- Put your marriage first.
- Be open to your families, but learn how to define and set boundaries.
- Accept that anger toward your family is okay.
- Be willing to heal past injuries.
- Identify and share your feelings.

- Learn how to trust.
- Accept that your spouse may feel loyalty for his or her family.

Letting Go of the Past

Many of the coping strategies you developed as a child to handle various situations will be inappropriate as an adult. If as a kid you dealt with conflict by retreating to your room, you will find that behavior won't work in your marriage. If you managed to manipulate your folks into letting you have your way, you'll discover that manipulating your spouse will not bring the results you hoped for. These types of behaviors need to be left in the past.

Unresolved Issues

If you do have unresolved issues related to your parents or things that happened in your childhood, and you have family of origin issues that are haunting your marriage, now is the time to work on them. When you hold on to toxic memories from your past, you are letting others live in your head rent-free. Everyone has a lot of tapes still playing in their heads from their childhood. Many of the behaviors, both positive and hurtful, that exist in your marriage come from those family of origin tapes. Ask yourself if you really need to continue to listen to those tapes. Try to let go of the pain of the past if there is any.

Letting Go

When you hold on to hurt and pain, you will feel anger and bitterness. These feelings can eventually hurt your marriage. As you decide what you need to let go of, look at what has stopped you from doing it.

Letting go is an internal decision that involves only you, not really your spouse. It's a choice you make to both feel the anger and hurt, and at the same time to forgive. Letting go doesn't mean you have to burn all the bridges to your past if you can make a distinction between the behaviors and situations that hurt you and the people involved.

You don't have to personally confront your parents if you don't want to. You could write yourself a letter that expresses all the pain that you remember. As you write, be honest with yourself and make sure to affirm your own good qualities. When you've finished writing the note, read it, and then burn it. Making the decision to let go is not condoning what's happened. It is kicking them out of your head, and allows you to move forward in your life.

You can't change the past. But you can change the effect that the past has on you and your marriage today. Letting go of old problems will help you face your partner and marriage with a fresh start.

Two Me's Becoming a We

Being married doesn't mean that you lose your individuality or that the two of you have to become one. When people speak about unity, they aren't talking about sameness; you and your partner are two different, unique people in one relationship.

Your two "me's" become a "we" when you both want to understand each other better, and you have an appreciation of your spouse and what your partner brings to your marital relationship. There is a sense of being a team and working together as you plan your future, make decisions, have fun, deal with conflict, and communicate your feelings and dreams with one another.

You do have to be in touch with yourself before you can share who you are with your mate. One way is to do some journal exercises. Get those thoughts and feelings out of your head and onto paper so you can see it yourself.

Merging Family Cultures

Throughout your lifetime together, little memories will surface from your childhood. You may uncover some good times and the joy of having fun.

You might remember an incident that caused you to be extremely thrifty and you have a better understanding of that trait in yourself. As you take time to talk about your childhoods with one another, it is important to recognize that the discoveries you each make about yourselves will continue through the years. When a new awareness about yourself enters your life, share that with your spouse.

When you first married, you started to merge your two family cultures into one. It isn't easy to do—to sort through all the information to be discovered about one another and to make decisions so the two of you can end up with your own family traditions. To avoid a collision of cultures, you need to take time to discover how your pasts affect your marriage and your own self-esteem. Learn about the habits and customs of your spouse's family of origin. Ask each other these questions:

- What was your role in your family? What rules did you grow up with?
- How alike are your families? How different are they?
- What family traditions do you want to continue? Which ones do you want to let go?
- How has your family of origin affected you? Did you learn to hide or deny your feelings?
- Are you concerned about hurting your parents if you let them know your real feelings about your childhood? Is it hard for you to be yourself when you are around your family?
- What role does your family history play in your life?
- How does your family communicate with one another? Are there any possible misunderstandings in your family?
- What do you value about your family customs?
- What are the strengths and weaknesses of your family? What did you learn as you were growing up?
- Does your family medical history concern you?

Spend time with your spouse's family and view how they express their love for each other. Examine the relationships that the family members—parents, brothers, sisters, grandparents, and so forth—have with one another. Look at their ages and personalities. Talk about childhood memories. Talk about separations or divorces in the family, and problems like alcoholism or other addictions. Discuss religion and religious practices in the home.

Don't underestimate the importance of childhood memories, religious upbringing, and family backgrounds, traditions, values, and priorities. They become part of your marriage as soon as the two of you tie the knot. Learn who you are, believe in yourself, and be willing to share that knowledge with your spouse.

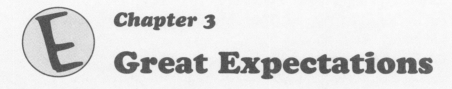

Chapter 3

Great Expectations

Buying into happily-ever-after scenarios and fairy tale myths, or looking for your one and only soul mate, can lead to unrealistic expectations that can cripple a relationship. Additionally, attitudes you've developed from your family of origin often lead to unrealistic expectations. It is critical to clarify your hopes, promises, plans, and attitudes with one another.

Myths of Marriage

Do you believe that life will be perfect once you're married? Do you think that all your needs can be met by your spouse? Have you decided that having children will be the icing on the cake? Are you hoping that being married will solve all your problems? Do you believe that happily married couples will never get bored with one another and that their lovemaking will always be passionate? These are just a few of the many myths that can set you up for a sense of failure in your marriage.

If you are looking for the Cinderella-like happily-ever-after storybook marriage year after year, you will be disappointed. It is perfectly normal for you as a couple to want and expect romance and happiness in your marriage. However, believing myths and expectations such as these will throw your marriage into a tailspin. Love is not enough. Life will throw mundane tasks and tough times at the two of you. How the two of you decide to deal with your expectations regarding life in general and your marriage, both spoken and unspoken, will determine the fate of your matrimonial journey.

Your Partner as Soul Mate

The notion of soul mates has been around since ancient times. Plato described a soul mate as a person's other half. Many folks believe that people can be drawn together by destiny or fate and that there is still a connection between soul mates even after death.

Others think that a soul mate doesn't necessarily mean someone a person marries. A soul mate could be of either sex and could be a family member, a friend, or a business partner. When people think of soul mates, they often think of couples that are temperamentally suited to one another, who have the same point of view, and have compatible dispositions.

The soul mate concept becomes a myth when couples search for someone to make them whole, or they believe that living with a soul mate would be easy and not require any work, or that a soul mate will accept and love every part of their spouse's personality.

Soul Mate Marriage Characteristics

Soul mate marriages are often described as well-balanced, strong, and positive. They have a lack of intimidation, manipulation, or abuse. A soul-mate partner feels like a mirror to their spouse. Other characteristics of a marriage to a soul mate include honesty, supportiveness, familiarity, mutuality, passion, harmony, acceptance, and friendship. These couples take delight in the growth of one another, relish their time together, and cherish the commitment they have made to their marriage.

You don't have to be predestined soul mates in order to have a marriage with these characteristics. You can have a relationship that feels like a natural fit, with a sense of being at ease and connected with one another by making your marriage a priority and spending time in working on having a great relationship. This type of partnership in marriage is able to handle difficult times because they are not only in tune with one another, they each take responsibility for their role in conflicts, and they are committed to making their marriage successful.

Whether or not you believe that your spouse is your soul mate, there are some things you should keep in mind:

- Don't expect your mate to feel and think exactly the way you do.
- Don't use the concept of searching for a soul mate as an excuse to walk away from your marriage.
- Remember, you can still have difficult times even when you are married to your soul mate.

Danger of the Soul Mate Myth

If you start looking for perfection in your spouse, or think that everything in your relationship should immediately click and that there won't be any problems, you are setting yourself up for a dose of heavy disillusionment. There can be temptation to bail out of an unhappy marriage because you believe your spouse isn't your soul mate. It is not realistic to think that marrying a soul mate will give you a life free from hard times and conflict.

Sharing Expectations

Expectations need to be verbalized with one another. Unspoken expectations create huge barriers in communication. Sharing your expectations with your spouse on a daily basis is one of the most important things you can do for your marriage. When expectations are unspoken or unmet, feelings of disappointment, anger, and resentment will surface. The issues don't have to be important ones. Often times, it is the little things that can cause the deepest hostility. People laugh about leaving the top off the toothpaste tube, or which way the toilet tissue roll should hang, or whether or not the toilet seat should be left up or down. However, it is these types of incidents that can build resentment, especially when they've been talked about once and then ignored.

What to Talk About

Discuss not only your expectations of a given day, but also talk about them before taking a trip, before going out for the evening, visiting friends, going shopping, or even when you have a quiet weekend together. Make an agreement that at least one of each of your expectations will be met. It can make a huge difference in how you perceive the experience.

When it comes to the holidays, don't assume that your partner wants to celebrate them in the same way that you do. Discuss where you want to be for the holidays, foods that are important to you during specific holidays, when you prefer to open gifts, your feelings about birthday parties and anniversaries, being with families for special events, financial concerns about holiday or birthday or anniversary spending, and time stresses.

Expectations in themselves are not the problem. Expectations are necessary. Expectations become a problem in a marriage when they are either too unrealistic or judged to be not that important, and are not shared or discussed on a regular basis.

Other topics filled with expectations include parenting beliefs, financial considerations, use of free time, emotional support, decorating and landscaping a home, sexual intimacy, types of meals to prepare and when to sit down to eat, exercise options, when to go to sleep, mattress comfort, temperature settings, music and movie likes and dislikes, friendship, housekeeping standards, punctuality, happiness, priorities, and on and on. Virtually every aspect of your life together has expectations to it.

The Test of Time

As a couple progresses through the stages of marriage, they will meet new challenges and will continuously have to make decisions. It is obvious that couples in long-term marriages experience a variety of life-changes throughout their years together. They may deal with having and raising children, ups and downs in their relationship with one another, health and financial issues, career decisions, and more. Expectations and hopes also change as life goes on. It is critical to be able to continue to identify and talk about expectations with one another.

Understanding Attitudes

Attitudes are different from expectations in that attitudes develop very early in life. Many of your attitudes are just defense mechanisms and a way to protect yourself, especially when your self-esteem is in the pits. Attitudes, especially deeply ingrained ones, aren't likely to change.

Take, as an example, a male chauvinist. Deep down, this husband believes that a woman's place is in the home where she should be cooking, sewing, cleaning, creating crafts, and raising children. He marries a strong-willed woman who has the attitude that a woman's place is in the world, and who thinks she has better things to do with her life than cooking, sewing, cleaning, and creating crafts. These two opposing attitudes are a heavy water bucket in this relationship. Although, over the course of their lifetime together, this issue will have been dealt with over and over again; however, it still exists and will be in this marriage when the couple has been married for eighty years. Since these attitudes aren't going to just go away, the couple needs to learn how to live with them by acknowledging them and knowing that their attitudes don't have to be defended.

Realize that although the attitude will be hanging around for a very long time, you can change the behavior that the attitude creates. If this guy lived alone, his male chauvinistic tendencies wouldn't be a problem for him. However, when he sees how detrimental this attitude and resulting behaviors are on his wife and on his marriage, he may realize that he needs to change his responses to his wife's choices in how she spends her time. She also recognizes that now and then, cooking him a gourmet meal and taking time to make sure the house is clean would be acts of love.

Attitudes by themselves don't hurt a marriage. It's the negative behavior or response to a person, issue, or situation that an attitude brings about that is damaging to a relationship. It is important to take responsibility for these hurtful reactions, and discovering and understanding your attitudes is a first step toward this.

You probably have some strong attitudes about money, debt, kids, Valentine's Day, gift giving, gender roles, honesty, trust, in-laws, pets, vacations, lifestyle choices, sexual intimacy, love, and marriage. If you haven't already done so, get to know your attitudes. Call them by name. Analyze them. Accept them for what they are.

Where do you think your attitudes about marriage and life come from? Why? Do you like any of them? Do you dislike any of them? What does your spouse think about some of your attitudes? Do you think your attitudes are the root of some destructive behaviors in your marriage? Share this knowledge with your spouse and examine how they affect your marriage.

Getting Beyond Unrealistic Expectations

The many marriage myths that abound in society often give couples unrealistic expectations. Having unrealistic expectations can, in turn, bring you to the point of wanting to call it quits. In fact, many experts believe that unrealistic expectations are the number one reason that marriages fail.

If you want an image of marriage that never ever was, watch television series re-runs and classic romantic movies, listen to love songs, and read romance novels. There's nothing wrong with any of these enjoyments. Just don't buy into the myths that they often portray. They often don't touch on situations dealing with prior marriage issues, unemployment, stepchildren, dropping out of school, physical abuse, political discussions, infidelities, drinking problems, drugs, severe economic problems, civil disobedience, and thoughts or threats of divorce.

In real life, you won't be able to solve your problems in a quick thirty minutes. Your hopes and expectations won't always come true. Your dilemmas won't necessarily have happy endings. But this doesn't mean that you can't have an exciting, fulfilling, and meaningful marriage. If you face unrealistic expectations individually, it can help the two of you develop realistic expectations together.

FACT

The television series *All in the Family*, which first aired in 1971, was one of the first television series to have story lines that went beyond simple misunderstandings, silly complications, and little white lies. It was the first sitcom to explore deeper dynamics of marriage and family relationships

It's okay to have expectations. Everyone does. However, your expectations must be achievable. Otherwise, the sense of disappointment, disillusionment, and despair from failed expectations will bring you to the point of divorce. Below are a few suggestions on ways to ensure that you are both aware of the expectations you have without being unreasonable.

- Ask for what you need, but don't expect your spouse to fulfill your every need.
- Be open to compromise.
- Don't avoid conflict in your marriage. Disagreements in a marriage are normal.
- Realize that some areas of disagreement may never be resolved.

- Accept that your marriage isn't perfect.
- Let go of your fantasy marriage myths and preconceived notions about marriage.
- Don't expect your spouse to read your mind.
- Talk about how you each define love and what being loving means.
- Don't let resentments and hostility build up. Don't play the role of martyr.
- Be open in sharing your expectations with your spouse, even your wild ones.

Athletes often use visualization techniques with their imaginations to create a positive momentum before they perform. You don't have to lower your expectations, but keep them appropriate and realistic. Having great expectations together can help the two of you have a balanced, fulfilling, and happy marriage.

The Art of Compromise

You can't always have things your way. Finding a middle ground is often a positive solution to a difficult situation. However, many people who believe in unilateral decision making believe that compromising is a weakness. It is not. It is a form of cooperation between spouses that shows that they consider one another to be of equal importance to their marital relationship.

If one of you feels short-changed a great deal of the time, your partnership may eventually deteriorate. To maintain a strong marriage, compromise is necessary so that each partner feels that his or her needs have been met part of the time.

Look for win-win solutions. If one of you loses, one of you may feel like a winner, but your relationship will be the biggest loser. There are ways to have this win-win approach and find solutions that you both will feel comfortable with. A compromise solution can often turn into a better choice than what either of you originally perceived.

Accept that just because the two of you have differing opinions on a decision, neither of you are right or wrong. Remember to place the highest priority on your relationship.

ALERT!

There are some issues where you should not compromise—including cases of abusive or addictive behaviors. It is critical that you don't compromise on any issue that goes against your own moral code or that puts you at risk legally, physically, or sexually. If you are in a situation like this, getting help from someone is the best choice.

There are many issues in a marriage that require compromise. Some are important topics like parenting styles, making financial decisions such as purchasing a car, taking a vacation, or refinancing a home. Others are minor compromises like which restaurant to eat at, or which movie to see, or where to plant the tulips. Whether it is a big issue or a small one, the key to compromise is listening. What is your partner really saying about their stance in a particular situation?

Suppose a couple has decided they want to visit their parents who live in separate states. His plan is to take about two weeks off from work, and to make a combined vacation/visit the folks type of road trip. Her plan is for him to take a flight to visit his folks, and she could take a flight to visit her folks on the same weekend. She sees her plan as saving both money and time and accomplishing the need to see their parents. He sees his plan as a chance for the two of them to get away, see some part of the country they haven't visited before, and have a more relaxed trip.

She's saying she just wants to visit her parents. He's saying he believes they need a vacation. A compromise would be to take the road trip, limit the amount of time spent with their folks, and to be budget conscious on the trip by packing lunches, staying at economy lodgings, and so on.

Be willing to give in a little. While listening to one another, look at possibilities for compromise. Working together in this manner can help you gain a new perspective about an issue.

On the other hand, a lack of compromise in a marriage can lead to hostility that is communicated in nonverbal ways, such as subtle moves to control a mate, or one partner withdrawing affection. Compromise can lead to growth and mutual satisfaction when married partners make the decision to be selfless, are willing to set aside defensive barriers and control tactics, and learn to listen to one another and adjust their expectations.

As previously mentioned, all marriages encounter rough times. But marriages can get through the moments of conflict, disappointment, and problems when spouses share their expectations with one another. You can have a successful marriage if you make time to talk with one another about how you get along, why you don't get along, how you see things the same, how you see things differently, and what you want out of life. Ⓔ

Chapter 4

Prioritizing Your Values

Each person brings to a marriage relationship personal goals and priorities that are based on their own values and ideals. Some believe that where you place your time and money is where you place your love. The two of you can stay on the same course throughout your lives together by knowing your values and making plans for your future based on those values.

Values versus Ideals

Many people confuse values and ideals—probably because both are important. A value is something you believe is good and worthwhile. You choose to have a value in your life when you willingly sacrifice other things for that value, for example, choosing to give up overtime opportunities and additional income because you value more time with your spouse.

An ideal is also something you recognize as good. It's something that perhaps you would like to achieve, but you aren't necessarily willing to sacrifice what's necessary to achieve it at this time. For example, you may think having an uncluttered home is an ideal, yet neither of you is willing to toss out or give away items you haven't used or needed for years. *The difference is the level of commitment.*

Just because you believe something is an ideal does not mean it has value to you. It could become a value to you, but if you don't do anything about it, it will just remain a nice ideal. For example, a woman really likes having fresh flowers in her home, yet she isn't willing to plant and weed a flower garden or pay money to buy fresh cut flowers. So it is an ideal for her. She has shared this ideal with her husband, who does plant the garden and cuts and puts beautiful flowers in vases throughout their house. For him, fresh flowers are a value with a high priority because of his love for his wife.

Good intentions only become a reality when you make your ideals into values by following through on your decisions. It is not a lived experience until it becomes a value. It is important that the two of you don't play games with semantics and that you are in agreement as to what your ideals and values are.

QUESTION?

Why is it so important to talk about values together?
Values determine how you deal with issues such as sex, companionship, religion, control, politics, money, affection, parenting, communication, time, roles, justice, independence, loyalty, and family.

Clarifying Your Values

The way you live your life together on a day-to-day basis is the key way to seek out your values. To recognize your own values, analyze money and time aspects of your life. These two important topics will help you discover your actual values. Do you know how you spend money? Where does it go? Look at the choices you've recently made regarding your finances. Perhaps you believe that you value having a home with really nice furniture. Yet when you've had money to spend on new furniture, the two of you usually spend the extra funds on a family vacation or on entertainment items like a new television or computer. So, in reality, having nice furniture is an ideal, and not a value, in your life.

The other way is to examine how you spend your time. Are most of your hours at work or at school or participating in a hobby or sport? How much time do you spend on chores around the house? How do you fill your time when you are not working? Do you bring work home with you? It is very easy to get caught up with things that need doing or things you want to do and to forget about spending time with the people in your lives who are the most important to you. Be honest in your answers. You may not like what they reveal to you, but they can help you discern changes you may want to make in your lives.

Communicating Values

Hopefully, prior to exchanging vows you had some conversations as to which values are most important to each of you. When you make assumptions about your partner's values, that is what your partner places a high priority on, you can end up with major misunderstandings, resentments, hurts, disappointments, and doubts about your marriage. You can avoid this miscommunication by making sure that you don't assume.

Ask questions. Clarify responses. Discuss reasons for priorities and values. It is possible for the two of you to have the same values, but different priorities. If you both believe in the importance of eating dinner together as a family, but one of you misses one or two meals a week due to other obligations, then your priorities on this issue are different. One of you is expecting to have family meals together every night, and the other expects being able to miss a meal now and then. If you don't discuss situations like this, feelings of defensiveness and hostility can surface.

ALERT!

Remember that having a difference in priorities will be part of your marriage forever. Knowing how to work through them and to respect each other's positions is essential to a good relationship.

Another example of differing priorities for the same value is when a couple decides to spend money on a large item. They decide that they create a value of having a newer vehicle with more space for their growing family. Her priority is on getting the most car they can for the best price. His priority is to get a specific car. Their value is the same—they both want a car—but their priorities are far apart. She's focused on the price and room for the kids, and he's focused on the horsepower of the engine and the amount of legroom.

Even joyful events such as anniversaries, birthdays, and other gift-giving holidays can turn into days of disappointment and stress rather than celebration when priorities about spending money haven't been talked out and expressed in advance. If your spouse is truly uncomfortable with receiving an expensive gift, then don't give such a present. If you aren't sure about your partner's thoughts in these areas, ask some questions. Don't assume that you know your spouse's thoughts on values and ideas.

Once you discover your values, then you can begin to set new priorities in your lives and together make plans to live them. However, you must be prepared to talk about your values and priorities over and over again. As we age, new life experiences and situations can change a person's perspective about their values and priorities.

Learning about Values Together

Here are some easy exercises that the two of you can do on your own: make a list of your values and priorities. Making these lists will help you in your discussions with one another to determine your values.

- Make a list for each of you of the following values: money/possessions, independence, education, spirituality/prayer, leisure time, careers, having children, number of children, owning a home, working at home, being active in church/community, living close to extended family, rural life, city life, vacations. Add more to the list if your values aren't included here. Put checkmarks next to the ones you consider to be your top five values and share them with one another.
- Prioritize (with 10 being the highest) how you would each spend money: home, clothing, food, education, entertainment, transportation, savings, medical, charity, recreation, personal needs, and so forth.
- Prioritize (with 10 being the highest) how you would each use time: chores, work, volunteer work, sports, time alone as a couple, visiting friends, sleep, television, recreation, visiting family members, vacation, time on the computer, "my time," reading, education, and so forth.
- Prioritize (with 10 being the highest) people you would like to spend time with: spouse, yourself, children, God, friends, relatives, parents, business associates, no one.

Go over your lists with one another and compare answers. Talk about why you responded the way you did, and listen to your spouse's reasons for his or her choices. This can help both of you understand where the other is coming from.

FACT

Many couples find that although they thought they knew one another prior to their wedding day, they are constantly amazed at how much they *didn't* know.

Re-evaluation of Values

The examination of your values will be a lifelong quest. Values are not formulated at just one point in time. They often change so you will need to re-evaluate them on a regular basis. It can be very easy to let some of your more important values take a back seat to some of the less important ones. New babies, sending kids off to college, fluctuating incomes, purchasing a home, retirement, illness, and vacations are just a few of the circumstances that can initiate the need for re-evaluation of your values and ideals.

For instance, many couples want and value a good marriage. However, when it comes to attending a marriage retreat or reading a book about marriage together, they don't have time for those activities because they are spending time on lesser values. Daily situations can point out discrepancies in how you live out your values. You both want couple time alone, yet because of your busy schedules, neither of you finds a babysitter for your planned date with one another. Together you agree that having an uncluttered home is important to your internal sense of peace, but neither of you is very concerned about picking up old newspapers or magazines left in the living room.

All of these situations can cause resentment to slowly build. That's why having plans is so important. Remember that re-evaluation is a key tool to use throughout your marriage. Don't be afraid to make changes in your priorities when necessary.

Making Plans for Your Life Together

Take time to share your dreams and visions with one another. Individually, write down your thoughts about where you would like the two of you to be in the next six months, next year, in five years, ten years, and twenty years. Be specific and make some plans. Set aside concerns about money when you are dreaming the big dreams.

Ask yourself whether the plans you have made will bring you closer together or will the plans leave you open to growing apart? Then, get together and share what you have written. Don't try to discuss all the plans at one time. Talk about the six-month plan one time, and the next-year plan another time. If you do one time frame per week, it will take you a month or two to discuss all your thoughts in detail and to merge your two plans into one. If either of you is having serious doubts about a decision regarding your plans, then trust in that doubt, and take another look at what you are planning.

Don't worry if you find that your plans aren't working out, or if you decide to change them at a later date, or if you realize one of your plans is totally unachievable. That is part of learning how to plan together. Some of your plans will work out great and others will be cast aside. Many of your plans will need to be re-evaluated. What is important is that you are fine-tuning your planning skills so that you can make workable plans together and know you are both on the same page.

Different Planning Styles

If one of you is a planner, and the other has a more spontaneous personality, you may find that making plans together will be a challenge. While you may think that long-term planning is unnecessary, your spouse will still have opinions about short-range plans. Some people like to think of themselves as free spirits, while their spouses see them as a boat without a sail drifting from here to there. An opinionated spouse may believe that his or her way is the only way and fight any plan that is a compromise. Different planning styles, along with having to make a choice between his plan and her plan, can make this a difficult process. The more you practice on making plans together, the more your different styles will merge together, too.

Vague or Rigid Plans?

One of the problems in making plans is getting caught up in plans that are either too vague or too rigid. A vague plan is one that has no true beginning or ending, or no set parameters. A rigid plan is just the opposite and can leave you feeling trapped. An example of a vague plan is going on a vacation without knowing what you want to see or do while on the trip. A rigid plan would be planning every detail of the vacation down to which restaurants you'll stop at, along with a complicated time schedule to have to deal with. It is best to find some happy middle ground.

Other Planning Considerations

If your plans are not in unison with your shared values it is unlikely they will succeed. Using the vacation scenario once again, a couple wants to take a particular vacation. It is clearly a high value for them. While working on their plans for the trip, they realize though that the extra hours spent at work for the funds for the trip would take time away from one another and their children. Since family and together time has a higher value, they make a decision to choose a less expensive vacation so they can avoid having to work overtime. Make sure that the two of you consider your values as a couple when making major decisions such as this one.

Planning Tips

Here are a few things to consider when you begin making plans with your spouse, whether they are short-term or long-range plans.

- Make sure that your plans are achievable and that they do not depend on some unlikely event (such as winning the lottery).
- Do your homework. Do the necessary research and obtain background information so that your plans have a greater chance of success.
- Take into consideration who and what else will be impacted by your plans. Will your children, parents, friends, careers, bank savings, and so forth be touched by your plan?
- If your plans are short range, set a time frame for three weeks to a month.
- Keep your plans specific.
- Write your plans down. Schedule them on your calendar.
- Reward yourselves when you are successful. Plan in advance what your reward will be.
- Re-evaluate at the end of the time period you specified in your plan. Decide if you want to continue the plan or create a new one.

Developing a Shared Calendar

Every couple needs a shared calendar. It becomes even more critical when you have children who are in school. A major stress in marriages and family is the pressure created by having too many things to do or being involved in too many activities. Not enough time together as a family and as a couple can literally kill your marriage.

The calendar can be a tool that you use when you are talking about your expectations of the day, week, or month. It will help you negotiate and agree on how you will spend your time together. It can ultimately help keep your marriage on the right track. Seeing your schedule in print will point out time-gobbling activities (e.g., overtime, clubs, hobbies, sports, social engagements, volunteering) that you may need to re-evaluate and limit.

ALERT!

Make sure that the calendar is posted where everyone in the family has easy access to it. An erasable one is a good idea, too.

Re-evaluation of Priorities

Don't be afraid to re-evaluate your plans and to change them. Re-evaluation is healthy and necessary. Keep a journal for a week or two and track not only your expenses but also your daily schedules. The results may shock you. Most people who do this discover that they are spending more money than they intended on unnecessary items, and they are spending less time than they thought with their children and partner.

The shared calendar can help you find or make more time to spend with your spouse and your children. If you both lead very busy lives, and your sexual life is suffering, you may discover that you need to schedule times for intimacy. Since priorities can shift overnight, it is important that at least twice a year, you sit down together and look at your financial budget and your calendar. This will keep your good intentions from going astray and turning into large disappointments or areas of contention between you.

Plans for the Two of You

You need to have some plans that involve just the two of you, don't take much time, and that won't cost any money. Here are some ideas.

- Work on your photograph album together.
- Give each other a massage.
- Light a candle at dinner.
- Exercise together once a week (even something as simple as a walk around the block).
- Create a gourmet meal out of what you can find in your kitchen cabinets, refrigerator, and freezer.
- Before going to bed, share one positive thought you had about your spouse that day.
- Spend time reading together. Take turns reading out loud.
- Plan a dream vacation together.
- Simplify. De-clutter a drawer or a closet together.

Handling Differing Values

Every married couple will find that they have values that differ somewhere, whether it's concerning work, education, children, money, or priorities. Getting to the root of these values will help in understanding your differences. Together, list your top four priorities in life. Priorities may or may not involve spirituality, God, fun, education, happiness, love, financial security, family, and happiness. Don't judge what is on your spouse's list or what isn't on the list. The purpose of the list is to get to know one another's values and not to judge them.

Talk about what you would like to be remembered for. Reflect back on happy times when you were children, teens, and young adults. Talk about why you think you were happy at those times. Was it because of the people you were with or where you were or what you were doing? As you share with one another, remember to have respect for one another's values and experiences. Be open to your spouse and listen with not only your ears, but with your heart as well.

FACT

Happily wed couples are ones who consider themselves as friends and who have compatible interests and values.

Intercultural Marriages

A couple in an international/intercultural marriage is likely to face even more differing values. This is due to cultural backgrounds and the way in which each of you was brought up. The first five years of an intercultural marriage are the hardest due to the family and cultural pressures. The family of origin issues need to be discussed in depth with one another. Some of the obstacles international/intercultural couples will have to learn to deal with include bridging the language barrier, cultural values differences, religious conflicts, sex role expectations, economic adjustments, political issues, and legal complications. Patience and understanding will help overcome these barriers.

Spouses need to learn how to communicate well in at least one language, discover one another's countries' traditions and societies, become aware of the cultural roots that go deep, focus on positives, seek out what they have in common with one another, and discuss family expectations and traditions.

The Rewards

Each new experience that you share is an opportunity to further understand one another's values and ideals. Although some of your values will be refined and changed through the years, many are your core values and they won't change. These core values usually involve basic beliefs such as freedom, value of friendship, and your spirituality. Throughout your lifetime together you will continue this journey of setting priorities by blending and adapting your values from individual ones to joint values and ideals.

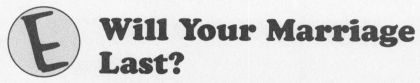

Chapter 5

Will Your Marriage Last?

Statistics are showing that nearly half of all marriages today will end in divorce. Additionally, fewer than half of married individuals say they are happily married. Hearing this can leave many couples wondering what they can do to keep their marriage intact. Couples can work together for long-lasting, meaningful relationships by looking at both what is right and what is wrong in their own marriages.

Knowing If You Are at Risk for Divorce

Although no two marital relationships are alike, the issues that can lead to divorce are fairly universal. The two of you could be considered at risk for divorce if you don't know how to resolve conflict in your marriage. If you don't know how to fight fair or to compromise or to bring a difficult issue to closure, your marriage relationship will ultimately suffer. Other factors that can lead a couple to divorce are poor communication skills, financial problems or disagreements about monetary issues, addictions and/or substance abuse, physical or emotional abuse, infidelity, failed expectations, a lack of marital commitment, and unmet needs.

Conflict

Being able to deal with differences of opinion and how to fight fairly is critical for a marriage to succeed. There are couples in satisfying marriages who claim that they don't get frustrated or angry and that they have no disagreements or conflict in their marriage. These couples are probably in denial and are hiding their frustrations with one another because they think the issues aren't important enough to bring up or they are fearful of rocking the boat. Such unresolved issues are not emotionally or physically healthy for either the individuals or the marriage. Conflict is normal in a marriage and not to be feared. The problem isn't the fact that a couple has disagreements or argues. The problem is that many couples don't know how to fight fair.

The word "fighting" is defined here as disagreeing or arguing. The term does not refer to physical hitting one another.

Poor Communication Skills

If one spouse is the type of person who talks too much or lectures, the other spouse may develop a habit of not listening as a way of coping. Couples also don't listen well when they judge what their partners are saying or are worrying about what their own responses will be. Let your spouse know if you've had a bad day so that your quietness or moodiness isn't taken personally. Communication is a two-way street. It involves both the sending and receiving of information, thoughts, feelings, and opinions. Good communication within a marriage just doesn't happen. It takes time and it takes skill to reach a point of not assuming what your partner is thinking or feeling.

Good communication is more than talking. It includes using all your senses, and being aware of actions, movements, and nonverbal clues.

The top four areas that couples have difficulty communicating with one another about are:

1. Possessions
2. Sex
3. Death
4. God

Finances

Monetary concerns fall under the category of possessions. The main issue that creates difficulty in marriages is finances. Couples have disagreements about monetary issues such as how much to spend and what to spend it on, how to save, who should pay the bills and handle the checking accounts, how many checking accounts to have, the pros and cons of individual accounts, and disagreements about allowances for kids. Add to this mix some financial difficulties, and a marriage can deteriorate quickly.

Abuse

If either or both spouses are having substance abuse or addiction problems, their ability to communicate well and to handle other marital issues is severely decreased. Although physical abuse is noticeable and you can see the outward signs of it, psychological or verbal abuse is just as damaging. Some marriages with an abusive partner will have a quick demise, and some will linger for years. However, any marriage with physical or emotional, or verbal abuse is likely to fail eventually. If you are trying to save a marriage with an abusive partner, don't attempt to do this on your own. You need help to maneuver this difficult journey.

Infidelity and Lack of Marital Commitment

Although there are many ways of betraying one's spouse, the act of being unfaithful is one of the most hurtful and harmful decisions a partner can make. Cheating fractures the trust in a marriage. Many marriages can survive infidelity and rebuild trust, but it takes time, an ability to ask for forgiveness, the willingness to forgive and let go, and a willingness of both spouses to build again with a new sense of commitment to one another. When a marriage has been rocked by infidelity, both partners will need to be totally open and honest with one another in order to move forward with their relationship. A solid marriage cannot be built upon a loose foundation.

Failed Expectations and Unmet Needs

Everyone has expectations. They play a big part in how people perceive life and the world around them. Expectations have to be brought into the light of day. When expectations are not shared, misunderstandings and hurt feelings will happen. It is also important that you ask yourselves if your expectations are truly realistic or not.

Failed expectations often occur in a marriage when these expectations are too unrealistic or are not discussed. Take time to examine whether you are placing the burden of your needs on your spouse when you can meet these needs yourself. Ask yourself how important a particular need really is, and how you can fulfill it yourself. Unmet needs are the result of poor communication and not sharing these needs with one another. Make a habit of sharing your daily expectations with one another.

Predicting Marital Satisfaction

Studies have shown that there are certain traits of a marriage that can be measured and used to rate the couple's satisfaction. Individuals in successful marriages need to have a good self-image, be assertive, be flexible, and enjoy being around other people. Couples need to have some similarities in things they like or enjoy doing, have known one another for a while, communicate well with one another, and know how to resolve conflicts in their relationship.

Other factors that increase a couple's chance of long-term marital success are waiting to marry and not marrying as a teenager or in the early twenties, having the approval and support of friends and family when they marry, having healthy family-of-origin experiences, coming from families with successful marriages, refusing to accept hurtful behavior early in a marriage, knowing how to talk about difficult areas with one another in a loving way, and being educated and rooted in their careers. Talk about these traits to see how firm a foundation your marriage stands on.

Qualities of a Successful Marriage

Couples in successful marriages respect, enjoy, support, and love one another, and have a solid commitment to their marriage. They also know how to communicate and handle conflict. They don't let disagreements drag on and on. They know how to bring closure to a difficult issue. They have a sense of humor, and can have fun together.

FACT

Allow your partner some time, say fifteen minutes, to be alone and to unwind each day before expecting them to be ready for togetherness with you or your children. This includes stay-at-home parents, too. They need a break from parental responsibilities each day.

Tolerance, caring, nurturing, having realistic expectations, interdependence, and having the ability to solve problems together are also critical qualities of a successful relationship. These couples are intimate with one another both sexually and emotionally. Their communication is enhanced daily by their willingness to share and express their feelings and emotions as well as their thoughts. They have realistic expectations of themselves, one another, and their marriage. Individuals in successful marriages are open to giving more than their "share" to their relationship with one another. They know how to reach a compromise.

Compromise as a Skill

Many individuals view compromise or collaboration as losing or giving up. It is neither. When a successful compromise has been decided upon in a marriage, a couple will find themselves in a win-win situation. Finding common ground will take active listening and an ability to ask pertinent questions. In order to resolve your differences and overcome the obstacles that are standing between the two of you, express your concerns for one another's opinions and feelings, and be open to new ways of handling an issue. Neither of you may get exactly what you wanted, but by blending your interests, you can discover the common ground that will keep harmony in your relationship.

Things That Can Kill a Marriage

Although there are many situations, experiences, and attitudes that can destroy a marriage, lack of respect, stonewalling, defensiveness, and an inability to forgive are the top four. If you notice any of these red flags in your marriage, realize that your relationship has problems and is in trouble.

Lack of Respect

If either of you is unable to show respect for one another, especially when arguing, you have set yourselves up for having a difficult relationship. Showing contempt, putting one another down, character assassination, name-calling, and not letting go of the past can create even more problems. Words to watch out for and not to use include "always" and "never." Hurtful teasing and sarcastic comments are other signs of lack of respect along with not caring if actions or behaviors hurt one another's feelings.

If you feel you may suffer from not treating your partner with enough respect, ask yourself what it is in you that keeps you from reaching out and loving your spouse.

Stonewalling

A spouse who refuses to talk or who shuts down emotionally is stonewalling. If either you or your spouse plays this game, you are increasing the negativity in your marriage. You will also discover that small molehills will turn into huge mountains. Refusing to discuss important issues or ongoing problems increases the distance between you and lessens the amount of trust and emotional intimacy in your marriage.

Being Overly Defensive

Sometimes it can be very difficult to hear your spouse say things about yourself or your marriage that are negative. Unless you have given your spouse permission to comment on your weaknesses or negative aspects of your behaviors in your marriage relationship, it is criticism and can be destructive. It is important though, when such permission is given and when the comments are not in the form of put-downs or severe criticism, to listen with an open mind and heart, and to not get defensive about what you hear. Defensiveness can only make a difficult situation harder to resolve.

Lack of Forgiveness

One of the main skills necessary for a successful and happy marriage is the ability to forgive. If either you or your spouse has a habit of holding on to grudges, you will find yourselves dealing with the same problems over and over again. Holding on to past hurts is a poison that will continue to create negativity in your relationship. Unless you both learn how to forgive, the accumulation of hurts and issues will get bigger and bigger and the negativity will intensify. The inability to forgive or to ask for forgiveness can turn negativity and hurts into a vicious, damaging cycle. Remember, too, that saying you are sorry, asking for forgiveness but then not changing inappropriate or hurtful behavior is the same as breaking a promise.

Characteristics of Long-Lasting Marriages

Couples in long-term marriages share common traits. They trust in their love for one another, allow each to be who they truly are, and can accept that it is normal for them to each need some alone time. They believe in the old adage that actions do speak louder than words and they show their love for one another both through the verbal expression of their love and through their actions.

They enjoy experiencing new things together and they look forward to watching their marriage evolve through the years. They learn from their mistakes, they support one another during a crisis, and they deal with conflict in a constructive manner. They enjoy candlelight dinners, romantic surprises, and time alone together. They respect and like their mates. They are able to share both their wild dreams and deep fears with one another.

In successful marriages, couples know how to attack a problem or an issue and not one another. They know how to affirm one another. Couples who have been married a long time didn't bail out when things got tough. They know how to fight fair and they work through the difficult issues together. They know how to compromise. They are open to being collaborators and not adversaries when dealing with difficult issues. They are not in competition with one another. They see themselves as a team and believe that their marriage needs and deserves to be nurtured and protected.

FACT

Couples who have long-lasting marriages enjoy being with one another and talking to each other. Even if their lives are busy and their schedules are crowded, they make time to be together.

Happily married couples work at romancing one another through the years. Aren't you touched when you see an elderly couple holding hands or kissing one another? They recognize the importance of showing their love, devotion, and caring. These couples cherish one another. You know what lights the fire between the two of you . . . keep doing it.

Keeping Your Marriage Together

Along with a sense of commitment that can help a couple get through the tough times, being friends with one another is key to having a great marriage. Spend time together. Keep romance and lust alive in your relationship. Place a high value on having time for just the two of you. Think positive, work at accepting your spouse and not trying to change him or her, and show empathy when it's most needed.

Be Friends

Loving your spouse is very important. However, just as important as loving your spouse is being able to say that you like your spouse. Don't underestimate the importance of companionship in a marriage. Keep your friendship with one another alive. Treat your partner as you would a very good friend, and you will not only be lovers, you will be friends as well.

Friends are thoughtful and sensitive of one another, unselfish, and take personal responsibility for their own behaviors. Friends show their appreciation and gratitude for each other. Other qualities of friendship such as flexibility, understanding, and honesty are also important in a marriage. Be willing to admit to making a mistake. Share your spirituality and prayer life with each other. Encourage both yourself and your mate to continue to grow emotionally and intellectually. Talk about the changes you experience with one another. Be there for each other and don't keep score.

Other qualities important to both a friendship and a marriage include being:

- Dependable
- Nice

- Helpful
- Respectful
- Sincere
- Happy
- Forgiving
- Open
- Friendly
- Genuine
- Supportive

Focus on the Positive

Pay attention to the good aspects of your marriage. Make sure that you share with your partner what you enjoy about your relationship and when you notice the two of you being in sync with one another. Particularly during difficult times, remind yourselves of why you fell in love. Remember the importance of praise and validation.

Studies have shown that happily married couples make five times as many positive statements as negative ones about their marriage and one another. When there is a lot of negativity in a relationship in the form of put-downs, criticism, making demands, constantly bringing up old hurts and issues, negative attitudes toward life, and a lack of positive feedback, a marriage will quickly deteriorate. The negative energy can subtly continue to drain the other partner of any feelings of love and commitment. It is important to not let negativity affect your own self-esteem or to take it on personally.

If you do encounter negative energy, try to divert it past yourself. Remind yourself often that your spouse's negativity has nothing to do with you as an individual. You can lessen negative energy in your marriage by being playful and affectionate, by seriously listening to one another, and by making sure that you compliment your spouse.

Sense of Commitment

Having a deep commitment to one another and placing a high priority on your marriage is critical to making it through the tough times. This type of commitment is a decision and requires one or both of you to make decisions based on what is the best thing to do for your marriage and not for yourself. Placing a high value on your marriage may call for spending less money, which could mean spending less time on your work or on some individual interests.

Couples who are committed to one another handle difficult times and crisis situations more effectively. They are able to solve problems and can cope with challenges together because they believe in the strength of their marriage and in one another.

Making Time for Each Other

Everyone needs some alone time, however, and the freedom to pursue individual interests. Therefore, a balance is needed between too much couple time and too much personal time. Lack of quality time with one another can weaken even the best of relationships. In order to prevent this, busy couples may have to actually schedule time to be together. If that's what it takes, then do it. Take walks together. Have a picnic in the back yard. Schedule time for lovemaking. Plan on having a mini-vacation for just the two of you at least once each year. What you do or where you do it isn't as important as just being together.

QUESTION?

I don't have enough time to get everything done—how can I find more time for my spouse?
To make time for one another, schedule "time for us" appointments in your organizer, in your computer calendar, and on your family schedule calendar. Treat them with the same importance as you would any other appointment.

Empathy

The quality of empathy is shown in a marriage when a person tries to truly understand what their spouse is feeling or experiencing. This is another two-way street. A spouse can't understand his or her partner's feelings if they aren't openly shared and communicated.

Acceptance

Along with the importance of respecting each other is the importance of accepting one another. When you accept your spouse, you are saying it is okay for him or her to be who he or she truly is. Demanding change or not accepting individual differences is a sure way to create a huge wedge in a marriage. You are tearing down your spouse's self-image and saying he can't be who he is when you are being critical and asking him to change. You can't change anyone but yourself.

People often do change their behaviors, but not because they were told to do so. Changes come from within. People change because they feel loved and they can see that their behaviors are having a harmful impact on those they love. They want to give more to their relationship so they work on changing behaviors that have a negative effect on their relationship.

Working on Your Marriage

As the adage goes, "love is not enough" to make a successful marriage. So many other skills are involved in creating a good marriage. You need to pay attention to one another. Learn how to fight fairly. Share your expectations and needs with one another. Listen with understanding when your spouse talks with you. Communicate on a daily basis about your feelings and thoughts of the day. Decide to remain faithful to your vows and commitment to one another. Don't lose touch with one another. Don't wait for your spouse to make the first move.

Keep your romance alive. Lighten up. Show respect for each other. Learn how to balance your various roles in life and place your role as spouse, friend, and lover as a high priority. Place a high value on your friendship with each other. Learn what makes your partner tick and what causes your spouse to feel aggravation or calm. If you aren't sure what your spouse desires or needs, then ask that question. If your marriage is in distress, seek help. Be willing to forgive and to ask for forgiveness. Do the obvious things that you know in your hearts you should be doing for one another. Ⓔ

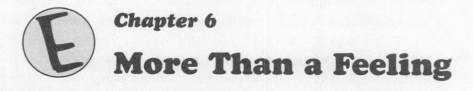

Chapter 6

More Than a Feeling

Love means more than just romance. Every marriage relationship will go through cycles of romance, disillusionment, and joy. It is important to understand this cycle and recognize each stage for what it is, remaining committed to each other throughout even the disillusionment phase. As this chapter shows you, love is a *decision* that takes work.

What Is Love?

Writers, theologians, and lovers have been trying to define love since the beginning of time. There is an abundance of books, movies, songs, and poems that attempt to explain and describe the emotion of love. Love is intimacy and passion but more than sexual attraction and lust. Love is friendship and commitment, not just a sense of obligation and duty. Love is maturity, trust, and openness to growth and change in behaviors. Love is a willingness to put one's self aside for another. Love is a passionate, ever-growing friendship. Love warms one's heart. Love accepts and understands imperfection. Love can be sustained even though miles apart. Love is often thought of as a feeling. Love is also a decision.

Love as a Feeling

Love is a deep, wonderful feeling that can be here one day, and missing the next. This is because feelings regularly come and go throughout your lives. They can overpower you quickly. You cannot control what you feel. However, you can control your reactions and behaviors as a consequence of a feeling, but the feeling itself just appears without your consent. As a result, feelings have no morality. They are neither right nor wrong. You will always be called to cope with your feelings that are ever-changing. What becomes right or wrong, good or bad, is how you *respond* to your feelings.

For instance, Paul is a married man who enjoys the sight of a pretty woman. He feels delight when he sees an attractive woman. He may even feel lust. There is nothing wrong with either of these feelings. They are not immoral. However, if Paul were to obviously leer at women, or harass them, or make obscene gestures at them, or try to make a date with one of them, then these behaviors would be judged as inappropriate and wrong. But his feelings just *are*.

Many times, asking yourself the question, "Is this the most loving thing I can do right now?" will help you keep your behaviors from creating wedges in your relationships.

Mary may have feelings of protectiveness and cautiousness about her teenage children. The feelings are okay, but if she begins stifling her children's activities, watching them every minute, and never letting them out of her sight, then these behaviors in response to her feelings are creating problems with her kids.

All feelings will fade at one time or another, including love. Any feeling can be refreshed and intensified by focusing on it. When you cannot let go of a hurt, or you talk about an injustice you felt, or you complain bitterly about your anger, those feelings will last longer within your heart and mind. The same holds true for the feeling of love.

When a marriage is based just on the *feeling* of love, it will have a rocky journey. By focusing on being loving, and making the decision to love on a regular basis, a married couple can experience the depth and feeling of love throughout their marital journey together.

Love as a Decision

Some people want to romanticize their marriage and wish to believe that they don't have to work at having a successful marriage. Others want to believe in the myth of happily-ever-after and think that making a decision to love is being phony. But love is also a decision and not just a warm, fuzzy feeling.

All marriages will go through rough times when feelings of love are overshadowed by other events and emotions. If you've based your marriage solely on how you feel toward your spouse, your marriage won't last. It won't have a chance. Since feelings often follow behaviors, acting kind or lovingly toward your spouse can revitalize your amorous feelings for one another.

You are probably already making the decision to love many times every day without realizing it. You made it when you got up earlier than necessary so you could say goodbye to your spouse. You made the decision to love when you put aside watching the news on television to go for a walk with your partner. Your partner made that decision to love you by not snapping back when you were grumpy and difficult to be around. You both make the decision when you set aside time to truly communicate and connect with each other. You often make the decision to love when you are open to compromise and listen to one another without bias. When you both are able to make a decision to love in spite of your feelings, the two of you can keep your marriage on an even keel throughout your lives with one another.

The Cycle of Feelings

Disillusionment isn't simply a stage that you go through once in your marriage. In other words, it's not something you survive once, and then go all uphill after that. The constantly recurring cycle of romance, disillusionment, and joy can happen every day, or even several times a day in a marriage. Some periods of disillusionment may last only a few minutes, while other periods may last for several weeks or months.

Who Experiences These Cycles?

Every couple will go through these phases. It is a natural aspect of marriage. As you become closer to one another, you are inevitably going to know the good and bad aspects of each other's personalities. This knowledge can set you up for disillusionment. You know one another's most vulnerable spots, and you know how to hurt. This cycle isn't like being caught in a squirrel cage, though. Think of it more like a spiral, because as a couple you are never in the same place emotionally or intellectually. You are constantly changing, growing, and discovering new things about yourself and one another. The cycle of romance, disillusionment, and joy can be a roadmap to help the two of you see where you are in your relationship. When you recognize that you are in disillusionment, you can then make the decision to love so you can move out of that sense of despair or disappointment.

FACT

This cycle of disillusionment is different from stages of marriage. All marriages go through predictable stages—honeymoon, parenting, midlife, empty nest, and widowhood—related to age and experience. The cycles of romance, disillusionment, and joy are ongoing and are repeated many times.

When Do the Cycles Occur?

Realistically, this cycle occurs in all sorts of situations. You've probably experienced it at work as you become tired of your job itself or with working on a new project. Initially, there is the rush of the excitement of the newness of the experience. Then you are hit with some negative feedback, or the hours are longer than you expected, or the people you are working with are difficult to be around. You have a choice of quitting the job or project or of making some decisions to improve your situation at work. Once you make the decisions that enable you to once again enjoy your work, then a sense of joy will return.

Becoming a parent and coping with all that having a child entails can bring about moments of romance, disillusionment, and joy as a parent. What parents haven't been thrilled and amazed at the new creation that has become part of their lives? Yet, nights of no sleep, the sense of extra responsibility, and feeling trapped can trigger feelings of disillusionment. Then a smile or a gurgle from your baby can bring back the joy.

When a child misbehaves or does something embarrassing, the disillusionment may return. Feelings of being unappreciated, or taken for granted, may possibly surface. Making the decision to love with no strings attached can help you, as a parent, deal with the many conflicting feelings that you will experience as your children grow both physically and emotionally.

Even something as simple as purchasing a new car or computer can create this spiral of feelings. The first dent on a vehicle or the first time a computer drives you crazy can send you into disillusionment. Seeing the new models coming out each year can deepen a sense of disillusionment. Making a decision to re-examine your priorities can help bring about the sense of happiness with these objects. People experience this cycle of romance, disillusionment, and joy throughout their lives, and in all their relationships. Knowing how to make the decision to love makes coping with the cycle easier.

The Romance Phase

Generally, when people think of romance, they think of falling in love, starry eyes, passionate sex, racing heartbeat, feeling light-headed, candlelight dinners, presents, and being with one another as often as possible. When it comes to romance, folks are influenced greatly by novels, magazines, and movies.

However, there is more to romance than that. It is more than a romp in the hay and great sex. Romance is having great conversations with one another, always having something to talk about, and enjoying being with one another even when doing the dishes together or grocery shopping. Romance happens in difficult times as well as easy times. A simple glance across the room, whether you are in a crowd or alone, can be a romantic moment.

Romance is different for every couple. What one husband and wife consider romantic, another couple will consider to be boring. It is critical that the two of you continually discuss the romantic aspects of your relationship. Be specific with one another. Talk about your romantic expectations and desires. Some couples have romantic traditions in the way they say good morning or good night to each other, or in scheduling regular dates, or remembering anniversaries and other important events. Being romantic is another decision to love.

QUESTION?

What's a thoughtful way to be romantic?
Think back to your dating days. Remember how you acted and where you went when you were first dating each other. Are you still doing any of those things with one another? If not, plan to surprise your spouse with a trip down memory lane!

When you want to be romantic, think about being caring and sensitive. In order to keep romance alive in your marriage, you need to make time for one another. Time together may need to be scheduled by having a date night at least once a month, or getting together for lunch once a day each week. You can have inexpensive babysitting by arranging to watch another couple's children now and then and have them reciprocate for you. A romantic notion doesn't necessarily involve a big expenditure on a gift or an elaborately planned evening. Romance can be giving a wildflower plucked from your yard, or watching a romantic movie together. It can be a small note expressing love and desire that your spouse will find in his or her lunch tote or on his or her favorite chair.

Here are a few other ideas for ways you can be romantic:

- Telephone your spouse during the day.
- Hold hands while walking.
- Get dressed up for each other.
- Spread a blanket in the backyard and watch the clouds or stars together.
- Do something different or surprising.
- Go somewhere you haven't been before.
- Pick out a romantic card to send to your partner.
- Whisper sweet nothings in your partner's ear.
- Compose a love letter.
- Rent a motel room for the afternoon.

The Disillusionment Phase

You will know you have reached a moment of disillusionment when you find yourself being critical of little things—for example, when your spouse doesn't replace the roll of toilet paper, or when you see the toothpaste tube has been squeezed from the middle. Often times, a quality or behavior that first attracted you to your spouse will end up being something that really bothers you.

Disillusionment is that sense of being stifled, of feeling in a rut, or thinking that your marriage is going nowhere. You may feel as if you are walking on eggshells. Neglect may be the order of the day, and winning is what counts. When blame, put-downs, anger, criticism, resentment, and sarcasm invade your relationship, this bumpy road in your marriage is in disillusionment. Feelings of hopelessness and despair will drown out any positive thoughts about your spouse or marriage. Fear and confusion may paralyze you both. Disillusionment will happen to every married couple. It is important to remember that neither of you is perfect, and neither is your marriage. Any married couple that says they have never been in disillusionment is in denial.

Thoughts and Feelings of Disillusionment

The grass starts looking greener on the other side of the fence. Your marriage isn't what you expected it to be and you feel disappointed. You judge that other marriages aren't experiencing the same feelings of boredom, desperation, and loneliness. You may be thinking about leaving your marriage. You wonder where the happiness went. You overreact to your partner's perceived insensitivity and your spouse gets impatient with your apparent inability to be somewhere on time. The two of you fuss and nitpick over all kinds of insignificant issues. Spontaneity and joy are missing in your life and seem to be replaced by resentment and a sense of drowning. Like the lyrics in the song that Peggy Lee sang, you ask the question, "Is this all there is?"

Signs of Disillusionment

Along with focusing on the negativity in your marriage or spouse, signs of disillusionment include an unwillingness to show affection, a sense of distance and alienation, a lack of communication, a desire to do things individually rather than as a couple, a belief that your spouse is unresponsive, and a general attitude of not caring about one another or your marriage.

Every couple should make time to enrich their relationship with one another. There are many marriage enrichment seminars and workshops available. These are generally private experiences that will enable the two of you to reconnect with what made you fall in love with one another in the first place. They also help couples learn how to improve their communication skills and how to fight fairly.

Some red flags to watch out for are:

- Lack of respect
- Sexual problems
- Disinterest in having fun together
- Lessened moments of intimacy and romance

- Not wanting to share
- No desire to deal with trouble areas
- Increased conflict
- Overscheduling of time commitments
- Surfacing of unrealistic expectations
- Tendency toward physical/emotional abuse

Common Mistakes

Disillusionment can be caused by a variety of situations and experiences. Here are some of the most common mistakes one or both partners can make that may lead to disillusionment:

- Poor listening, interrupting, and ignoring of body language
- Lack of sex
- Needing to have the last word or always wanting to be right
- Loss of respect, lack of affirmation, and badmouthing your spouse
- Being mean, inappropriate teasing, and inconsiderate behavior
- Lying
- Not keeping promises
- Angry outbursts and temper tantrums
- Selfishness and greed
- Being gross in personal hygiene

What Disillusionment Means

Being in disillusionment doesn't mean that you should divorce. It doesn't mean that you don't love one another. It doesn't mean that your love for one another has lessened.

It may mean that you aren't spending enough time together, or that the two of you are taking your marriage for granted. You both may be spending too much time on other important obligations like your children, work issues, or furthering your education. Experiencing disillusionment in your marriage *does* mean that you are a normal couple going through life's ups and downs. Disillusionment is natural. It also means that you both need to be making the decision to love one another more often.

The Joy Phase

Joy in a marriage is more than just being happy with one another. Happiness can be dependent on having things, being financially secure, and achieving goals. The sense of true joy in a marriage relationship stands apart from that. It doesn't require money in the bank, bills to be paid on time, having disciplined kids, achieving success, creating a nice home, or obtaining a college degree.

True joy in marriage is experienced often but quietly and with a great deal of thanksgiving. Marital joy resides deep in the hearts of married couples who have weathered the storms of life together, embraced the good times with one another, relished the quiet times both together and individually, and accepted the moments of heartache by holding tight to each other. The sense of true joy in a marriage can often be seen in the faces of an elderly couple as they help one another make it from the store to their car, in the way they hold hands with each other, or in the look of delight as a couple shares their hopes and dreams with one another. There is happiness, fun in being together, deep passion, and intimacy.

The joy that a couple feels in their marriage is a very unique experience. It is difficult to express the sense of closeness and the sense of being glad that you are together. The joy phase is when you realize you are in a good place in your marriage. When you experience it, you know it.

This isn't to say that newlyweds can't experience true joy in their marriage. They can and do. However, the true joy of marriage is a more grounded feeling of peacefulness and contentment than a couple typically feels during the honeymoon stage of their marriage. Couples who experience joy in their marriage know that no matter what happens they will be able to deal with it together and remain best friends. They cherish one another, have respect for their marital journey, and relish the life and memories they have created together.

Making the Decision to Love

When making a decision to end a marriage, many people cite their reason for getting a divorce is because they are no longer in love with their spouse. What has happened to these couples? Did their love for one another just go away or evaporate into thin air? No. They no longer feel love or loving toward their partner because they have not made the decision to love. They base their sense of being in love only on how they feel. Through their years together, the absence of making the decision to love has widened the distance between them.

Living It Out

As mentioned earlier, love is a decision. The key to breaking a period of disillusionment and moving on to joy in a marriage is to make the decision to love even when you don't feel like it.

This decision is a willingness to give more to your marriage than you may be receiving from it. It is a decision to give 100 percent. It can be an easy decision such as having at least one meal together daily or walking with one another for exercise and communication. Or it can be difficult like moving to a new location in order to allow your spouse's career to prosper or to take in an aging parent.

What the Decision Means

Making the decision to love means deciding to fight fair, to not lash out at one another, to show that you care for your partner in little ways—in short, to put your marriage relationship first. It is accepting that when either one of you or your marriage is under a great deal of stress, that things won't always be perfect. It means making the decision to not snap at our spouse or lose your cool because you are tense. When you make the decision to love you decide to not allow a minor disagreement blow up into a major fight. Often, it is a daily decision that requires both of you to decide to make time for one another, to decide to apologize, to decide to forgive, and to decide to put the other's needs first.

The Benefits

If a couple is unable to make the decision to love, or they don't want to make the decision to love, their marriage won't last. The negative feelings and behaviors that are created out of long periods of disillusionment will ultimately destroy a marriage. The finger pointing of who is at fault, the sense of resentment, the lack of seeing anything positive in the relationship, and the hostility between the couple will only increase.

For a marriage to succeed, when things are difficult, both partners must be willing to decide to love and do whatever is necessary to make their marriage whole again. Making the decision to love puts you in a place to see what's good in your marriage and helps you change your focus, giving you power over negativity.

Make the decision to spend at least ten minutes each day in meaningful conversation with each other.

Chapter 7

Something to Talk About

Good communication and listening skills are vital to keeping a marriage relationship strong. As it only widens the gap between partners, operating only on assumptions or guesses puts your marriage at risk. One of the main reasons couples divorce is because they have lost the ability—or never had to begin with—the skills to communicate with one another. This chapter explains how to communicate effectively and overcome the roadblocks you may face to understanding what your partner is telling you.

The Impact of Noncommunication

Classic movies have romanticized the idea of being married to the quiet, little woman or the strong, silent type of guy. However, in real life, these noncommunicative partners can make a marriage very difficult to endure. When a couple isn't communicating with one another, the result will be all kinds of misunderstandings, conflicts, and hurt feelings.

Any time that a spouse refuses to discuss an issue, clams up and won't share thoughts or feelings about a topic, or plays the game of distancing themselves from their partner, noncommunication has taken place. A lack of communication turns married partners into little more than combative roommates in a toxic environment. Being non-communicative erodes any sense of closeness and intimacy that may have previously existed. Additionally, trust, openness, and the sense of being a team is wiped out by closed or lack of communication.

Listening to Each Other

There is a huge difference between hearing what your spouse has said and truly listening. You can listen to what is being said, but not hear what your spouse meant. For instance, you come home from work and discover your husband washing the dishes that have piled up. He says, "This is something I wanted to do, so don't worry about it." You hear the words, but did you hear what he meant? His comment could mean he recognized how busy you've been and he wanted to help out, or it could be sarcasm. You can tell what he actually meant in the way he said the statement, in his nonverbal communication, or by using feedback.

Not hearing what was really said can lead to unnecessary conflict. Although some people think they are being a good listener if they are quiet and seem to be paying attention to the speaker, that's not always the case. Effective, active listening requires skill.

Keep Listening a Priority

In our fast-paced society, people have been trained to do two or three things at one time. This busyness is often counterproductive to good listening. Listening is about presence. Listening is doing just one thing, and that is giving your full attention to your spouse during a conversation. Work on listening fully so that you are not planning on what you are going to say in response. Don't try to address your agenda (if you have one) while you're listening—let go of that and just focus on what is being said. Keep eye contact with your spouse. Just listen. Don't glance at the television or fiddle with the newspaper or start washing the dishes while your spouse is talking with you.

Don't Interrupt

Let your spouse finish what he or she is saying. If this is difficult for you to do because you are fearful that you will forget what you want to say, write down your thoughts as you listen. Interrupting can be a serious problem that can push your spouse away from you. If this is something you do a lot, find some way to remind yourself to keep quiet until it is your turn to speak. Some people put their chin in their hand as a sign to themselves to not talk until their partner has finished talking.

FACT

Men tend to interrupt women more than they interrupt other men. Women usually respond to being interrupted by a man with silence.

Keep an Open Mind and Show Respect

Imagine that the two of you are standing in different areas of your backyard when a deer wanders into your yard. You will each see this deer from a different perspective. Both of your views are correct. There is no right or wrong in what you have each seen.

Some people will insist that their view is the only one. This can happen in a marriage relationship, too. It is necessary to keep an open mind when listening to your spouse. Don't judge. Try to not jump to conclusions. Looking for the right or wrong in what is being said will prevent you from truly listening. Think before you say anything in response, especially if you have an emotional reaction. Respect your spouse's point of view, even if you disagree with what is being said. Showing respect for your partner's opinions, thoughts, and feelings is extremely beneficial to keeping the lines of communication open between the two of you.

Use Feedback Technique and Stay Focused

Although many folks joke about the feedback technique in communication, it is a valuable skill to keep the two of you from misinterpreting what is being said. You don't need to restate everything your partner says. However, saying something like, "I hear you saying . . ." when you want to clarify what you heard can prevent major misunderstandings.

Feedback verifies what you have heard and also tells your spouse that you are listening. This is especially important when the two of you are discussing a sensitive area of your relationship. Be open to the possibility that you didn't hear clearly what your spouse was saying. You can also put your partner's statement into your own words. This shows that you are paying attention, and want to hear what your spouse is saying. Focus on the main points that your spouse is talking about. It's okay to ask questions to clarify what you thought you heard.

Communicating Nonverbally

The oldest language on earth is body language. Watch for nonverbal signs and clues of both yourself and your partner. These can include:

- Shrugging shoulders
- Expressive movements, such as nodding or crossing arms or legs
- Tone of voice (sarcastic, loud, soothing)
- Spatial arrangements
- Cultural differences
- Eye contact or looking away
- Facial expressions like a smile, rolling eyes, tears, surprise, frown, shock, boredom, disgust, and so on
- Mannerisms, such as twisting a lock of hair, fiddling with papers, or tapping fingers

Defensive body language clues include crossed legs, having your body turned away from the speaker, stiffening up, and folding your arms. Also note that your eyes are in constant communication. If your spouse looks down or away, it could be a sign he or she doesn't like what is being said. If, when speaking, your spouse's eyes never move upward to retrieve information, it could be a sign that what you are hearing is a lie. Gestures can be friendly, angry, a warning, threatening, secretive, embarrassing, and obscene.

FACT

Couples from different cultures must recognize that the meaning of a gesture in one country could mean something entirely different in another locale. For example, the typical American thumbs-up gesture is considered an obscene gesture in the Mid-East.

If you notice a difference between what your spouse is saying and what nonverbal actions he or she is conveying, trust in what you see. It is difficult to manipulate one's gestures, but fairly easy to lie. A nod in silence, a groan, or encouraging sounds can be appropriate responses to what your spouse is sharing and shows empathy. Hugs are great nonverbal communication! Nodding can mean, "I hear you" or it could mean, "I agree with you." If you are unsure about what you sense your partner's nonverbal communication is saying to you, ask to see if you are reading the clues correctly. Discuss your concerns about your spouse's nonverbal language to clarify what you are sensing.

Gender Differences

There are both similarities and differences in the way men and women communicate. The differences can create major problems in the way a married couple talks with one another. Men often share only when they want to give information or solve a problem. Women tend to communicate to develop relationships or to get information. It is important for a husband to realize that what his wife needs from him is to just listen, and not to fix or solve the problem that she has shared with him.

Men are often more concerned about details than women. Women usually talk more about feelings than men. Men dislike asking questions or getting directions. Most men would rather wander around in the desert for forty years just like Moses. The usage of words can also create misunderstandings between husbands and wives. For example, what he means when he says "play" can be entirely different for her. Learning how to interpret differences is not necessarily easy. But realizing that gender differences can create misunderstandings is a first step toward understanding one another.

FACT

During communication, 7 percent of the message is communicated verbally, and 93 percent is conveyed through nonverbal signs. Of the nonverbal message, 38 percent is communicated through vocal tones and 55 percent through facial expressions.

Blocks to Listening

Everyone at some time or other is distracted from truly listening. You can get caught up in wondering what your spouse really means, or in thinking that you are in the right, or perhaps your mind is focused on all the errands you have to run. If you catch yourself not listening to your spouse, or only half-heartedly listening, say so. Ask your partner to repeat what was just said. You will be showing that their comments are important to you and that you do care about what they think and feel. There are several major blocks to listening that you can learn to recognize and overcome.

Rehearsing

This is also often referred to as having your answer running. Your mind is speeding along and preparing and rehearsing what your response is going to be instead of really listening to what your partner is saying. You may look as if you are interested but your focus is on what you'll say when it's your turn to speak.

Comparing

This block occurs when you are busy deciding which one of you has talked the most, or accomplished more. You could also be assessing who is more intelligent or competent. It's impossible to be a good listener when this type of comparison is happening.

Daydreaming

Daydreaming is when you find yourself drifting off into other thoughts when your spouse is talking. It's not that you aren't interested in what is being said, but rather that something you hear triggers something in your mind that sends you zoning off into a different world. Everyone does this now and then. However, if it becomes a pattern in your listening, your spouse may believe that you don't care about what he or she has to say.

Mind Reading

You have the habit of mind reading instead of listening when you assume you know what your spouse is going to say. This block also includes missing most of what is being said because you are busy trying to guess what they are saying. Mind readers are often distrustful of what they do hear. This can create a great deal of frustration in a marriage.

Placating

Do you find yourself saying a lot of "yep," "uh-huh," "you're right," or nodding your head in agreement? People do this type of half-listening so that they won't have to face conflict or because they want to appear as nice and supportive. Agreeing with everything your spouse says is a form of noninvolvement and is unfair to your marriage.

There's an old adage that says you should listen twice as much as you speak because you have two ears but only one mouth. This is sage advice.

Identifying

Telling your own stories is an important aspect of communicating. However, when you are more involved in sharing your own experiences than you are in allowing your spouse to finish telling his or her story, then you are identifying. This block occurs when you relate everything shared to your own life. If you hear a comment about having a flat tire, you interrupt and start talking about when your vehicle had problems. If your spouse starts talking about a difficult time in childhood, you jump in with your own story. One of the results of this block is that you never really get to know your spouse.

Filtering

Folks who filter a conversation hear only what they want to hear. Everything else is screened out. You may find yourself listening in a conversation to figure out if your spouse is unhappy or angry or threatening. The true meaning behind your spouse's words can be greatly misinterpreted because you haven't heard all that was said. You could also filter out things that you consider unpleasant, uninteresting, or negative.

Judging

When you prejudge what your spouse is going to say, you aren't listening. You've already decided that their words don't carry any weight or will be boring or will be in conflict with what you want to hear. Writing your partner off in this way is a sure way to close all communication between the two of you because you are saying that your partner has no value to you.

Sparring

Sparring is dismissing your partner's point of view as having no merit or being quick to disagree with everything your spouse has to say. This involves put-downs, sarcasm, and hostile comments. Your spouse is never understood because you spend your time looking for things to argue about when your partner is talking.

Having to Be Right

Having to be right all the time is the most damaging of all the listening blocks. Folks who practice this will not accept their spouse's viewpoints, won't stand being corrected, and will shout their way through excuses and accusations to make sure they don't appear to be in the wrong. It is a closed mentality that focuses on a spouse's past mistakes, twists the facts, and rationalizes behavior. This is a "my way or the highway" attitude that destroys any attempt at true communication.

Changing the Subject

Also known as derailing, folks use this listening block when they are uncomfortable with what is being said, embarrassed by the conversation, or just plain bored with it. The easiest rail to derail a conversation is to change the subject. Derailing can occur by turning the conversation into a joke. Although your level of discomfort may be alleviated by this tactic, it is sure to create hard feelings with your spouse.

Stonewalling

Stonewalling builds walls between partners instead of bridges. This listening block is a sign of contempt and can create a complete breakdown in communication. Although time-outs and space from one another are necessary now and then, withdrawing and ignoring your spouse through the silent treatment only creates distance and hostility between the two of you.

Advising

If you try to be like a superhero, solving everyone's problems in a single bound, you are caught up in the block of advising. Once you've heard the first few comments, you stop listening and jump into the conversation to start offering your own words of wisdom. Your spouse's feelings will be misunderstood and not acknowledged. Your advice will be premature and based on incomplete information.

Sharing Yourself with Your Spouse

As you share with your partner, talk in such a way that your spouse won't have to guess what you are talking about. A way to ensure that your message is being heard, both the facts and the emotions you have, is to share your feelings. Feelings are the core of who you are. The sharing of feelings is a gift and should be treated as such. Feelings should not be put-down or criticized.

Identifying Feelings

It can be difficult for some people to identify and name their feelings. They have worked so hard throughout their lives to hide their feelings that they aren't sure themselves what they actually feel. Remember to accept that feelings are neither right nor wrong and that feelings come and go quickly and change often. It is important that you not judge either yourself or your spouse because of the feelings you both have.

A way to recognize the difference between your thoughts and your emotional feelings is to apply the "I think versus I feel" rule. Anytime you can substitute the words "I think" for "I feel" in a sentence, you have expressed a thought and not a feeling.

Describing Feelings

Be descriptive as you share your feelings. It is best to stick with just one feeling at a time. Use words to paint a picture of your feeling to give your spouse a better opportunity to understand and experience that feeling. One way to describe feelings is to mentally put yourself in an activity or place with a feeling. Use colors, textures, past memories or events, foods, and how you see yourself experiencing this feeling.

As with any new tool, you may find trying to describe your feelings to be cumbersome. However, this descriptive tool does work, and the more you practice describing your feelings, the more natural it will be in your communication with one another. Identifying and describing your feelings to one another on a regular basis will improve your communication and bring you closer.

Some examples of using visual images to describe your feelings are:

- Serene as when watching waves on a beach
- Quiet as snow falling
- Agitated like a cornered cat
- Tender as when holding a baby
- Relaxed when having a hot cup of chocolate.

Think of words like *trapped, boxed in, caged, soft, joyful*, and *calm*. Remember situations where you have felt strong feelings such as the sense of anxiety as you planned your wedding, the anticipation you felt as the time grew near for the birth of your baby, or the worry and fear when your spouse doesn't arrive home on time and is several hours late.

Daily Communication Efforts

The time the two of you spend in conversation with one another is invaluable. This communication helps you stay connected with what is happening in your lives, allows you both to be supportive of one another, and gives you two an opportunity to brainstorm and solve problems.

Responding to Your Spouse

It's important to remember that just because your spouse doesn't take your advice to heart, it doesn't mean he or she wasn't listening to you. It means they disagreed with what you had to say. Communicate this fact to your spouse. Letting your spouse know that you understand her or his perspective, even though you don't agree with it, will help the two of you stay on the same track communication-wise. It will help the two of you reach a point of compromise on difficult issues.

It is important to not overreact to what your partner has shared. Make sure you did not misunderstand what was being said. If you think you are being misunderstood, explain that to your partner. Don't reject your partner's feelings. It is the same as rejecting your spouse.

Daily Dialogue

Daily dialogue is a communication tool in which both of you write a letter about your feelings on a selected topic or question and then share those feelings with your partner. Spend no more than ten minutes writing this note. When the two of you get together to read one another's letters and talk about them, limit this time to ten minutes also.

It is important during the sharing time to not try to change your spouse's feelings. This is also not a time to try to make things better. When you share your feelings, you are sharing the intimate core of who you are. During these sharing times, listen to your spouse with respect, understanding, and love.

What topics should you write about? When your relationship is going through a difficult time, it is best to not try to tackle tough topics. Select questions that focus on the positive aspects of your relationship. This can be accomplished by centering questions on remembering good times while on a vacation or a date. You can also have questions that ask what qualities you like about one another or simply about your feelings of the day. The twenty minutes you spend communicating this way can make a tremendous difference in how you both feel about yourselves and your marriage.

One question that can be answered over and over again in the daily dialogue technique is, "How do I feel about my day today?"

Difficult Topics

Throughout the years of your marriage, it is of vital importance that you discuss the problems and issues that are important to both of you and to your marriage. If you don't make it a priority to talk about difficult and important topics in your relationship, your marriage will stagnate and you will slowly grow apart from each other. As previously stated, the most difficult topics for couples to communicate about are possessions, death, sex, and God. Additionally, you should be talking about each of your dreams, hopes, fears, and your thoughts about your future with one another.

Don't expect to come to a complete understanding or agreement every time the two of you talk with one another. When you use communication skills and techniques, keep an open mind, and listen to your spouse with sensitivity, the two of you can deal with difficult topics in a positive way. Keeping the lines of communication open in your marriage is the key to keeping your marriage vibrant and alive.

Chapter 8
Do Opposites Attract?

Everyone is different. Along with differences in religion, culture, ethnicity, income, and parenting styles, couples often have to deal with different preferences in room temperature, foods, eating habits, movies, music, body clock, where to vacation, politics, planning, pet preferences, bedding textures, spending money, and more. It isn't necessary to try to minimize your differences. They can make your journey together more interesting! Don't let differences get in the way.

Why Opposites Attract

The old adage of opposites attract has some truth to it. The reason opposites attract one another has been the subject of many classic romantic movies. Think of Spencer and Hepburn in *Adam's Rib* or Ryan and Hanks in *You've Got Mail*. Many people choose their marriage partner based on things they have in common such as their ethnic background, age, social or economic status, values, likes and dislikes, beliefs, and education. While there is truth in the saying that "birds of a feather flock together," similarities such as ethnic background, age, social or economic status, and education don't guarantee happiness. Couples can have different tastes in movies, clothes, books, TV shows, foods, drinks, hobbies, sports, temperature of the room, size of dog, height of mirror, furniture styles, vacation choices, and more. Your marriage isn't doomed because you have a lot of differences.

Dealing with Differences

Generally, people fall in love because of traits such as spontaneity, creativity, ambition, generosity, humor, intelligence, honesty, and so on. People tend to look for partners who have personality traits and qualities that they lack in themselves; it is a way of completing themselves. This is why a goody-two-shoes woman may be attracted to a bad boy type of guy, or a slob pairs up with a neat freak, and introverts seek out extroverts.

Later, they may begin to resent this. The sense of humor that she loved about him becomes embarrassing. The predictability that he relied on in her becomes boring. Her need to have a clean home that was so refreshing at first turns into a real annoyance. His take-charge attitude feels more like controlling behavior.

The key to dealing with differences is to talk about them with one another. Express your expectations and feelings. It is not fair to expect your spouse to change. In reality, most of you really don't want that change to occur. She really does value his spontaneity, and would be upset if he lost that trait. He relies on her dependability and would feel lost if she didn't take her responsibilities seriously.

Coping Skills

Remember that you weren't attracted to one another by what you preferred to eat or which movie you liked best. It can be fun to list what attracted you to one another when you first met, as well as what you continue to appreciate in one another. This can be an enriching and fun thing to do on a chilly day when you can relax together, share some memories, and talk about your love for one another. Through the years, you will learn how to complement each other's strengths and weaknesses. Don't try to force your partner to undergo a personality change, because the result will likely be rejection and it isn't fair to your spouse.

Making Decisions Together

Acknowledge that you are different and let go of the need to always have things your way. Everyone is self-focused. Marriage requires that two, distinct personalities learn how to be giving not only to themselves, but also to one another. The concept of "we" needs to take priority over "me." That's not to say that individual needs shouldn't be met. It is saying that neither spouse's needs are more important than the other's needs.

Decision Making How-To

Since you can't change your spouse, deal with your differences by deciding which differences you can live with and which ones will drive you up the wall. You will need to find ways to compromise on the big differences, and let go of some of the small ones. Only the two of you know when a laid-back attitude, generosity, ambition, neatness, spontaneity, humor, and so forth has turned into a big issue and is creating conflict between the two of you. As you come together to make a decision, focus on what you love about each other. To effectively make decisions together, you need to make sure that you are listening to one another, understanding what is being said, and that you both have an openness to compromise.

ALERT!

Trying to always have things your way causes you to lose the sense of partnership and being a team that marriages need. This is a symptom of having unmet emotional needs. Step back and ask yourselves, individually, why you are digging in on particular issues. Express those problems as feelings, such as by saying, "I feel lonely when you work late every night," and you will be able to find ways to resolve the real problem without feeling like you are having to "give in."

Make sure that you show respect for your spouse's opinions, talents, skills, and intelligence. When making a decision take time to research your options. Once you have made a decision, agree to accept mutual responsibility for that decision. If things don't work out like you planned, don't fall into the trap of saying, "Well, it was your decision." You both take the glory and you both take the blame. Be willing to revisit your decisions and to re-evaluate them to make sure that your original goal is being accomplished.

Different Genders, Different Needs

Generalizations about the difference between the sexes are just that—generalities and stereotypes. However, exceptions exist for every generalization made. For every man who wants space during times of stress, there is a woman with the same need. Yet, understanding the gender gap between the two of you can help you cope with attitudes and behaviors.

The starting point is admitting there are differences. The second point is recognizing that being different doesn't make either one of you less significant. Keeping the lines of communication open in your relationship can help you avoid a battle of the sexes in your home. Bringing the differences between you and your spouse into the light of day will help you see how you two can more effectively work as a couple without competing with one another.

Some general differences between men and women in our society include the following.

- Men seek space; women seek closeness.
- Men look for sexual fulfillment; women need affection.
- Women share experiences and feelings; men talk about achievement and information.
- Men read for information; women read for enjoyment.
- Men focus on the future; women focus on the present.
- Men want to feel needed; women want to feel cherished.
- Men place a lot of importance on the size of a gift; women view all gifts as important.
- Women value conversation; men need someone to have fun with.
- Women talk about problems; men like to solve them.
- In dealing with grief or loss, men tend to feel anger sooner than women; women tend to feel sadness sooner than men. Men want to "do" something to make things right again; women just want to "be."
- Men look for an attractive wife; women are attracted to honesty and openness in a spouse.
- Men either handle conflict with intimidation or silence; women either ignore conflict or assume responsibility for it.
- Men seek admiration from their mate; women desire a commitment to family from their spouse.

FACT

Men have a larger hypothalamus than most women. This small organ near the brain stem can increase rage, desire, thirst, and hunger. Women generally have a larger corpus callosum. This bundle of nerves in the brain helps the right side of the brain to communicate with the left side. Having a larger corpus callosum allows women to be more two-sided in their thinking.

Interfaith Marriages

When two individuals of different religious traditions marry, they will need to learn how to reach a consensus on how their differences and some potentially irresolvable conflicts will be handled. If they don't, their marriage will suffer.

Many of the conflicts in an interfaith marriage are culturally embedded. It is vitally important for any couple in an interfaith marriage to share what is important to each of them as individuals. Talk about why something is important to you along with discussing how you can support one another's needs in this area of your relationship. Recognize and identify the outside pressures on your marriage so that you can cope with them in a positive way.

FACT

All religions are seeing an increase in and acceptance of interfaith marriages. Approximately 60 percent of Jews marry non-Jews. Greek Orthodox persons have an intermarriage rate close to 80 percent. Many Catholic dioceses are reporting that nearly half of the marriages performed are interfaith.

Stress Points

Compromise can become difficult for some couples in an interfaith marriage. If one spouse has to give up some of their beliefs, chaos can result. Parental expectations can be a major stress point, as well, especially if the parents have negative feelings about your marriage. You may have already dealt with family conflict related to faith in planning your wedding. However, parental expectations and family traditions can continue to clash, leaving the two of you in the middle of a war.

The holidays are another time when outside pressures from families, friends, and religious traditions and rules can envelop an interfaith married couple in feelings of confusion, misgiving, anxiety, and mixed loyalties. A couple can feel as if they are being torn apart.

For an interfaith couple, continued stress will exist around decisions they need to make throughout their marital journey together: where to worship, birth control, parenting styles, diet, unresolved religious conflict, and how to make decisions together. Other issues that will impact an interfaith marriage include societal pressures, religious rules and traditions, finances, continuing education, sex, extended family relationships, interdependence, and communication styles. The challenges facing an interfaith couple are never-ending.

FACT

Although many people believe that there is a lower divorce rate among same-faith couples, these claims are unsubstantiated.

It isn't the religious or denominational differences that cause a marriage to fall apart. It's the way the couple handles (or doesn't handle) the differences. When a married couple can share and live their religious lives individually without trying to change one another, their marriage can be stable.

Coping Strategies

Face the facts and be realistic about your faith differences not only before you marry, but throughout your married life with one another. Don't ignore the differences. Waiting until after your wedding to tackle your different beliefs can lead to more complex problems later on. It's important to learn about one another's faith traditions. Consider having something from both of your religious traditions in your wedding ceremony. In some cases, couples choose to have two separate ceremonies.

Make a decision about where the two of you will worship—either separately or together. Discuss tithing expectations. Talk with one another concerning your children's religious education so you know if you are going to teach your children about both faiths or only one. Know how you will handle your in-laws if they are having a problem with your attitudes about religion. Keep talking with one another about both the common aspects and differences of your faith lives.

Without continual discussions, religious differences can be a major contributor to a breakdown in your marriage. It is vitally important for the two of you to set some ground rules regarding religion in your marriage. Do remain nonjudgmental and find ways to brainstorm solutions together. Withdrawing from either of your churches or faiths is usually not an effective option. It is only a temporary fix. At some point in time, and often when children enter your life, one or both of you may want to become involved in your religious tradition again.

Conversion of one spouse to the religious faith of the other works only when the change is something that is truly desired and is done without pressure. Although not a workable compromise for many, some couples seek out a third, different religion for both of them to join.

Another alternative is for a couple to stay active in both of their faith traditions. In this scenario, they support one another in their faith activities. This multi-faith approach requires time and commitment to honor and appreciate both religions. Other couples merge both their religious traditions and become a united ecumenical unit. Another approach is that of total separateness when it comes to religion. Only you as a couple can decide what works best for your relationship. Whatever that is, do it with love and respect for your spouse.

Although some couples do nothing and just let things slide when it comes to religious issues, this is not a recommended approach. It is bound to create problems at some point—you might as well face them head-on now so you are prepared to deal with the differences.

Handling the Holidays

The holidays don't have to be times of stress because of your different faith traditions. Although your faith traditions are important, your marriage and your relationship with your spouse need to come first. In thinking about the holidays, reflect on what is important to you, why it is important to you, and what isn't important to you—then write it all down. This way when you share with your spouse about this aspect of your life you will have specifics to discuss.

Be supportive of one another. Look for what your two faiths have in common. You can create new traditions by building on existing ones or by blending the ones you have together. Realize that you don't have to celebrate the way your families have always celebrated, and brainstorm solutions for the two of you.

Flexibility, too, is important. If you can work it out without too much stress, try to be willing to spend some time with one another's families. If you have difficulty with this, create a secret password between the two of you that you can use to signal that you've had enough and it is time to leave. Make sure that your children are taught about the rich heritages that you each brought into your marriage. In doing so, discuss your remembrances of the holiday seasons when you were children. Work at having that type of joy and awe in your current celebrations.

QUESTION?

Shouldn't husbands and wives who share the same faith have it easier?
Same-faith couples can have the same religious related problems of interfaith couples because where they are on their faith journey and how they practice their religion may be very different. It's important for all couples to communicate carefully with each other about their faiths.

The key to enjoying the holidays as an interfaith couple is to keep communicating with one another by learning from one another and continuing to ask questions. Realize that you can't have everything your own way. And don't let your extended families make the decision as to how you two will spend your holidays.

Developing Traditions

Family traditions are those rituals and celebrations that create positive memories for a family. They give children a sense of who they are, a feeling of belonging, an understanding of their roots, and can convey values. Don't you enjoy the familiarity of returning to something that you've done for a long time?

For traditions to be important, they need to be understood. The story behind the tradition needs to be told so it has meaning. Have you heard the story of the Easter ham? A little girl is watching her mom prepare the Easter ham. Mom cuts off both ends of the ham before putting it in the pot. The little girl asks why both ends are cut off. Her mom responds that she doesn't know. It's the way her mom always fixed the Easter ham. So they call grandmother and ask her why both ends of the Easter ham are cut off before putting it in the pot. Grandmother says she doesn't know either. It's the way her mother always prepared the Easter ham. So they call great-grandmother. When asked, she laughs and says, "It was the only way I could get the Easter ham to fit the only pot I had!"

Some traditions can get outgrown, but if you tell the story about them, they may be resurrected when your kids have little ones.

Creating new traditions involves seeing things in a new way, letting go of things you thought you couldn't live without, being flexible, respecting the traditions of others, telling your stories, and trusting one another's opinions.

Intercultural Marriages

Although every marriage requires dedication, work, and a deep commitment, if you are in an international/intercultural marriage, you will both need to give your relationship even more attention because of the many obstacles that you will face. Make time to learn as much as you can about your partner's lifestyle and culture. Don't be blinded by thinking that your love for one another will get you through the challenges and obstacles you will face with an intercultural marriage.

You will need to become very familiar with your partner's culture and to have an understanding of where you are different and where there are similarities. Make sure you can find a way to handle the differences before they impact your own self-esteem as an individual. An example of this type of stress in a marriage is when a strong, self-reliant woman marries someone from a culture where women are treated as second-class citizens with fewer privileges than men.

ALERT!

The biggest mistake you can make in an intercultural marriage is to assume that your partner will change.

Cultural Obstacles

The obstacles facing an intercultural couple flow from family, friends, personal values, expectations, and bureaucratic procedures. Some of the problems these relationships may face are discussed here.

Different Value Systems

Value systems are derived from your own upbringing and family of origin issues: your whole approach to life in terms of how to spend your time, making decisions regarding finances and raising children, roles and responsibilities, where you want to live, and involvement with extended family members.

Extended Family

Oftentimes, the extended families of intercultural couples can exert subtle pressures that can undermine your relationship. Even when extended family members are creating difficulties for you, having respect for your partner's parents is important. Having respect doesn't mean you do what they tell you or that you agree with what they have to say. Be open and honest with your families.

Communication Difficulties

If you have a language barrier, it is important that you work on having one language in which you can both communicate effectively. Topics you will need to talk with one another about include possible religious conflicts, finances, expectations about sex and roles in your marriage, political issues, complications arising from immigration requirements, and so forth.

Hints for Making It Work

As you talk about your differences, make sure that you focus on the positives and notice what you have in common with one another. Realize that the cultural roots in each of your pasts go deep and that your partner probably won't change. You each have to ask yourself if you can live with that fact. If either of you answer "no," your marriage will have difficulties. Make sure you discuss your expectations about holidays, traditions, finances, sex, chores, education, careers, roles, mealtimes, vacations, recreation, and in-laws. It isn't always easy to cope with the heritage that you've grown up with. Your ethnic, religious, and socioeconomic backgrounds will impact your relationship throughout your married life together.

ALERT!

The first five years of an intercultural marriage are said to be the most difficult. Developing understanding, patience, and good communication are keys to making this type of relationship grow closer together.

The important thing to remember when the two of you talk about your differences is that neither of you is right or wrong. It's okay to be different; in fact, this is probably part of the reason you were drawn together in the first place. By understanding your differences, and making plans around them, your differences can enrich and deepen your marriage. Those differences can also make life together more interesting!

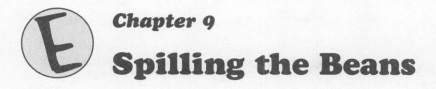

Chapter 9

Spilling the Beans

Is honesty the best policy in marriage? Not always. How do you know when and what to tell your spouse? You may need to seek outside help from a counselor to determine this. Life is a journey full of surprises and unplanned moments. Although sharing what you think and feel is vital in a marriage, it is important to know when honesty could hurt your relationship.

Honesty as a Moral Value

Being honest shows you have a sense of morality. Certainly, truthfulness is a necessary part of every marriage. However, too much honesty or inappropriate honesty can be a double-edged sword. (This is a controversial statement. What is being talked about here is the sharing with your spouse of your own history and family of origin issues that may have become a burden to you as an individual.)

Honesty for the Wrong Reasons

Honesty can also be manipulative: Phil believes that Georgia is a bad cook. He thinks that he needs to be honest with her and tell her about his perception of her cooking. "Hon, I'm just being honest" is really a criticism disguised as being honest. This type of honesty, whether it has to do with weight issues, personal hygiene, interests, or how your partner drives, keeps house, entertains, spends time, takes care of the kids, handles finances, makes love, and so on can be extremely hurtful in a marital relationship.

If you share old, painful situations with your spouse, it could be detrimental to your relationship. Your mate could take on responsibility for it or want to cure it, or solve it, or make it go away. The newly discovered knowledge from long past could create a situation that could divide you rather than bring you together. There is no easy chart to follow or specific guidelines to help you in knowing what to do in a case like this because each relationship is different.

Some aspects of your lives and memories are better worked through with a counselor or a minister. Let him or her help you discern if something should be shared with your partner. For example, Mike had an affair early in his marriage. Twenty years later, the guilt is still eating him up inside, and he decides to confess it to his wife, Helen, now that their relationship is going well. Helen is rocked by the news, and although she forgives him, she takes on the burden, becomes depressed, and begins having doubts about her own self-worth. Their marriage starts to crumble under the strain. Was Mike wise to suddenly be honest with her about this?

If sharing something out of the past with your spouse could be detrimental to the relationship, then don't share it. If you need to talk about this type of situation, it is best to seek counseling, or go to your religious leaders to talk about it.

Every individual has aspects of their lives that are private and secret. This isn't something you have to defend. This sense of autonomy, this sense of private space, both emotional and physical, is important to your mental health. Some people disagree with this belief. They believe that any type of secret in a marriage will eventually create problems, prevent intimacy, and cause difficulty and isolation between spouses. However, this reasoning doesn't accept that honesty can be an immoral act when it creates a shift of the burden of guilt from one to the other.

Is Honesty Always the Best Policy?

There can be valid reasons for keeping a secret from one's spouse. Many long-time married couples have things they haven't told one another. Some things could be embarrassing moments from childhood or the teenage years. Some secrets may involve someone else who has asked that the confidence not be shared.

Keeping a private journal of one's inner thoughts and feelings doesn't do any irreparable harm to a marriage. Many people need this type of space, this sense of the private self. Although honesty and trust are vital to the success of a marriage, it's a thin line between what secrets are acceptable and which ones will haunt an individual and hurt a marriage. If you begin to feel distance or avoidance in your marriage, and you think it may be the result of a secret, then it is time for you to consult a professional counselor.

Keeping Secrets

There is a difference between private things or thoughts and secrecy. One way you can tell if you are keeping a secret that should be shared is to look at your physical responses when trying to hide a secret. If you notice increases in your blood pressure, blinking rates, perspiration, and breathing, this is probably a secret that needs to be shared.

Another approach is to ask yourself why you are keeping the secret. Is it because you fear being seen as a fool, or you are afraid of being rejected by your spouse? Is keeping the secret truly best for your marriage? Is your intimacy with one another being enhanced or hindered by this secret? You need to carefully weigh the pros and cons of not sharing something with your spouse. If you don't ever take a risk in your relationship, how will you know how much love and trust exist between the two of you?

What Are Secrets in a Marriage?

When you think that something in your past or present is negative and unacceptable to your spouse, and you keep this to yourself, it is a secret. People may have secrets both in their current lives and in their past. Usually, a secret is about a situation or an experience where one's own ethical or moral boundaries have been crossed and feelings of guilt, shame, confusion, and fear are strong. Some types of personal secrets are embezzlement, shoplifting, addiction to pornography, sexual abuse, abortion, drug addiction, lying about something, cheating, an affair, incest, sexual orientation, or letting a child be adopted.

FACT

A person's attitudes about keeping secrets in a marriage often reflect this issue in their parent's marriage. If your mother and father often kept secrets from one another, then you may be more prone to do the same in your own marital relationship.

Why Secrets Are Kept

Oftentimes, people keep secrets because they don't want to face the consequences of the secretive behavior or they don't want to see the reaction of someone they love when they hear the secret. People who keep secrets worry that they won't be loved or respected if the truth is known. Secrecy can also be a way to avoid responsibility in a relationship. People keep secrets out of fear of being judged. They withhold information as a way of manipulating their spouse or protecting themselves. Some rationalize a secret by saying doing so protects a spouse from being upset over the contents of the secret. Depending on the amount of stigma attached to their secret, they may have concerns of having a tarnished reputation or of being ridiculed if found out.

Consequences of Secrets

Secrets cause people to build protective walls by avoiding specific dates, people, or situations that are connected to the secret. The emotional energy that is required to keep secrets from unraveling is huge and can cause major problems in a marriage. Keeping secrets with the intent of deluding or hurting a spouse is a sign that the marriage is in trouble. Some examples of secrets that are harmful to a marriage include hiding job problems, seeing relatives and friends on the sly, not paying bills and spending money on other items, not revealing an illness, lying about a previous marriage, being quiet about future plans, or having an affair.

Sharing It All

Having an expectation that full disclosure will be part of a marriage is quite possibly an impossibility because people often don't realize the depth or importance of their own past experiences, feelings, thoughts, fears, and more.

Knowing What to Reveal

Some people don't share things because they just don't think sharing their past will have any positive impact on their marriage. Married partners may often share that they've had sexual relationships prior to their marriage. However, going into detail with names, dates, and descriptions can create damaging images in the mind of a partner. Spouses should not have the role of being one's moral guardian.

Additionally, if George has a one-night stand while on a business trip, feels guilt and shame and knows it was a stupid mistake, should he tell his wife? What if he gets tested for an STD, and finds out he wasn't infected. Should he still confess this episode that he knows in his heart he will not repeat? The important question for George to ask himself is why he would be telling her. If he does tell his wife, she then has the burden of responsibility for deciding whether or not to forgive. Telling her can be a very selfish act. What purpose is served by telling her?

This kind of secret is a heavy burden filled with pain, guilt, and shame. Some people say they'd want to know, some say they wouldn't. These situations aren't black and white. This is another example of a person who should seek the counsel of a therapist or minister.

Knowing When to Hold Your Tongue

Being intimate with your spouse doesn't give you the right to say what you think all the time. On the other hand, that's not saying you have to walk on eggshells and watch everything you say. However, there are times in a marriage when it is prudent to be quiet and to refrain from speaking. Discord can result from saying things without thinking first. Never bring up old history when you're angry.

FACT

Being able to postpone a discussion shows that the two of you have confidence in your marriage and have the ability to resolve issues. However, it is important that you don't fall into the habit of postponing important talks. That type of continued avoidance can undermine your relationship, intensify your scrabbles, and shows a lack of confidence in one another to deal with difficult topics.

Some partners need time to mull their thoughts over before discussing a situation further. When a partner needs to vent, the proper response is to listen without responding. Some issues and problems may need to remain unsettled and unsolved for a short time. Times to hold your tongue include:

- Before going to bed.
- When intoxicated.

- In very stressful situations.
- If either of you are in a bad mood.
- When very angry or in a rage.
- While tired or ill.

Privacy Concerns

Although secrecy can be detrimental to a marriage, privacy does not need to be feared. Some believe that individual privacy can create a barrier to intimacy since becoming a married couple means the two shall become one. This sense of "oneness" that some proclaim as necessary to a solid marriage relationship can create hostility. You can't become a couple or have that sense of oneness if what you share causes division and distance.

When spouses don't honor the sense of individual privacy in a marriage, they limit their intimacy with one another. In order for a person to be intimate with another person, the inner core of who they are must be personally known first.

What Is Privacy?

Everyone has a need for some privacy in his or her lives. This type of privacy includes having alone time and getting to know yourself. Privacy does not create incompatibility.

Being intimate with one another doesn't mean you have to divulge all your thoughts, all your dreams, all your fears, or all your fantasies. It doesn't mean you have to blend or meld into one another. It takes two complete, unique individuals to be intimate with one another. Your spouse was attracted to the person you were. Losing your identity by letting go of your interests, friends, and aspects of your personality is denying yourself and your partner of the gift of your individuality. Privacy isn't about secrets.

The Importance of Privacy

As a teenager, you probably valued your privacy. Most teens place a great deal of importance on having their own room and being able to close their door to keep the world at bay. Time alone was necessary for you then, and it is still necessary as an adult. Being married doesn't take away the need for being able to shut out the world now and then.

People enjoy reading romance and spy novels because reading is generally a private experience. They enable an escape from the trials, concerns, and routines of everyday life. Allowing one's partner emotional space and respecting your partner's privacy is a deep form of intimacy and trust in itself. A certain amount of privacy is necessary for being mentally healthy. There are times when there are inner thoughts, artistic creations, and self-revelations that need time to ferment in your hearts and in your minds. Most everyone keeps some aspects of their life private, such as bathroom habits, bodily functions, and the way they keep their dresser drawers sorted.

Again, balance is needed. Too much aloneness or private time can be detrimental to a marital relationship.

Garbage Dumping

There is a great difference in sharing something important like a recent infidelity in order to rebuild a marriage and sharing information from the past that is shared only to hurt the other person or to relieve one's guilt. The latter, dropping a bomb from the past or continuing to rehash old issues, is garbage dumping. This sort of sharing is *not* healthy for a marriage relationship.

When a spouse feels compelled to reveal all, although it may seem honest and open on the surface, in reality it may not be. If you have a deep, dark, hidden secret from many years ago, think twice before sharing it with your spouse. Seek counseling, individual therapy, or visit a pastor or priest first. Otherwise, you could be transferring a burden from one set of shoulders to another. The guilty partner may feel justified for past behavior if a spouse's reaction is either one of anger or of acceptance. It can become a no-win situation for the spouse doing the listening. This is a difficult concept for many couples.

The revelation of an action or event is a confession and shouldn't be confused with trying to be more open and honest with your spouse. The difference is that confession or garbage dumping involves past behaviors and openness deals with feelings, thoughts, and situations in the present.

FACT

The term *garbage dumping* means bringing up things from the past in order to hurt one's spouse. It does not mean talking about an infidelity so that a couple can begin the healing process and hopefully rebuild their marriage.

Garbage dumping is throwing mud from your past and telling about something done many years ago to relieve your own guilty feelings. Knowing about your spouse's past and family of origin issues is important, of course. It helps bring an understanding and perspective to the present. However, garbage dumping is an issue in which even marriage counselors and therapists disagree. Some maintain that complete honesty at all costs is necessary, with every juicy detail revealed. Others believe that such revelations could be used as a weapon during conflict or become a roadblock to intimacy. Look at the why, when, and how when making the decision to tell.

Trust Issues

Even when a spouse has felt betrayed or lied to, trust can be rebuilt. But it takes work—lots and lots of work. It also takes time. The time required will vary from individual to individual.

Trust requires forgiveness. It requires healing. During the process of rebuilding a relationship the level of trust may be quite low. As time passes, if a couple can grow to know one another more deeply, and on a feeling level, the decision to trust will be easier for both partners to make.

Although infidelity, lies, or broken promises can severely damage a marital relationship, both partners making the decision to work on rebuilding trust can save the marriage. Here's how:

- Let go of the past. As with disillusionment, this will take a decision to love. Don't obsess about what *was*. Focus on what *is*.

- Make a decision regarding forgiveness. One of you will need to decide to forgive and the other will need to decide to be forgiven.
- Show that the errant behavior is a thing of the past by changing behaviors. Actions do speak louder than words.
- Set some specific goals for your marriage. Do this as a couple. Include a renewal of the commitment the two of you have to your marriage and to one another.
- Share your pain and give your spouse a chance to acknowledge your feelings.
- Work on your listening skills. Make sure you listen with your heart, and not just with your ears.
- Be honest. But avoid using words that you know will trigger conflict. Use nonblaming "I" statements and don't say, "always," "must," "never," or "should."
- Be open to seeking counseling to gain better insight into what caused the trust to be broken.
- Remember that rebuilding trust takes time. It won't happen overnight. It's okay to remember the incidents and the betrayal.

When it comes to betrayal or being lied to, you shouldn't expect your partner to "get over it" quickly or in your own time frame. Allow your spouse all the time needed.

Along with individual space and privacy, honesty is essential in a healthy marriage. Since lies can create enormous problems in a marriage, it is better to say that you can't talk about something than to lie about it. Rebuilding a relationship after a betrayal takes work, time, honesty, vulnerability, openness, and courage.

Don't demand to know everything about your spouse. Trust one another to tell what needs to be told. Some secrets can destroy a marriage by not being shared, and some secrets can destroy a marriage when they are shared. You may need to have a third party—again, a therapist or a minister—help you in making the decision to share something from your past. Being open and vulnerable to one another does increase intimacy along with remaining faithful through the tough times.

Chapter 10

Dealing with Disagreements

Every married couple will experience conflict. In fact, conflict in a marriage is normal and doesn't mean a marriage is in trouble. Sometimes the disagreements may be over something that seems insignificant, whereas other times it may be over something much more difficult to work out. Couples in successful long-term marriages have learned how to handle their disagreements effectively—with respect for each other and themselves.

Who's Right?

More often than not, everyone likes to be right. Being right means that you have the right answer, or are able to solve a problem successfully, or get to do things your way. Being right makes a person feel validated, important, superior, smart, exonerated, and clever.

The Other Side

However, there are times in a marriage when it is more important to be in a relationship with your spouse than it is to be right. This means that even though you feel you are right about a particular situation or issue, you don't push this fact. For instance, Mary and Hal are discussing how to spend their weekend together. Mary wants to drive to a neighboring small town and check out antique stores. Hal wants to go hiking in the mountains. Mary truly dislikes trekking through the woods, but recognizes the nice weather is calling Hal to the outdoors. He had previously agreed to go on the antique shopping trip, but she has made the decision that the topic isn't worth fighting about and places her relationship with Hal over proving that she is right (about his previous promise to shop). Additionally, she knows that what she really wants is time alone with Hal, and she will be receiving that whether it is doing it her way or his way.

When you have a disagreement, often the best way to deal with it is to compromise. People compromise because being reconciled in their relationship breathes life into their sense of being.

Control is an elusive behavior. You don't need to control your spouse, and in reality, you can't control your spouse forever without destroying your marriage. Neither can a marriage succeed when ideas and feelings are met with contempt or rudeness.

Doormat and Control Issues

There is a danger in living out the concept of preferring to be in a relationship versus being right. If one partner is the one who always backs down, then that spouse can turn into a doormat. This isn't a healthy way to handle conflict in a marriage.

When one spouse prefers peace at any price, a marriage is in trouble because one mate is taking control and holding on to it. Control usually comes from fear, a lack of trust, or a sense of insecurity. Giving up control is often perceived as a sign of weakness, yet winning a battle due to the submissive behavior of a spouse is in fact losing. Spouses whose partners stop giving in all the time often feel confused and angrier.

Shirley is a submissive spouse who thinks that keeping the peace in her marriage with Tom is the right thing to do. She doesn't understand why Tom is becoming more agitated with her and seems more distant. Tom is less attracted to Shirley because she is no longer the enthusiastic, feisty woman he married. Although Tom wants Shirley to be the way she was when they first met, he also doesn't want to relinquish control. In order to change from being a doormat, you must determine which issues are just too important to back away from.

The Importance of Handling Conflict

When a couple doesn't effectively handle conflict, they are doomed to repeat behaviors that hurt each other because they haven't found solutions or reached closure on the issues that are tearing them apart. The problems, like a snowball rolling down a hill, continue to accumulate and overwhelm their love for one another. Additionally, the negativity between the two of them will increase and create even more unresolved conflict. It becomes a vicious circle that will drive a wedge between the spouses and ultimately destroy a marriage. This happens because the negativity and anger will overshadow any good actions or memories the couple may have had.

The impact of marital conflict on children is another reason why couples need to learn how to effectively confront one another. Children who live in families full of hostility generally experience low self-esteem, scholastic and social problems, and higher levels of stress. Parents owe it to their children to be role models for healthy problem-solving skills.

For every action, there is a reaction. When you throw a pebble into a puddle of water, rings will flow out from the pebble's point of impact.

Then they return back to where the pebble originally hit. Your actions and decisions in your marriage work the same way. They all have reactions or consequences. Consider how your partner responds to romance, praise, anger, and hostility.

FACT

Unhappy spouses experience more physical illness and emotional problems than individuals in successful marriages.

For instance, a consequence of a husband ignoring his wife during the day is that she is not likely to be receptive to sexual intimacy that night. A consequence of negativity is blaming one another and lowered self-images. The consequence of spending money you don't have is you will find yourselves in debt.

Throughout your married life together, the two of you will face consequences of your decisions and behaviors in a variety of areas such as legal, emotional, health, financial, and lifestyle consequences. Having children, growing older together, and dealing with change all affect a marriage and all are potential areas of conflict. Being aware of the consequences your choices have on your relationship helps you to keep love, trust, and mutual respect a top priority in your relationship.

Guidelines for Fighting

The term *fighting* as used here refers to a discussion about opposing viewpoints. It is referring to an argument, not a knockdown, physical type of conflict. Psychologists can tell more about a married couple from the way they fight than from what they fight about. Healthy, fair fighting and conflict, when done correctly, can strengthen a marriage. It is a form of communication that can be used to clear the air.

Sticking to the Subject

Know what you are arguing about and make sure that you both stick to the subject and leave unrelated problems out of your discussion. If you think that you are drifting into other issues, say so. The two of you may need to actually define what it is you are fighting about. Don't attack your partner. Remember that your fight is between the two of you. Keep your in-laws and friends out of it.

Hitting below the Belt

Don't hit below the belt or call one another names. The better you know one another, the easier it is to target sensitive areas or weak spots in one another's self-esteem. Don't use endearing terms or pet names in sarcastic tones. Make sure that you aren't rude in the way you speak to your spouse. It is also important to not be overly sensitive or defensive, either.

Teasing

Although having a sense of humor is important, it is important that you be cautious when using humor in an argument. Your partner can misinterpret some teasing. Even if said in jest, some comments just aren't funny. Inappropriate teasing can be offensive and can hurt a relationship. Cutting remarks can wound deeply.

If you think you or your spouse are using teasing as a smoke screen, or as a way to say something negative through insulting put-downs and supposedly funny remarks, think twice about this behavior. Don't make malicious comments about your partner's appearance, weight, a perceived physical flaw, or capabilities. If a spouse doesn't like to be teased, accept it without making accusations about being a poor sport. If you are the one being teased, and don't like it, tell your partner. Ask your spouse why he or she would say something that is so hurtful.

Teasing can be an effective tool in building strong relationships if the teasing is good-natured and playful. But at the first sign of hurt feelings, stop.

History

Don't bring up past history or issues that have already been discussed and settled. If you find yourselves fighting about the same things over and over again, you need to realize that you haven't reached a livable solution on that issue. Face the issue together, and deal with it by making a decision to bring it to closure. You can set a time in a few months to re-examine the troubling situation and to see if your decision has helped solve the problem. Rehashing mistakes and hurtful behaviors of the past is wasted energy and benefits neither you nor your marriage.

"48-Hour Rule"

If you find yourself angry about something and don't bring it up with your partner within forty-eight hours, you will have to let it go. This will help you both understand the urgency and seriousness of dealing with problems right away. Although it can be difficult to do, remembering the "48-hour rule" will prevent having bothersome little things build up and explode into a larger fight.

Set an Appointment

If the two of you need a time-out or if your spouse isn't ready to discuss the issue, set an appointment within the next twenty-four hours to have your fair fight. This may sound silly, but it works. Both of you will have time to collect your thoughts, and you will be calmer as you work together to solve the problem or issue.

Listening

Make sure that you listen fully to one another during a fight. Don't interrupt. Try to use "I" sentences instead of "you" sentences. As previously discussed, look at one another while you talk and be aware of nonverbal signs of distancing, being closed, or apprehension. Watch the tone of your voice. Being loud can intimidate your spouse and make it more difficult to listen to you. Make sure that you are free of distractions such as the phone ringing or the television playing in the room.

Blaming and Reconciliation

Don't play the blame game or accuse one another. It can be very easy during a fight to pay more attention to your spouse's weaknesses and bad or unusual habits than it is to look at your own faults. If you believe that it is your partner who is the cause of your conflicts, and the only one who needs to change, remember that the only person *you* can change is yourself. Blaming one another serves no purpose because in most relationships, both partners need to take responsibility for their role in the problems of their marriage.

ALERT!

If the source of conflict is physical or emotional abuse, or involves an addiction, then a different approach is needed. Seek professional help as soon as possible.

Your spouse is not responsible for either your personal happiness or unhappiness. Be open to asking for forgiveness and being willing to forgive. Although forgiving may be difficult, not being open to reconciliation can cause great emotional harm to both of you, and to your marriage.

Holding Hands

Hold hands while talking during your fight. It will help you to remember that you are not fighting to win, but for the good of your relationship. It puts your focus on what's at stake—your relationship. The gesture of holding hands can also communicate to your spouse your willingness to have an intimate conversation and your willingness to be open to all viewpoints. It's an additional way for the two of you to stay connected and respectful of one another.

If either of you are too enraged to be touched, then don't try to hold hands. Respect the need for some personal space until there is less anger.

Going to Bed Angry

Although going to bed angry is unhealthy physically, continuing a fight when overly tired or too angry isn't a good idea either. If it is getting late, and it is obvious that you are still far apart on any type of compromise or solution, call a truce, agree to continue the discussion the next day, and get some sleep. Keep that appointment with one another to finish the fight. It is important that the fight not be left unresolved, or resentment can grow.

Common Areas of Conflict

Conflict in marriage is often sparked by disputes over some common issues and areas in a relationship.

- **Money.** Financial disputes can occur within a marriage when a couple is broke as well as when a couple is doing well financially. Disagreement over how funds are managed, spent, and saved are common.
- **Sex.** There are many reasons that sex is a topic that raises conflict in a marriage. Differing expectations and libidos, along with a sense of embarrassment, can lead to avoidance in talking about needs and desires.
- **In-laws.** Although having a problem with one another over in-laws is more common in the first few years of marriage, it is an issue that can haunt a couple throughout their relationship. Generally, people have difficulties when in-laws are critical or controlling, or when one partner feels uncomfortable visiting or being visited by in-laws. When dealing with this issue, avoid being critical of your partner's parents.
- **Parenting.** Differing views about how to raise kids, along with the stress and worry that children can bring to a relationship, can create a great deal of disharmony in a marriage.

As the two of you work on communicating, make sure that you don't try to read each other's minds or jump to conclusions; each of you should have equal time to share your thoughts and feelings about the issue. If one of you is monopolizing the conversation, it isn't a true attempt at communicating. Watch your own body language and try to refrain from rolling your eyes, crossing your arms, sighing big sighs, speaking in a sarcastic or loud tone, and having facial expressions that could signify your lack of interest or obvious disagreement. Showing that you are really listening to what your spouse has to say is a sign of respect and love.

Although every couple needs to learn how to deal with the big potential conflict areas such as finances, parenting, in-laws, sex, religion, and time, couples also need to know how to handle disagreements over smaller issues. What color to paint the bedroom, how clean the house needs to be, what brand of coffee to purchase, who has control over the remote, and how to stir the spaghetti sauce can also turn into serious areas of conflict.

Problem Solving

If it is obvious that the timing of your argument is detrimental to being able to have a healthy outcome, say so. Don't fight just before going to bed, or if either of you are drunk, in a bad mood, overly tired, or ill. If you find yourself in the midst of an argument and realize that the two of you need a time-out due to extreme anger or frustration, state this concern. Asking for a time-out or setting an appointment to finish your fight is a sign of your commitment to finding a workable solution you can both live with. The appointment should be set so forty-eight hours don't pass without resolution.

Setting an appointment to get together to discuss a specific problem ensures that both spouses will be prepared both mentally and emotionally to talk about the same topic. When you two are faced with a difficult problem to solve, it is important for each of you to have opportunity to say what you want to say about the issue. Don't rush through the process of discussing the issue so that both can feel understood. Brainstorming without judging the comments can help a couple come up with a compromise solution.

Anger Management

Reacting to your spouse in anger can impede your judgment and makes communication more difficult. Anger can cause people to yell, throw things, become tongue-tied, cry, stomp out of a room, and even leave. This type of anger can also lead to physical abuse.

All of these inappropriate behaviors accomplish two things. They intimidate the other spouse and they create an environment where the disagreements are not resolved. If either of you are overreacting or having difficulty in maintaining your composure when buttons are pushed, it may be time to seek professional help. Some other recommendations for managing your anger include:

- When listening to your spouse during an argument, make sure to listen for common ground between the two of you, and give feedback as to what you are hearing your spouse say.
- Make sure that your arguments take place in person. Telephone calls, e-mail, notes or letters, and answering machine messages hide nonverbal communication and can create additional misunderstandings between the two of you.
- If you find yourself becoming defensive or wanting to run away from the conflict, communicate these feelings rather than defending yourself or walking away.
- Don't let aggravating situations build up. Talk with your spouse about what is bothering you. This will keep your arguments on the topic being discussed and you won't drift off into other issues.
- Be open to hearing your partner's side of the issue. Don't enter the conversation with a closed mind.
- Don't blame your spouse for your feelings. What you feel is your own responsibility.
- Accept that it may take time to learn how to maintain emotional self-control in tense and controversial conversations with your partner. If you aren't doing well at this on your own, look for anger management courses taught in your locale.
- If either of you gives yourself permission to yell, throw things, and show great anger and rage when you are arguing with one another, your spouse will be fearful and distant. Don't allow yourself to behave in this fashion.
- If either of you are to the point of rage, remember to call a time-out. You may need more time to research the issues you are dealing with in order to be more objective about them.

ALERT!

The amount of unresolved conflicts in marriages is nearly 60 percent. Many long-term married couples find themselves still arguing over the same issues.

Again, conflict in a marriage is not the problem. All married couples have disagreements. What creates major difficulties in a marriage is not being able to effectively argue.

Conflict can be a positive aspect of a marriage as the honesty and openness can enhance a relationship. When you fight for your relationship instead of fighting to win individually, you will find yourselves in a better place as a couple. Knowing how to fight fairly, on a win-win basis, and how to reconcile and heal is one of the most important things a couple needs to learn.

Chapter 11

The Nitty-Gritty of Finances

Although couples promise "for richer, for poorer," money matters are the number one reason couples divorce. Regardless of whether a couple has money or doesn't have money, finances can be a major point of contention in a marriage. The major marital disagreements about money are how much to save, how to spend it, and who has to take responsibility for paying the bills.

Setting a Budget

The thought of having a budget shouldn't send you running for the hills. A budget is deciding what you are going to do with the money that is coming in. It is a financial plan that takes a look at how much money is coming in and how much is going out. It should be a flexible plan that you feel comfortable adjusting and revising.

It is important that when you are making a decision about having a budget, you both can claim ownership to it and both of you are willing to accept responsibility for it. Although the thought of setting up a budget may make you think of a restrictive lifestyle and penny-pinching, a budget can actually free the two of you to handle your finances more effectively. Some people think they don't need a budget because they don't earn enough money. If they can pay their bills each month they feel successful. This is a myth. Having a budget can help any couple manage their finances regardless of how much they have.

If you've been married for some time and haven't had a budget, consider putting one together. This has to be a couple's decision. Having one spouse decide that this is what needs to be done will only create more hostility and uneasiness with the budget and in communicating about finances.

ALERT!

It will probably take you two years to settle on a workable budget. It will require negotiation and compromise. The first year you will be figuring out how much you are actually spending and want to spend. The second year you will be putting into practice what you discovered the first year.

Keep It Simple

Your budget is your money plan. Keep it simple and realistic so you won't be tempted to abandon your plan. Make it achievable so that you two can be successful in living within your budget. When you feel successful it will be easier for you to continue to work on your budget. List your income, and routine necessary expenses such as your rent or mortgage, utilities, food, transportation costs, and insurance. List other items you spend money on such as cable TV, Internet access, clothing, hobbies, gifts, and so on. Also list savings and include a slush account for unexpected expenses. One way that couples devise a realistic budget is to for each to develop a budget. They then take the two "my" budgets and develop an "our" budget.

Budget Advantages

Your budget will reveal if you may be charging more to credit cards than you can cover each month or if you are spending too much in certain categories. It will help you set goals for yourselves so that you can have an emergency fund and savings for future goals. The reality is that using credit cards is using money you don't have. A budget will help you see more clearly the areas where you are overspending. If you find that you are relying on credit cards, consider cutting them up or putting them in a lockbox to be used only in an emergency.

Budget Resources

Many computer software programs will make the budgeting process easier, but you can make a very good budget with pen and paper. Libraries and bookstores are full of resources to help you develop your budget. Many localities also offer financial workshops that provide valuable information and help. Don't let excuses stop you from taking this important step together.

FACT

Money is the number one reason couples argue. It's also the main reason that couples divorce.

Financial Differences

Having different spending habits, savings goals, fears about being poor, and views on investing will create tension in a relationship. When financial problems surface in a marriage, a power struggle may occur and the one making the most money may become controlling.

It's important to realize how your financial differences can affect your marriage. She may be perfectly happy packing an inexpensive lunch to take to work each day, while he believes his reputation in his profession is damaged by brown-bagging it. She thinks nothing of spending money on new clothes for herself and the kids, and he sees only closets already bulging at the seams with clothing. She can't understand his need to spend money on fishing accessories, yet he disdains her wanting to spend money on a vacation every year.

You learned most of your attitudes toward money when you were a kid. It is critical that the two of you talk about your monetary attitudes and expectations. Define what is important to you financially, and help your spouse understand what you value when it comes to money. How you handle your money, in spite of your differences, is a decision that the two of you should make together. Without knowing where one another stands on these issues, you will be making decisions with blinders on.

His/Her/Our Checking Accounts

A big decision that married couples must make is where to keep their money. It is important to realize that what works for some people may not work for others. Some couples pool all their resources and income into one joint account, others keep their funds separate in individual accounts, and many couples have both a joint and individual accounts. It is not recommended that only one spouse have access to the funds.

QUESTION?

Should I maintain my own bank account separate from my spouse?
Financial advisers generally recommend that when a couple is on a firm foundation financially, they should each have their own account.

One of the reasons individuals desire to have their own separate checking accounts is a concern about what they would do if their relationship falls apart. They want to have their own emergency fund to fall back on. Another reason is so that they can buy gifts for their spouse or others without taking money out of a joint account. Having separate accounts allows them to do what they want with their funds, whether it is to save it or spend it. They can also spend money without having to justify the expenditure to their spouse.

Some couples divide up the bills and make decisions as to who is going to pay what. Others pay all the household type of bills through a joint account into which they put equal amounts or an equal percentage of their individual incomes. The number of accounts that a couple has isn't as important as how much communication about money is taking place between the spouses. If the system that you develop isn't working, change it and try something else.

Financial Personalities

Many people, regardless of how they spend or save money, define their own self-worth on how much money they have access to. Generally, people fall into roles when it comes to money. Do you see yourselves in any of these roles?

- Spenders are folks who buy things without thinking about the consequences of their purchases.
- Hoarders save everything, throw nothing away, dislike spending money, and love budgets.
- Worriers nag a great deal when it comes to money issues.
- Planners want to track every penny.

Problems often surface when spenders marry hoarders, worriers, or planners. Even when two spenders or two hoarders marry one another, conflict over money issues can still be intense. Differences in their financial attitudes will surface eventually when a monetary crisis hits. The best way to handle differences in financial personalities is to honestly admit to your attitudes and behaviors about money. Together, set some guidelines as to how to handle spending or saving, or planning or dealing with the fear of being poor, so that neither of you carry these behaviors to the extreme.

It appears that many women place financial security high on their priority lists and that some are natural savers. Building a nest egg is an age-old practical, female tradition that is becoming more open and acceptable in today's marriages.

Stash Money

Having a stash of money hidden away is not necessarily a sign of a failing relationship nor does it necessarily show a lack of trust in one another. Women in past generations did not have easy access to cash. In order to have money for a personal indulgence or a special gift for a loved one, they learned how to save here and there, and to earn "pin money" on the side. (The term "pin money" originally referred to money that women earned on the side to add to their clothing funds.)

Many individuals feel a need to have money tucked away for a rainy day. These funds often provide emotional comfort and a sense of security. The funds are often diverted in small amounts from paychecks, bonuses, reimbursement accounts, household allowances, or even spare change or money earned by moonlighting at a part-time job.

FACT

When *Redbook Magazine* did a poll on pin money or a secret stash, the results showed that about 34 percent of women keep some money, generally less than $500, hidden away.

However, hiding money from your spouse isn't a good practice. Having your own account that your spouse knows about is a more honest approach to handling this need for some separate funds.

Paying Bills

Although it is not recommended for one spouse to have complete control of the finances, in many relationships, one spouse does write all the checks and pay all the bills. This happens because one spouse may have more skill at this than the other, or one spouse may have more time to commit to this chore. When this is the case, it is important that the other spouse knows what is happening with the finances. This will also make it easier during an emergency situation for the other partner to pick up the ball and take on this responsibility if needed. Many couples successfully write the checks and pay the bills together by setting aside one or two evenings each month to discuss and handle this aspect of their lives together.

When You Don't Have Enough Money

The first thing to do when you realize that you don't have enough money to pay all your bills is to not panic. The second thing is to not go into avoidance mode. Not dealing with the financial crisis will only make it worse.

Together, prioritize which bills need to be paid so that you can keep a roof over your head, utilities kept turned on, insurances paid, and food on the table. Contact your creditors before they contact you and explain that you are having financial difficulties. If having bill collectors calling you adds to your stress level, request all contact be through the mail and that they not call you. Educate yourself about your rights in debt collection. Find out what resources for short-term help are available in your community. Many local food banks don't require proof of need. Discern what you could sell to increase your cash situation. Decide what you can live without for a few months, such as cable TV, packaged foods, renting videos, other expenses pertaining to hobbies, and new clothes.

If a financial crisis hits during a holiday season, it can be even more difficult to deal with. Become creative in your gift-giving by making handmade gifts, giving gifts of your time, or visiting secondhand shops and thrift stores.

Continue to stay in communication with one another about whether your financial situation is improving or getting worse. If things aren't improving for you financially, seek the help of a financial consultant, planner, or accountant.

Frugal Living

For some couples, frugal living is a choice, whether they are having financial difficulties or not. There is a sense of beating the system when they can find a great deal on something they need or want. Living a frugal lifestyle does not mean living without.

There are numerous resources in books and on the Internet on how to live in a frugal, but nonrestricting or nonsacrificing way. Some items that are readily obtained at less than retail prices are clothing, books, baskets, suitcases, CDs, DVDs, VHS tapes, old records and cassette tapes, knick-knacks, pots, pans, dishes, drinking glasses, toys, stuffed animals, jigsaw puzzles, linens, holiday decorations, jewelry, furniture, and appliances. Check out local thrift stores and garage sales. This is another area that requires an agreement between the two of you so that one of you doesn't feel stifled by the decision to live frugally.

Planning for the Future

Without a financial plan, your life together will be like a sailboat without a sail, drifting aimlessly at the mercy of the wind and water currents. Sure, you may have an interesting journey, but wouldn't it be more fun and rewarding to have some control over your destination?

Before you can plan your financial future together, you both need to recognize and understand your feelings and thoughts about money. Know what your own dreams are for your future, and share that with your spouse. Who you are and the dreams you have will have a very large impact on the financial goals you choose to set. This is another situation where individual goals must be listed and then merged together to create a united plan for financial goals for the two of you.

Divide your goals into short-term and long-term. Long-term goals encompass plans that are five years or more into the future. Any financial goal that you hope to achieve within a year is considered short-term. Mid-term goals are those that fall in between, and from a planning perspective, they should be treated like a short-term goal.

Long-Term and Short-Term Goals

Your long-term goals could include items such as your retirement plans, funding your children's higher education costs, and home ownership. When you are hoping to take a special vacation, or are thinking about purchasing a new car, or are considering continuing either one of your educations, or you realize that you need to increase your emergency fund, these are short-term goals.

Crisis Planning

A major part of future planning is also being prepared for a financial crisis. It is important to have a game plan as to how you would handle an extended illness or loss of employment. A monetary crisis can also result in the short-term by an unexpected expense such as having to have major repair work done on your vehicle or home, or having to relocate. A gambling problem or other addiction can also trigger an economic disaster. Ask yourselves what you would be willing to do to survive a severe monetary crisis.

Yearly Checkup

It is important that the two of you know where you stand financially. At least once each year (January is a good month for this), set aside a couple hours of undistracted time to sit down and discuss your finances in depth. Another positive aspect of this financial checkup is that if you find yourselves in a financial crisis, you will be in a better position to handle it. Make sure you include these topics in your discussion:

- **Budget.** Talk about how your money is being spent. Perhaps you can find some expenses to cut back on. If either of you is surprised about the amount of expenses in a specific category, discuss why you think this is happening. Make sure your budget is workable.
- **Debts and Assets.** Although it isn't always an enjoyable task, knowing how much you own and how much you owe will help in your long-range financial planning.

- **Location of Important Documents.** Make sure that you both know where you keep important papers and documents such as wills, tax information, bank account numbers, insurance documents, investment information, and so forth.
- **Financial Vulnerability.** Overspending, having too much debt, low income, gambling, and lack of job security could be situations that jeopardize your financial stability. Deciding together how to strengthen your financial position will lessen the stress that being financially at risk can place on your marriage.
- **Paying Bills.** Re-evaluate if the system you are using for paying your bills is not working.
- **Financial Differences.** Continue your discussion with one another about how your upbringing, culture, and gender influence the way you perceive and deal with monetary issues. Talk about how your parents managed their money and what you liked about it and what you didn't like.
- **Financial Planning.** Look at the financial goals you made last year and see if you are making any progress in achieving them. Develop new goals for the next year, both short-term and long-term.

Money can either be a tool that strengthens your marriage or it can turn into a wedge between the two of you. No matter how difficult it is to face into your thoughts and feelings concerning your finances, it is critical that the two of you talk about your attitudes toward investment strategies, spending money, having or not having a budget, your expenses, and monetary goals.

When you make financial goals together, make a commitment to follow through on the goals until you decide together to change the goals. A budget can help you live within your means. Realize that having more money won't necessarily solve your financial problems. Communication is the key to marital success when it comes to money issues. (E)

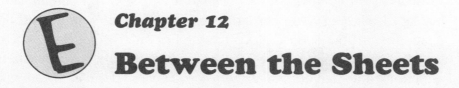

Chapter 12

Between the Sheets

Sex usually isn't a problem in the beginning of a marriage. The enjoyment and excitement of being with your new spouse seems to automatically keep sex frequent in a marriage. Throughout the years, however, the intimacy and sense of desire may lessen. As with other issues in marriage, communication with one another is the key to a healthy sexual relationship. Great sex starts in the morning with intimacy and continues with communication throughout the day.

Intimacy

There is a difference between sex as communication and sex as exercise experience. When sex is communication, the real sexual foreplay starts in the morning and continues throughout the day. When sex is just an activity, communication may be lacking in other areas of the marriage.

Intimacy in a marriage is more than having sex with one another. Intimacy is sharing your heart and feelings as well as your thoughts and opinions with your spouse. If a marriage has only sexual passion and a false notion of romance as a foundation, it is doomed from the start. You are having a degree of intimacy when you share information with your spouse about your past, or your thoughts and opinions on a topic. But there can be more.

What makes intimacy deeper and more meaningful in a marriage is to also share the current feelings that surround the factual information you are communicating. These emotions can change from moment to moment and day to day, so there is always something fresh and new to share with your spouse. A long-lasting marriage requires this type of deep intimacy to keep it alive and growing. A great deal of your deep happiness with one another will be rooted in your moments of intimacy. Being intimate with someone is a very human experience. People aren't intimate with their pets or their cars or their televisions or their bank accounts.

What Is Marital Intimacy?

There are many aspects to marital intimacy, and all are needed in order to have a strong, fulfilling, long-lasting marriage. Having sex with one another is not the only way to be intimate. Many people struggle with wanting to be close to their partner because at the same time they are fearful of being too close. Sharing our values and what we believe in and stand for, and where we've been and where we hope to be, and what we hold close to our hearts and enjoy, is being intimate.

Unconditional love can help bring a couple to being able to freely reveal themselves to each other and to experience true intimacy. You are intimate when you can appreciate the beauty in our world together and when you work side by side to create a meal, decorate a room, build a patio, or plant a garden. There are times that being aware of your spouse's thoughts and feelings can bring you closer. Some couples first notice this type of intimacy when they are coping in the midst of major problems, hurt, or loss. Enjoying one another in fun activities and hobbies is another type of intimacy. Couples who share a religious faith often can connect with one another through a spiritual intimacy.

> Schedule dates with each other. You don't have to have expensive dinners out, but it is important that the two of you have some time alone to just be there for one another.

The more intimate a couple is in all these aspects of their marriage, the more passionate and enjoyable their sexual intimacy will be. Their closeness with one another will be natural and not forced. Partners who are open to an intimate relationship are other-oriented and not self-focused. They have the ability to be open to what their spouse has to share. The sense of connectedness will allow both partners the freedom to continue to discover and be who they are. Intimacy is an empowering experience that is derived from knowing yourself.

Barriers to Intimacy

Some of the roadblocks that can get in the way of your intimacy with one another include:

- Trust issues with your spouse
- An inability to communicate
- Differing intimacy needs or a misunderstanding of what intimacy is all about
- Not spending enough time together as a couple
- Privacy concerns and gender roles
- Desire for power, sex, or money
- Self-doubts, poor self-esteem, fears, and feeling either superior or inferior in your relationship

A fear of being rejected is a giant barrier to intimacy. The possible consequences of being verbally attacked, rejected, not accepted, or possibly being forced to change can make a person not want to share the totality of who they are. Anytime either partner puts a higher priority on things outside their marriage, their intimacy with one another will suffer.

Ways to Improve Intimacy

On a daily basis, the two of you should be able to find a way to let one another know how much you appreciate something they have done or who they are that day. An additional beneficial exercise is to daily share with one another your current feelings. Whether you are talking about a difficult issue or a run-of-the-mill daily experience, share your feelings with each other. Take time to reflect on your memories of your good times together. Make time to discuss your dreams, hopes, fantasies, opinions, values, goals, misunderstandings, hurts, fears, and attitudes. Work on your listening and communication skills. Don't avoid conflict, but make sure you fight fairly. If spirituality is part of your lives, make time to pray together.

It is important to have the positive aspects of your marriage like caring, good conversation, having fun, sex, and being appreciative outweigh by five times the negative aspects like feeling bored, angry, critical, distant, and lonely.

Frequency of Sex

Even though there are lots of surveys done about the frequency of sex in a marriage, comparing your sex life to the sex lives of other couples is not recommended. It has been proved, though, that frequent sex in a marriage does produce some positive benefits other than the enjoyment of the sexual activity.

Couples who have regular sex also have better self-esteem, lower mortality rates, a more positive view of life, and are more connected to their spouses emotionally. From an emotional perspective these couples feel younger, calmer, and are less irritable. They have lower levels of insecure feelings and increased commitment levels. Medically, regular sex is said to relieve menstrual cramps, improve digestion and memory, help folks sleep better, lower fatigue and cravings, and has a therapeutic effect on the immune system. Frequent sex also stimulates new dendrite growth in the brain.

What Gets in the Way of Sex

There are many things that may cause you to have less frequent sex than you might like:

- **Children.** When babies come along, couples discover they are more tired, have more things to do, and less privacy and time alone as a couple. The combination of less time and less energy along with hormonal changes in a woman after childbirth can deprive a couple of a satisfactory sex life with one another.
- **Familiarity.** Predictability and a lack of spontaneity can dampen sexual passion and excitement. However, no matter how many times a couple has made love, the wonder and awe of mutual attraction can still be there. Sex in a long-term marriage can deepen and become a richer experience.
- **Growing older.** When hormone levels decrease, libidos will decrease too. Studies are showing the old adage that "use it or lose it" is true.
- **Conflict.** When a couple isn't effectively handling conflict or problems in their lives, the stress of the hostility and resentment will negatively impact their sex life.
- **Poor self-esteem.** If you don't see yourself as being attractive or sexy or worthy of your partner's love and attention, this can detract from your ability to have a fulfilling sex life.

Giving Your Sex Life a Jump Start

The key way to jump-start your sexual relationship is to talk with one another. If you want a healthy and active sex life, talk with one another about your sexual desires, what turns you on and what turns you off, and your lovemaking expectations. List what is important to you as an individual when it comes to sexual intimacy. Don't worry if books or other people say something is a turn-on and it isn't for you. What you find exciting and what turns you off are very individual issues.

After you've each shared these desires and dislikes on paper, exchange your lists with one another and discuss them. Your marriage will be hurt by unrealistic or unmet expectations. Remember that your sexual intimacy with one another is a continuing process of discovery throughout your years together. Sex is great when there is true intimacy through communication.

Busy lives and hectic schedules may make it necessary to plan for your sexual encounters with each other. It is important to make sex a top priority. You can set the mood in advance by starting the foreplay in the morning. Leaving notes in the house, whispering sweet nothings, giving hugs, sending e-mails, and making phone calls throughout the day lets your spouse know that you are thinking about him or her. Be attentive, kind, and sensitive to your spouse's needs and feelings throughout the day.

It is important to realize that sex isn't going to be perfect each time. Don't compare your sex life to the ones you read about in magazines or in romantic novels or see in movies or on television. Abstinence now and then for a week or so can be beneficial to your relationship if you start to lust after one another more.

Differing Sex Drives

When a couple has differing sex drives, they may find that their intimacy with one another is compromised. If differing sex drives is something that is bothering you, do more than dropping a hint now and then or making a joke about it. If it is a serious problem in your marriage, then it needs serious attention.

Why It Matters

Tremendous frustration, anxiety, and heartbreak are the consequences of discrepancies in sexual desire. When not dealt with either medically or emotionally, this issue can destroy a marriage. The lack of physical attention from a spouse with low sexual desire can leave a partner feeling like an unattractive, unloved, rejected loser. The rejected spouse may develop low self-esteem and think the lack of interest is somehow his or her fault because he or she is too fat, too skinny, or not attractive enough. In addition to anger, feelings of sadness, vulnerability, and confusion surface.

FACT

Therapists define a nonsexual marriage as being sexual with one another fewer than ten times a year. It is estimated that one in five married couples has this type of relationship.

Some marriages appear to be the perfect marriage because the couple shares similar interests, has love for one another, and rarely argues. Yet they've slept apart for most of their marriage and the sadness from the lack of intimacy turns the marriage into a sham. Because it is an embarrassing and humiliating experience, many couples refuse to get professional help. The consequences of lack of sex in a marriage can be a downward spiral. Less sex causes less talking and the communication gap in a marriage will invariably get wider.

Possible Causes of Low Sex Drives

You shouldn't try to diagnose low libido on your own. There are numerous possible medical and emotional causes for this condition including:

- Childbirth
- Diabetes
- Hypothyroidism
- Hormone deficiencies (especially low levels of testosterone)
- Fatigue
- Stress
- Family worries
- Not enough sleep
- Working long hours

- Emotional problems
- Marriage problems and unresolved conflicts
- Depression and anxiety disorders
- Incontinence
- Anger
- Antidepressants, tranquilizers, and other medications
- Past sexual abuse
- Diminished blood flow to the vagina or uterus
- Injury to nerves and blood vessels after a hysterectomy
- A desire to control or punish spouse
- Sexual orientation conflict or confusion
- Too much alcohol consumption
- Use of heroin, cocaine, or marijuana
- Cardiovascular disease
- Arthritis
- Parkinson's disease
- Anemia
- Endocrine or neurological disorders
- Chronic pain
- Infidelity

ALERT!

It is important that you seek the advice of a physician or other qualified health providers with any questions you may have regarding a medical or psychological condition.

Different Sexual Styles

If you really want a fulfilling sexual relationship with your spouse, you must, throughout your marriage, honestly communicate your expectations, your fears, your desires, your concerns, and your preferred sexual style.

Many couples never talk about this aspect of their sexual relationship. Most couples find themselves using all of these styles or moods at some time in their married lives. Everyone has a preferred style but enjoys experiencing other styles to spice up their sex life.

- **Funny.** If you enjoy teasing one another, having fun, and much laughter while you are enjoying sex, this is your style.
- **Spiritual.** When you are aware of an intimate union of your minds, bodies, and souls, and have a deep appreciation of your love for one another, you are experiencing the spiritual style.
- **Lusty.** The lusty style includes feeling a bit wicked, having "quickies," and wanting sex with your spouse just for the sake of having sex.
- **Fantasy.** Although some individuals prefer to keep their sexual fantasies private, this style involves the two of you cooperating with one another in acting out your fantasies.
- **Tender.** This healing style includes light touches, massages, stroking, and a gentle ministering to each other.
- **Angry.** Another form of healing sex is when you make love to one another even when you are angry with each other. (Just be sure that the conflict and issues are resolved according to the "48-hour rule.")

QUESTION?

How important is good sex?
When asked to rank factors that contribute to marital satisfaction, most couples rank good sex lower than respect, honesty, empathy, emotional intimacy, and companionship.

When There Are Problems

If you are having sex problems, be honest with yourselves and check to see of there are other problems in your marriage that are contributing to your sexual dissatisfaction.

Unless a sexual problem is caused by medical or psychological issues, it is generally a symptom of other difficulties in a marriage. If pornography or cyber-sex is creating problems in your sexual relationship, these need to be talked about. It is important to accept that you can't change your spouse. You can only change your own responses to this situation. Do not blame yourself for your partner's low libido or sexual problems because this has nothing to do with how much you weigh, your sexual performance, or the way you look.

Masturbation Concerns

The discovery that a spouse masturbates can create a major problem in a marriage and lower a partner's sexual self-esteem. Although this type of sexual stimulation is a normal, natural activity, myths about masturbation are still believed by a lot of people. Masturbation does not cause hairy palms. It does not shrink a penis. It does not cause acne or cancer or blindness.

Masturbation can relieve sexual tension and can be a coping mechanism for couples that have differing sex drives. For men who can't have sex due to a wife who is sick, late in pregnancy, or absent, masturbation helps prevent congestion of the prostate.

FACT

Nearly 90 percent of men and 67 percent of women masturbate from time to time.

If masturbation is taking the place of having sex with a spouse, then it becomes a problem that needs to be addressed. Since masturbation is quick and lacks responsibility toward intimacy, obsessive masturbation could be a symptom of other issues in a marriage such as repressed anger. Generally, masturbation shouldn't be a problem in a healthy marriage where communication about needs and desires are taking place.

Possible Solutions and Treatments

Along with convincing your spouse to see a physician or counselor, eating healthy foods, and making time together a priority, there are a few other things you can try to solve your sex problems. Try testosterone creams, vaginal lubricants, exercise, reduction of stress, loss of weight, marriage counseling, behavioral therapy, chocolate, exercise, get seven or eight hours of sleep per night, stop smoking, and drink in moderation. It is important to not expect immediate results.

Having no sexual desire is *not* normal. Refusing to get professional help or refusing to work on this dilemma is saying that the spouse is not interested in saving the marriage. If either of you is withholding sex, and it isn't due to medical or mental problems, you are acting out anger and aggression. Trying to find a quick fix such as Viagra won't help. The two of you need to address the underlying problems first.

Surface Sexual Problems

These are not as serious as differing sex drives or low libido. If a couple can't agree on when to have sex, or where to have sex, or even how to have sex, their problem isn't sexual. Their problem is their inability to communicate and resolve issues. These minor disagreements can snowball into deeper resentments, frustrations, and hurts resulting in more damaging, controlling, and punishing behaviors such as withholding sex or sleeping on the couch. A couple shouldn't allow surface issues such as these to have a negative impact on their marriage.

Sexual Orientation Issues

It is estimated that there are more than two million mixed-orientation married couples. The phrase mixed-orientation refers to a relationship where one spouse is lesbian, gay, or bisexual. More than 80 percent of these relationships will end in divorce.

Although most straight spouses have their suspicions, learning that their spouse is a homosexual turns their world upside down. As the gay partner comes out of the closet, the straight spouse often goes into hiding with feelings of isolation and shame. Some hints that you may be coping with a sexual orientation issue in your relationship is when your normal sexual desires are judged as excessive by your mate, your partner is repulsed by sexual activity with you, is secretive and moody, and appears to be noticing people of the same sex in a different way.

FACT

Scientists believe that chocolate stimulates the production of dopamine in the brain and increases a woman's sex drive. Now you know why chocolates are such popular gifts!

Along with the obvious sexual rejection, a straight spouse faces questions about his or her own sexuality, has massive self-doubts, concerns about their children, confusion about whether to try and save the marriage or not, and fear of being exposed to sexually transmitted diseases including AIDS. Feelings of hurt, rage, fear, shock, devastation, repulsion, anger, bitterness, despair, and betrayal will surface when a spouse faces the depth of the lies he or she has been living with.

The first thing you need to do if you find yourself in this situation as the straight spouse is to not isolate yourself. This family crisis needs professional help and support. Don't make any quick decisions and don't assume your marriage is over. Some couples can handle differing sexual preferences and some can't. Check with a physician to see if you have any sexually transmitted diseases even if your partner denies being unfaithful.

Take care of your own needs as you go through the grieving process of realizing that your marriage as you knew it has changed. It will never be the same. The trauma of being a straight spouse can be overwhelming, especially during the first year after the sexual orientation is revealed. Keep reminding yourself that it isn't your fault. Realize that you didn't cause your spouse to be gay.

If you are the spouse who has decided to reveal this aspect of your life, be prepared for the hostility and hurt that your partner will feel after years of deception. You have created a life-changing situation, not only for yourself and your spouse, but for your children as well. Hopefully, you will be able to ask for forgiveness for the betrayal. It is important that you both be able to let go of the past and make decisions together for your futures, whether you stay together or not.

Keep your communication on this area of your life open and honest. True sexual intimacy comes from one another freely giving to each other by being more concerned about the desires of each other rather than their own. When the two of you are sharing deep emotional feelings about who you are it creates the icing on the cake for sex.

Chapter 13

In-Laws and Out-Laws

Your parents and other extended family members can run the gamut from being wonderfully supportive to devastatingly destructive to your marriage. Realizing that you will be spending time with them may bring either joy to your heart or a deepening sense of dread. This chapter helps you deal with the issues that sometimes arise when two families are joined together by your marriage.

Putting Yourselves First

Making the decision to put yourselves and your marriage first over your parents can be a difficult decision. Even when you know it is something you should do, the influence of your parents can be very strong. It is especially important to stand your ground with your in-laws when they are critical, invade your privacy, or demand a lot of your time.

Even when your spouse's family is being difficult, don't speak critically of them. This can make the situation worse, creating defensiveness and distance with your spouse. When your partner vents or shares negatively about his or her own family, just listen. Getting into an in-depth discussion about how horrible you think they are will only create problems for you down the road. Everyone needs to vent now and then, but knowing and sharing your feelings about extended families will have a much more beneficial impact on your own relationship.

Accept that both of you will feel some loyalty toward your families. Such loyalty is acceptable as long as it doesn't place a spouse in second place. Show respect for your in-laws even if you don't believe they deserve it. Recognize when you've had enough and end the telephone call or visit at that time.

Relationships as Circles

As you develop your relationship with your respective in-laws, it helps to remember that each of you came from families with different structures, customs, traditions, and coping mechanisms. These family systems are like a circle. The two of you are forming a new circle, but the two other circles in your lives have strings attached. These strings continually pull at your new circle, and if pulled the wrong way or too strongly, your new circle could be torn apart. It is up to you and your spouse to make decisions on setting boundaries so that your circle stays intact. You must put your own circle, your own relationship, first.

Your Efforts Count

When you marry, if it is possible to have the approval of both sides of your families, do so. However, if this isn't possible, move on with your life together. Be open to possible reconciliation with upset parents at a future date.

Be polite, civil, and respectful when dealing with your in-laws. Talk with your in-laws about what they preferred to be called. Refrain from telling the typical mother-in-law jokes. Write thank-you notes. Offer to help with special meals. Don't forget their birthdays and anniversaries.

Look for activities that both you and your in-laws enjoy doing. Schedule time with them for these experiences.

If you find yourselves focusing on the negative aspects of your relationship with your in-laws, try to discover some things you do like about them. If they seem to be critical of you or are openly hostile toward you, back off for a while. Try not to take their comments personally.

Living with your extended families can be taxing. The sooner you can establish your own separate residence, the better.

Keep your privacy when talking about your jobs, finances, children, plans, and so forth. This doesn't mean you shouldn't ever ask your in-laws for their opinion or advice. It does mean that your lives shouldn't be an open book. However, do keep communication with your respective parents open and don't tell stories or do any lying to cover up your spouse's inappropriate behavior. It won't pay off in the long run.

Establishing boundaries with your in-laws is extremely important. If you don't want them dropping in for a visit unannounced, say so. If they are making too many or too long phone calls, tell them. If you think that getting together every weekend for dinner and board games is just too much, share this with them.

Don't be afraid to have some time alone with your in-laws. Invite your mother-in-law or father-in-law out to lunch or to go for a walk. Ask about their memories of growing up, where they lived, recollections of what type of a kid your spouse was. Get to know your in-laws as people.

If you are having difficulties in your marriage, don't ask your in-laws to be your mediators.

Establishing Boundaries

Knowing where to draw the line and how to draw it with extended family members is critical in keeping both your sanity and your marriage a priority. If you didn't already do this before your wedding, sit down with one another and make decisions so you can define and set boundaries with your in-laws. These limits should include the holidays, vacations, visiting both at their homes and at your home, time with grandchildren, financial issues, and privacy concerns. Once the two of you have made decisions on these matters, the expectations must be shared with all of your parents.

Keeping the Door Open

Have you been in a motel room with a connecting door to the adjoining room? When you open your door, you can see that the door behind it has no doorknob. You have no control over the other door. You can knock on it, or push notes under it, but you can't open it. Your relationship with estranged or difficult family members is the same. You can keep your door open a bit, but unless they open their doors there is nothing more you can do. Keeping your door slightly open is showing your willingness to be in a relationship with these family members.

Knowing Your Limits

Everyone has his or her limits in how much he or she can take when it comes to someone they clash with. When you are in the midst of dealing with a difficult in-law or extended family member, and you've controlled your own responses and behavior for as long as you can, and you know you've reached the limits of how much you can stand, then leave. Get out of the house, leave the restaurant, end the shopping trip, or jump off the boat. Do what you need to do to keep your own sanity, but don't escalate the disagreement into a full-blown battle. It's simply not worth it. What you have to say won't be heard anyway.

FACT

Difficulties in your relationship with your in-laws may be over any topic, but generally politics, bigotry, religion, parenting, spending money, health, and privacy issues are the most troublesome.

Being on the Same Team

If you are having difficulties with your mother-in-law or father-in-law, the only way things will change is if you and your spouse are both on the same team. You need to reach an agreement on how you will handle the situation. Oftentimes, feeling neglected, controlled, unloved, disliked, manipulated, or avoided can distort being reasonable or practical in solving your in-law problem. In order to effectively find a workable solution, you two must communicate with each other your feelings such as distress, worry, frustration, anger, disappointment, disbelief, and so on. Your loyalty to each other must be strong, and you need to stand firm as a couple.

Handling the Holidays

Whether it is your first holiday together or your fiftieth, the decision of whom to spend time with during the holidays can be a difficult one to decide if both of your in-laws are hoping to have you for a visit. Although being with extended family at special times is an important value, it is also important for couples to create their own seasonal traditions. Talking about your plans for the holidays needs to be an ongoing discussion throughout your marriage. Each year will be different. Be open to new solutions and ideas.

Being Honest

Ask yourselves how you truly want to spend your holidays. Are you enduring long hours of driving or traveling, or hopping from one house to another, and forcing yourselves to eat two big meals on special days? Are you and your children really having an enjoyable family celebration?

Be honest with your attitudes, thoughts, and feelings when discussing visiting either of your families. If there is a tradition that you really dislike, say so. The holidays should not be a time of stress or a tug of war. Make a decision concerning the holidays that is best for the two of you and your children. If your families don't accept your decision or have problems understanding, they may be difficult to deal with, but realize that ultimately it is their problem that they have to come to terms with, not yours. They will eventually get the message that your own traditions are important. Do what you two need to do so that you can experience a meaningful holiday season.

Strategies for Staying Stress-Free

There are a few ways you can help the holidays and the decisions that surround them go as smoothly as possible:

- Talk honestly with one another about your expectations, hopes, and fears in dealing with your in-laws and the holidays. If you don't share what is in your heart and in your mind, and you are miserable during the holidays, it is your own responsibility.
- Try to anticipate some problem situations you may have to face and develop plans for handling these potential problems. Anticipate difficult areas such as finances, time constraints, and misbehaving children. Brainstorm some solutions to these areas of conflict.
- Develop a secret code that only the two of you know. If either of you says the secret phrase or word it means that it is time to get away from the family. Take a walk around the block together, or a drive around the city.
- Consider renting a motel room that is close by so you have a private place to retreat to if tensions get too high at the family homestead. You are not obligated to stay 24/7 at your parents' home. Having your own space can also be beneficial for your children as they can become overwhelmed by large family gatherings.
- Plan to do some sightseeing, exploring, hiking, or other activity so you or your kids don't become bored or start feeling in the way at the family home.
- If you find yourself falling back into the child role while visiting your parents, take a step back and stop the behavior. You aren't five years old. Keep your relationship with your folks on an adult-adult basis.
- If your extended family has members with a variety of opinions regarding politics and religion, keep conversations away from these topics. It's okay to say that you don't want to discuss certain topics. If other members insist in having heated debates, stay out of the conversation, and don't try to be the peacekeeper for everyone.

- Work at creating good memories during the holidays. Some families keep a journal through the years of their holiday celebrations. This helps remind them of what worked and was enjoyable and what they should avoid doing again.
- Don't overschedule yourselves. When planning your holiday schedule, build in some quiet time or time to just be free of having to be somewhere or with someone.

Alternative Celebrations

If you celebrate Christmas, consider celebrating the Twelve Days of Christmas (December 26 through January 6) and using some of this time to visit your families. There is such stress around all the holidays to celebrate on one particular day. Your lives will be less stressful if you are more open and flexible about celebrating special days on alternate dates.

Some large, far-flung families have made a joint decision to not try to get together during Christmastime. They plan a family reunion during the summer months instead. This type of gathering allows younger families to remain home with their children during the holidays, yet enables all the family members to join together at a less hectic time.

Holiday Marital Stress

When you are both having increased worries about finances, having too many things to do, and finding yourselves disagreeing with one another more, you are experiencing holiday stress. Here are some other danger signs of holiday stress in your marriage:

- Irritation at everyone and everything—barking at one another
- Roller-coaster relationship—one moment everything is fine, and the next you are fighting with one another over insignificant things
- Retreating from each other
- Overtiredness from not getting enough sleep or sleeping too much to avoid spouse or tasks
- Defensiveness and making too much of simple comments
- Feeling lousy physically, along with recurring headaches or illnesses

- Poor eating habits from being too busy to cook or loss of appetite
- Forgetfulness
- Depression
- Escaping into drinking or other behaviors to distract from current reality

It is important during stressful times such as the holidays to drink plenty of water, eat healthy meals, cut back on caffeine, do breathing exercises, exercise, stick to your holiday budget, realize it is okay to say no—in short, to make reasonable plans for the holidays. When your marriage is being hurt by your in-laws and holiday expectations, take a step back and look at all that the two of you have accomplished and at the positive aspects of the season. Realize that no holiday is ever perfect. Remember to schedule at least a fifteen-minute quiet time each day for yourselves, both as individuals and as a couple.

Problematic Behavior

It may help to remind yourself that your in-laws are the people who raised your delightful spouse. Be open to understanding the changing dynamics of your family of origin issues. As you age, understanding your cultural roots and your childhood will become more important to you as you experience your own self-actualization issues. This openness can also help you deal with past hurts from your families. Be open to reconciliation and healing with extended family members.

Flawed Parents

If you are having in-law difficulties, at some point in your marital journey together, you need to face these problems and deal with them. No one is trained to be a parent. It isn't something that is taught. More likely the parenting style of your mom and dad was what they caught from *their* family of origin. One of the critical skills that parents are not taught is how to let go and cut the apron strings. Some parents never teach their children how to fly their own kite. They don't let go of the string, and they control their children by flying the symbolic kites in their children's lives for as long as they can.

This type of controlling behavior is not necessarily a conscious decision, but their offspring will still find the control very destructive to their own relationships. Some of the common manipulative behaviors you may see in your in-laws as they try to influence your spouse include:

- Being controlling
- Being overly generous in providing monetary support and in gift giving
- Having all the answers and being know-it-alls
- Clinging, smothering, being over protective
- Whining or being helpless
- Asking lots of questions and being nosy
- Making offspring feel guilty
- Criticizing
- Demanding

Mother-in-Law Problems

So often when people speak of in-law problems, they mention the troublemaker as being their mother-in-law. It makes one wonder if father-in-laws ever create problems. Of course they do. However, in families where the home was controlled by the mom, the entrance of another woman to that territory can cause hostility. Men often don't feel this same sense of intrusion or invasion. Problems with father-in-laws often center on finances or wanting to be overprotective.

ALERT!

Before you let your parents care for your babies, make sure they realize that a few things have changed in childrearing. They may not realize that babies shouldn't be placed on tummies to sleep or be covered with lots of blankets.

Benevolent Strings

Sometimes you or your spouse won't admit that your parents have strings attached to their relationship with you. These uncut strings may seem like good things initially. However, you need to be aware that free babysitting, expensive presents, help with education or travel expenses, and their desire to have you with them during the holidays can eventually create difficult situations where you feel that you are being manipulated or controlled.

That's not to say that you can never accept gifts from your parents nor allow them to be babysitters for your kids. Just be aware of a pattern or of growing expectations that your folks may place upon you in these situations. If you keep your line of communication open and honest with your parents, although they may be disappointed by your decisions, hopefully they won't be hurt.

Coming Full Circle

As you grow older, you will find yourselves becoming in-laws to your children's spouses. Hopefully, what you learned from dealing with your own parents will help you to not repeat any mistakes that they made. Being in-laws can be a tremendously rewarding experience when you are open to letting your children live their lives. Be invitational, not demanding. Don't do all the talking. Listen to what your adult kids have to say. Remember that doing things differently from the way you did them doesn't mean that they don't have respect for you. They just have another perspective.

You are preparing your children for the day when they will be making independent decisions as an adult. Your adult children need the space to learn and grow through their own marital experiences. Sure, they will make mistakes, just as you did.

Don't criticize your child's spouse. Do not freely give advice unless your kids ask for it. Make sure you don't nag, even when you see them going astray. If you think you need to warn them, share your concern from your own lived experiences. Doing this occasionally, in a spirit of love, will be accepted and not resented.

When your children come to you for advice or a serious discussion, ask up front what role they need you to take. Are they asking your advice as a parent, a friend, a business mentor, or do they just need you to listen?

Caring for Aging Parents

One of the most difficult roles a person cam take on is that of taking care of one's parents. It is important to remember that not only must you maintain your own life, but you also need to help your parent keep a life of his or her own.

Make time to discuss with your in-laws and parents their expectations about their care. Don't leave out practical concerns such as health and financial issues, living arrangements, and so forth. If you have made the decision together to be caregivers for one of your elderly parents, you will need to work at maintaining your own privacy and individual space, as well as providing that for your parents. Always be up front with your parents. Don't beat around the bush. Keep them in the loop of what is happening in your family life regarding visitors, daily schedule, who's going out, and so on.

When you marry your spouse, you also marry your spouse's family. In-laws can be a tremendous joy and support in your marriage, or they can be a real burden. As with other major topics in a marriage, communication is the key to having a successful relationship with your in-laws. The communication needs to be between you and your spouse, and between the two of you and your in-laws. Ⓔ

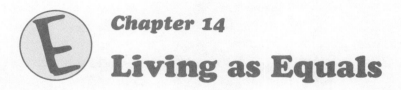

Chapter 14

Living as Equals

When individuals are too independent or too dependent on their spouse, problems can surface. Interdependence is the key to being in a relationship because you want to be there, not because you have to be there. Couples in relationships based on mutuality are willing to give of themselves and are not worried about losing their individuality, because they have mutual trust with their spouse.

Are You Too Dependent . . .

Humans are all born as very dependent beings. Their survival depends on someone else providing their basic physical needs. As they grow physically and mature emotionally through the years, that dependence usually gives way to independence. The disengagement period during adolescence is a natural process that enables young people to discover their own values and to make a life for themselves.

Most folks look for a balance between independence and dependence in their lives. A spouse who is extremely dependent in a marriage will eventually feel trapped, hostile, insecure, frustrated, and helpless. The partner who shoulders most of the responsibility in a marriage will likewise feel trapped, hostile, and used. Spouses should be with one another because they want to be united, not because they *need* to be together. Dependence isn't love but need. Too much dependence in a relationship leads a marriage to divorce.

Some marriages can be described as a master/slave relationship where one spouse is superior and the other is inferior, or one is in charge and the other is not. Many believe that the submissive role is a slap in the face to women and a way to limit the role of women in society. Others view submission as good advice for keeping a solid marriage and point to traditional and biblical roles supporting such a lifestyle.

ALERT!

If you are in this type of a dominant-submissive marriage and want to change the dynamics of your relationship, don't attempt to do this without help from a therapist. The interaction between the spouses is often toxic. If one partner gets emotionally healthier, the other partner may become troubled and attempt to be more dominant by striking out either verbally or physically. A therapist can help keep the focus on building the relationship through communication skills.

However, submissive spouses will often find themselves in a relationship led by a controlling mate. Over time, they will find that their individual choices, relationships with friends and extended family, knowledge of family finances, and opinions are severely limited. If a woman wants to work outside the home, but her husband doesn't agree with that, she can't take the job she was offered. This "my way or the highway" attitude builds distance and lack of respect in a marital relationship.

Or Are You Too Independent?

Being self-sufficient, both emotionally and financially, is important in having a positive self-esteem. However, when a couple makes their independence or self-sufficiency a priority in their lives and is unable to meld any aspects of their lives together, the marriage is little more than a legal right to have sex.

Couples who place a high value on personal and financial independence also believe strongly in individual autonomy to do their own thing and to be their own person. These attitudes do not promote strong marriages. The idea of each person doing his or her own thing and meeting together now and then when it is convenient doesn't build a strong marriage.

Having self-confidence in one's talents and gifts, and desiring some autonomy, is healthy in a marriage. However, having a fierce desire for doing whatever you want can eventually tear your marriage apart because these thoughts tend to undermine an individual's commitment and dedication to marriage.

What Is Mutuality?

Putting two lives together is one of the greatest challenges that anyone can face. It isn't easy dealing with solving problems together, remembering to communicate and to not just decide things alone, compromising to meet differing needs, and handling conflict so a relationship isn't torn apart. You may have mutuality in your marriage and not realize it. If the two of you as a couple enjoy doing things together, both fun and chore-wise, and you make your decisions together after respectfully listening to one another's opinions, mutuality is part of your relationship.

Mutuality in marriage is the spark of universal energy that enables a couple to reach great heights together, and to share both burdens and joys in their marriage.

In a mutual and equal relationship, both spouses accept equal responsibility for one another. Their marriage is strengthened by their mutual decision making and respect for one another. When a couple truly cares about each other and lives out that caring in their day-to-day interaction with one another, they have mutuality in their marriage. It also includes loving, empathy, cooperation, respect, and verbal and nonverbal (and non-game playing) communication. It's the way a couple positively relates to each other.

Mutuality in a marriage relationship is love in action. It is acknowledging the wholeness of both spouses and having a true dialogue of openness and honesty with one another. Mutuality is also when the two of you have a deep respect for one another as individuals. You know and appreciate your spouse's tastes and choices. Mutuality involves vulnerability and an agreement to not attack or destroy one another's self-esteem or integrity.

A couple in a mutual relationship is aware of each other's needs and wants, and they work hard to balance the differences between them. Mutuality calls a couple to not want to change one another, but to accept each other, on a daily basis, as an equal partner. When there is mutuality in your relationship, you then have the freedom to love and give of yourself fully.

Mutuality Through the Years

Hopefully, when a couple gets engaged, they share their expectations and agree to some ground rules for their relationship before they marry. It is important to realize though, that as they mature together, both in love and respect for one another, their opinions, behaviors, values, and expectations will change. As a result, the expectations and ground rules they made early in their marriage will need adjusting throughout their years together.

This re-evaluation is normal and healthy. So many aspects of a marriage change as the years go by and a couple moves from one stage of marriage to another. The chores that need to be done during the parenting stage are much more numerous and intense than the chores of an empty-nest household. The financial concerns and responsibilities fluctuate through the years as employment changes take place.

How a couple spends their leisure time will also vary as they age. Health issues and physical concerns may force couples to change how they get exercise. Some retired couples may find that they need to develop some individual interests and activities to offset being together all the time. Other couples may find that having a great deal of time together in their aging years challenges them to find things they enjoy doing together. Making adjustments and being flexible won't be a problem when a marriage is based on mutuality because they realize that there will be times and situations along their marital journey that call them to set aside what was—and to respond to what needs to be done.

The ability to make mutual decisions and accept mutual responsibility for those choices is key to the success of a long-term relationship.

The Role of Mutuality in a Relationship

Mutuality in a relationship affirms the role and presence of both partners. If a couple decides one spouse is going to stay home to take care of the children, then both partners must respect the responsibility that that work entails, even though that spouse isn't earning a paycheck. Any time one partner feels inferior, or believes that they are being taken care of, then the other spouse isn't fulfilling the responsibility to be affirming and supportive of the value that the stay-at-home spouse provides.

Mutuality doesn't measure how much money each spouse earns. Mutuality calls a couple in a strong marriage to personal obligations and responsibilities without nagging or defensiveness. Each spouse needs to continue to grow mentally and emotionally through the years to reach a point of self-actualization. A relationship based on mutuality rejoices when a spouse develops a talent or skill or achieves a personal goal. There is no sense of competition in this type of marriage, but rather an environment that encourages and invites accomplishment.

Individuals who believe in interdependence and mutuality in a marriage do not have an attitude of watching out for number one or for putting themselves first. They believe in building up one another's self-esteem and being a source of encouragement when the other is down or struggling.

The Challenge of Mutuality

The main challenge of putting two lives together in an interdependent relationship is being willing to focus on what you can give to your marriage, and not on what you receive. Making the decision to love and the decision to trust, along with fine-tuning communication and conflict skills, will enable a couple to build a marriage based on mutuality. Respect, caring, compatibility, honesty, and dependability are additional benefits of living as equal partners.

Mutuality means building up your spouse, making time to listen to dreams, thoughts, fears, and hopes, and being willing to compromise in order to achieve mutual goals.

Lack of Mutuality

A marriage relationship is weakened when mutual sharing and decision making is lacking. Being focused on "me" rather than "you and me" or "us" loses the interdependence and connection with one another that mutuality provides. Living a lifestyle of being basically "married singles," and passing one another like ships in the night, only leads to disillusionment and frustration.

Interdependence and mutuality are not the traditional forms of marriage that have been practiced throughout the world for many centuries. Many people still believe in the type of marriage where the husband is the head of the household by making all the decisions and handling all the finances, with the wife staying home, taking care of the kids and house, being submissive, and not asking questions. This type of living can create major problems in a marriage. Statistics show a larger divorce rate in traditional role marriages. A person can remain a doormat for only so long. Self-preservation will ultimately rise to the surface.

A marriage is lopsided when mutuality is missing. A couple misses out on the joy and delight that results from a partnership based on respect and trust in one another.

The Friendship Component

For a marriage to be long-lasting, a couple needs to find the balance between too much independence, and too much dependence. The answer is *interdependence*. This is a balance between the two extremes of independence and dependence.

Many brides and grooms use the theme of "This Day I'll Marry My Friend" on their wedding announcements and programs. It's a good theme if they can build on their initial friendship with one another and continue to be friends throughout their lives together.

Think of what it takes to be a good friend. Friends allow one another to be themselves without any pressure to be someone they are not. Friends keep secrets and promises. Friends tell the truth and pay attention to you. Friends stand up for one another when things are tough, and they know how to take turns and share things. A friend makes you feel special and doesn't give up on you when you make a mistake. Friends quiet your fears and touch your heart. A friend walks beside you and doesn't make fun of you. A friend affirms your goodness and praises your talents, yet keeps you rooted in the reality of life. A friend understands and accepts your feelings. When you need help, guidance, and support, the person you turn to is your friend. A friend lets you know that you are cared about and calls you, writes notes, and sends you unexpected gifts.

Take a look at your relationship with your spouse and see what type of friend you are. Friendship between a husband and a wife is a major part of a firm foundation for a strong marriage. One of the signs that a couple has an interdependent relationship is that they are friends. Marital friendship goes beyond the notion of conditional love and having strings attached to the level of commitment that a couple has for one another. True friends, especially when married to one another, try to make life better for each other.

Achieving Interdependence

Interdependence is taking responsibility for yourself without trying to change your spouse. Interdependence is mutual submission to your marriage. Interdependence is going with the flow of your marriage.

Couples in an interdependent relationship are partners in many aspects of their marriage. It is feeling secure enough in your relationship that you don't need to know where your spouse is every second of the day. It is being in a relationship because you want to be there, not because you need to be there or have to be there. They can handle the good times and the bad times, and the boring times, and the exciting times with a sense of support and joy. They are able to reflect on the past and they look forward to the future as they continue their growth as individuals and as a couple.

FACT

An interdependent lifestyle is not giving up and it is not giving in. It is trying to live up to your promise of saying, "I do/I will" at your wedding.

Letting Go

Interdependence requires that both of you let go of the myths of marriage and realize that the perfect marriage is unattainable. Ask yourselves why did you marry one another. Was it because you wanted children? Or did you feel a connection and sense that this person you were physically attracted to was your soul mate? Did you marry because it was the only way to have sex? Or were you looking for economic security, or companionship and friendship? It is critical that you both let go of false expectations about marriage.

Wanting to do absolutely everything together or everything on your own are both sure roads to disillusionment. Realize that no matter how close the two of you are, you can't read one another's minds nor can you make the other person always be happy. You both also need to let go of the quest for total personal independence. This doesn't mean you are letting go of your individuality or unique personality. It means you are letting go of having to always have things your own way. It means letting go of superior attitudes. It means letting go of competitiveness. It means letting go of wanting to be provided for. It means letting go of making decisions always entirely on your own or never having to make a decision.

Ways to Be Interdependent

There are many ways you can express your mutual love and respect for one another as equal partners.

- Treat yourself well.
- Tell your spouse what you need.
- Accept that your marriage isn't perfect. The rhythm of your marriage is ever-changing.
- Show affection for your spouse often.
- Let go of manipulative behaviors in general, and don't manipulate your spouse.
- When trying to make a mutual decision with your spouse, approach the issue with an open heart and mind and not anger, defensiveness, or hostility.
- Take time to know who you are as an individual and make quiet time for yourself to continue reflecting on your own life. Make sure you share your self-discoveries with your spouse.
- Focus on the positive aspects of being married.
- Set definitions or boundaries for your relationship to help each other understand how you can each keep your personal integrity and sense of freedom in your marriage.

Maintaining Individuality

When you marry it doesn't mean that you need to give up your own identity. In fact, it is very important that you hang on to the person that your spouse fell in love with. As individuals, you each possess unique qualities and strengths, along with some personality flaws and weaknesses. If your weaknesses create major problems in a relationship, then you need to deal with the behavior. Many couples strive for oneness in their values, goals, finances, and intimacy. This is a positive sign of strength and commitment. However, this type of oneness does not mean that the couple will meld into one being or that they will give up their individuality. Loss of individuality weakens a marriage.

Here are a few ways you can maintain your individuality within marriage:

- Make sure that you stay in touch with who you are.
- Continue to share feelings in a nonjudgmental way with one another.
- Don't nag each other.
- Avoid getting into any power struggles with your partner. Establish ways to work together to get chores done.
- Be willing to let go of some things that really aren't that important in the greater scheme of things.
- Continue doing activities that bring you personal enjoyment.
- Don't abandon friends just because your spouse doesn't enjoy their company.
- If you have different work shifts, make the most of the time you have with one another. Find ways to connect even if you aren't physically present with each other.
- Accept that your spouse may not be able to fulfill all your needs all the time. It is your responsibility to make yourself happy.

You don't have to be joined at the hip for the rest of your lives to be in a marriage based on mutuality. You do have to be friends and to allow one another to be who they are. A couple in an interdependent relationship believes in equal responsibilities and equal rights as they journey through life together Their sense of individuality is not lessened by what they give to their marriage.

Two people working toward mutual goals are much more powerful than one person working alone. When a couple reaches a place of mutuality, they can recognize that they will have some problems along their marital journey. They also trust that the security of their togetherness and the sense of belonging to one another will form a bridge to deal with those difficult times. (E)

Chapter 15

And Baby Makes Three

Parenting is a time-consuming task that requires huge amounts of energy. Having children will open new doors and create new challenges in your marriage. You must communicate with each other to be up for facing the issues that will present themselves to you as you enter this new phase of your lives called parenthood.

Family Planning

Making the decision to have children or not to have children, or deciding how many children to have, requires consideration of more than just the medical facts. The financial obligations are a big part of your decision. Look at what maternity benefits your health insurance will provide. If you don't have health insurance, educate yourselves as to the expenses involved with having a baby. Other costs include time away from work, maternity clothes, baby outfits, diapers, car seat, stroller, crib or cradle, and so on.

If you wait for the perfect time to have children, though, you may never have any. Strive for a balance between the realities of your financial concerns and your desire to have kids.

Lifestyle Changes

The sense of parental responsibility, and the feelings of awe and delight when you watch your child grow and mature, will stay with you for many years. Feelings of stress, exhaustion, frustration, disillusionment, and even incompetence will come and go. You may believe you need an extra vehicle to haul around all the accessories your kids seem to require. Everything you do—dining out, seeing a movie, taking a walk, visiting friends, raking leaves, buying groceries—will change when you have kids. It is important to keep your discussions with one another about being parents as an on-going conversation throughout your childrearing years. Although you will experience changes in your lifestyle, remember the importance of your relationship with one another. The love and respect you have for each other flows into your relationships with your children.

The impact of a child on a marriage begins at the moment of conception. The dynamics of the relationship are forever changed. A husband may even feel the physical and emotional toll that pregnancy puts on his wife's body. There is a lot going on in both the hearts and minds of parents. There is so much preparation and planning that accompanies the birth of a baby. Without talking it out, you may find that you have different ideas about the experience, rather than a joint plan.

Even choosing a child's name can be a source of contention. A new baby demands attention, and the focus can shift from one another to the baby. There's no denying it. Once you have a baby, your lives will never be the same. That doesn't mean that your lives will be boring, stifled, or restricted. It's usually just the opposite.

ALERT!

If parenting concerns are not discussed in a marriage, there can be a lot of misunderstandings between spouses that can erupt into feelings of being neglected and mistreated.

Creating Alone Time

Once the two of you are parents, you may discover that spontaneous sex happens less and less frequently. Quality time alone is critical for a healthy and happy marriage. Scheduling sex with one another may be the only way that you can keep passion in your lives. That doesn't mean it won't be enjoyable. It just means that you have to be a bit more creative and practical in your lovemaking.

Perhaps you can find other couples to swap date nights with. They watch your kids one night for a sleepover, and you watch their kids another night. Quality time isn't just about sex either. You know what can rekindle intimacy between the two of you. If it's a walk around the block, or going to a movie together, or taking a hike, or a dinner out just for the two of you, or snuggling together to watch a movie on the television, or going to a museum or an art gallery, or whatever it is, do it.

Parenting Style Conflicts

You and your spouse may have differing and conflicting views about how to discipline and how to parent your children. This happens because you were raised differently. It is very important that you both learn to compromise and negotiate on parenting styles.

Whatever rules the two of you make, or whatever decisions you decide, you must be united in front of your children. If you don't stand together as parents, your kids will sense this and learn how to play one parent off the other. This will create even more disharmony in your marriage.

The Peanut Butter Concept

Many things hold a marriage together just like peanut butter can keep two pieces of bread together. When the sticky stuff in your relationship is love, commitment, joy, devotion, respect, delight, and shared activities there isn't a problem. However, if the glue that keeps you married to one another is your children, debts, church, or organizational involvement, then it isn't a healthy situation.

In some families, the mom starts talking to the dad through the kids. The kids are the peanut butter between the mom and dad. If kids can only talk to their father through their mother, then the mom is the peanut butter. When a couple only communicates with one another through others, then they have a peanut butter relationship. Keep the lines of communication with those you love open, honest, and direct.

Parents Are Lovers

The greatest gift you can give to your children is for them to know that you love one another. It's a gift that will have a positive impact on their whole lives. Be romantic around your kids. Although they may act embarrassed, children do love to see you hugging, kissing, patting, squeezing, pinching, and smiling at one another. Let them see the love and affection the two of you feel for each other.

Traveling with Kids

Now that you have children, you don't have to put an end to the fun vacations you used to take as a couple. On the contrary. Family vacations can be a great way to spend quality time together. Some changes may be in order, though, to make your vacation with children more pleasant and less stressful for everyone. The key to having a successful and inexpensive trip when you are traveling with children is organization and planning. It's never too early for your kids to learn to pack for themselves. Let children have their own suitcase, backpack, or shelf in the RV. Make it clear that they can only take what will fit in the designated bag or area. If you have the space, let the kids have two bags—one for clothing and necessities, and one for fun stuff. Encourage them to pack the fun stuff one lightly so they can add treasures they find during their trip. (Just make sure they understand they can't bring home anything that is alive, such as snakes, fireflies, or frogs!)

If you're traveling by car, consider starting really, really early in the morning so the kids sleep a few hours while you are on the road. Stop at every rest stop so the kids can run laps or you can play imaginary badminton or hopscotch with them. These rest stops can also be breaks for the two of you. You two can have a private conversation while the kids run and play.

A great game to play in the car, on trains, and even on planes is the alphabet game. Everyone looks for something that begins with the letter A, then the letter B, and so on through the alphabet. But decide before you start playing if words you see on signs count. (Most parents usually said no until they get to the letter Q!)

When traveling by plane, teach your kids how to "yawn" or "swallow" to open their Eustachian tubes. Nurse your baby or give him or her a bottle or pacifier when you are taking off and landing so that pressure on the ears is relieved.

To keep pleas for souvenirs at bay, keep an envelope with each child's allotted funds to spend on the trip. That way you won't be tempted to give in to the "I want this" pleas and you and your partner won't be fussing with one another about money. Kids are often more conservative about what they buy when it is their own money they are spending.

And finally, don't make your days too full or too long. When you are at your destination, plan for an afternoon break for a nap or just some quiet time. This will be beneficial for your marital relationship, too.

Keeping Balance in Your Lives

The best way to avoid becoming an overstressed family is to have a family calendar that has empty spaces on it. Make sure there are plenty of dates when nothing is scheduled and at least one night a month for the two of you to be alone. It is certainly beneficial for children to be involved in sports, drama, scouting activities, and so on, but it is also a positive experience to be able to spend time by gazing at clouds, reading a book, listening to music, or writing in a journal.

When you overbook your kids, you overbook yourselves and put a strain on your marriage. You also miss out on time to play games with them, read to them, bake cookies with them, or do other spontaneous activities together.

Balance is the key to a successful family life. Teach your children that who they are is more important that what they can do or accomplish. One way you can do this is to teach by example. When either or both of you are open to volunteering, be aware that you can start to get asked to do more and more. This doesn't apply just to helping out at school or church. Your friends and family members can ask you to run errands, cook a meal, baby-sit kids, pick someone up or drop someone off, or attend a family gathering. Overscheduling and saying, "yes" to too many groups and people can lead to conflict and unnecessary stress with your spouse and your children. Make time to ask yourselves how you as a family and as a couple are spending time.

Look for ways that you can all volunteer together as a family or only take on tasks that have a short time frame. You must be able to discern together what you can and should refuse to do for others. Make an agreement that neither of you will accept another volunteer position without first discussing it with each other. People will accept your "no." There are times when saying, "no" is in effect saying, "yes" to your relationship and to your family.

Family Traditions

Keeping traditions is another way to de-stress not only your family, but your relationship with each other, too. Traditions in a family aren't necessarily just for the big holidays or birthdays. Family traditions are those rituals and celebrations that create positive memories for a family. They give children a sense of who they are, a feeling of belonging, an understanding of their roots, and can convey values. Don't you enjoy the familiarity of returning to something that you've done for a long time? Knowing what to expect and when to expect it gives time for preparation, which can reduce stress levels in your marriage.

Understanding Traditions

For traditions to be important, they need to be understood. The story behind the tradition should be told so it has meaning. Tell the story! Develop some traditions that have nothing to do with special days. Traditions can surface out of common occurrences such as taking a walk in the first spring rain, trying to find the end of the rainbow, picking strawberries together as a family, or having banana splits on the first day of summer. Having traditions in your family, and in your relationship, helps create positive memories. These memories can help sustain you through the tough times.

Keep Traditions Simple

For a tradition to have meaning and to be a positive impact on your family life, make it simple. The more complicated the custom, or the more time or money it requires, the more likely it is to fall by the wayside. Don't be afraid to discard traditions that no longer have meaning for your family. Feel free to dump a tradition that creates stress. Do communicate your desire to discontinue a tradition with both your spouse and your kids. It may have more meaning that you thought.

As your family cycles through the stages of little ones, grade school, teen years, and watching kids launch out on their own, your love relationship with one another can be one sense of home that your kids can rely on. If the two of you can be flexible in these changing situations, you will find that your family gatherings will continue to be times to tell family stories, laugh at inside jokes, remember special moments, and have fun together. Be open to new and exciting traditions as your family grows.

For a family activity that will link your past and future together, create a time capsule to be opened in twenty years. Include things like newspaper headlines or magazine covers; pictures of favorite toys, pets, your house, your town, and one another; advertisements for food, cars, clothing, toys, movies, or furniture of the current style; favorite family recipes; lists of favorite movies, books, TV shows, sports, and hobbies; and written notes with the hopes and dreams of each member of your family.

Facing Obstacles Together

The quest for parenthood can overwhelm your life together if you have difficulties in conceiving or experience the loss of a child. How you handle your grief over the loss of the dream of parenthood can either make or break your marriage. Realize that the stages of death and dying will apply to the loss of this dream, too.

Facing Realities

When dealing with infertility or the loss of a child, there are two realities that you as a couple must face. The first is that your families, friends, and acquaintances will probably not have a true understanding of your loss. They may also lack sensitivity when they talk with you about this issue. They will probably say some stupid things to you.

Relatives often try to hurry the grieving process in the misguided belief that it is better to move on quickly with your lives. The other reality is that the stress on your relationship from wanting a baby will be monumental. There will be many decisions the two of you need to make regarding treatments, surrogacy, adoption, or trying to accept life without children.

Coping Strategies

As with other important issues in a marriage, the desire to be a parent and coping with all that is involved with that desire requires a couple to have good communication skills. Make sure you have time to spend together so that you can create happy memories and moments.

If you have experienced a loss, it is important that you can accept that you will each grieve in a different way and on a different timetable. Demanding that your spouse "get over it" or "get on with life" will have a negative impact on your relationship. Keep talking to one another daily about your inner thoughts and emotions.

Chronically Ill Children

When the realization hits a couple that their child is chronically ill or will have special needs, they may become overwhelmed by their flood of feelings. It is not unusual to have feelings of sadness, worry, anger, embarrassment, denial, fear, guilt, resentment, confusion, and shock. Although their child hasn't died, many individuals will experience feelings in stages similar to those caused by death. These feelings of disbelief, bargaining, anger, depression, and acceptance can be felt in no particular order. Some people go through one or more of the stages several times before reaching a sense of true acceptance.

ALERT!

It is important to accept that the loss of the dreams you had for your child may cause you to experience grief. The danger in a marriage is when one of you refuses to recognize this sense of loss.

One of the realities a couple needs to face with a child with a disability or a chronic illness is that their lives are never going to be the same. Areas in their marriage that can be severely touched by this situation are sexuality, spirituality, social life, self-esteem, finances, parenting styles, recreation, and future plans. Disagreements can increase when one parent becomes overly protective of their other children, turns away from their faith, has no interest in sexual relations, doesn't want to make any future plans, has lost the sense of having fun, and begins to have self-doubts.

Communication Is Key

Make sure that the two of you regularly express your feelings and thoughts to one another. If you need some time alone, say so. If you need to vent, say so. If you need just to be held, say so. Don't keep feelings and needs bottled up inside. Having to deal with this issue does not necessarily destroy a marriage.

If you are a couple with an ill or disabled child, you will also need to be open to receiving support and help from others. Don't let embarrassment keep you isolated and coping alone. You can't just wait for the support to show up at your doorstep. You will need to make phone calls, ask questions, and seek out support. It's out there but you have to look for it.

Be patient with one another and accept that your lives will be disrupted. Talk about your individual needs and how they are affected, both from a practical and an emotional perspective. Remember to take care of your relationship with each other.

Having an ill or disabled child changes a marital relationship. This change isn't necessarily negative. A marriage can be enriched when a couple is able to openly share with one another both their feelings of sadness and frustration and their sense of joy and awe.

The role of parenting will add a variety of both positive and difficult situations to your marital journey. Keep the lines of communication open, not only with each other, but also with your kids. Good communication skills will help turn your childrearing years into a tremendous bonding experience of parenting your children together. Ⓔ

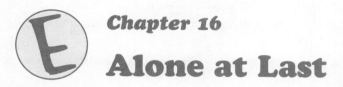

Chapter 16

Alone at Last

Life after your children have moved out can take some adjusting to. Your grocery bills are less. The house is quiet. Your home doesn't need cleaning as often. You can go to the refrigerator for leftovers and they are still there. After the daily exhaustion that comes with parenting young and adolescent children, this period of life is often dreamed about and looked forward to. However, the empty-nest stage creates new strains on your marriage. Here's how to embrace the golden years together.

Adjusting to the Empty Nest

If you don't want your relationship to join the ranks of the growing number of long-term marriages that end in divorce, it is critical that you fine-tune your communication skills and refocus on your life together. When your children leave home, it is time for the two of you to truly talk about your hopes and dreams for your future together. You will need to practically discuss finances, health concerns, retirement plans, aging parents, boomerang children, relationship with grandkids, household chores, and other role adjustments. This is an opportune time to re-energize your relationship.

Your empty nest years are the "re-years." This can be a time to refocus, recommit, review, reappraise, rediscover, rekindle, regroup, refresh, relook, renew, re-examine, re-emphasize, and reinvent your marriage relationship.

Divorce in the Golden Years

Some long-term couples divorce once the kids leave home because the only reason they were together was for the kids. Others spend so much of their time focused on their kids that there wasn't any time for their relationship and the marriage crumbles when the kids are gone. Troublesome issues that have been buried for many years often surface once the kids are out of the house. Fear of aging, confusion and uncertainty about the future, loneliness, depression, and health issues are other reasons that long-lasting marriages end.

FACT

The divorce rate among couples that have been married thirty or more years is steadily increasing. Statistics show the increase in the divorce rate among these couples is 16 percent. Many of these couples focused much of their lives on children and not on one another.

Too Much Togetherness

When spouses have been working separately for many years, being together for twenty-four hours a day can be overwhelming and frustrating.

He suddenly realizes how she actually does the laundry or grocery shopping and thinks she should handle these tasks differently. She thinks he should be more productive around the house and yard. Resentment, defensiveness, and hostility can erupt.

Marital burnout due to being around one another so much doesn't have to happen. You don't have to get on one another's nerves. Discuss the differing roles you are finding yourselves in and share your feelings with one another.

Facing New Issues

It shouldn't be a surprise that the major issues that older couples need to cope with are the same ones they had when they were first married. Dealing with conflict, being able to communicate, sexual concerns, finances, and children are still critical concerns. However, older couples have additional situations to consider. They need to deal with their own health issues and learn how to have fun together again. Making plans for their retirement and deciding what to do about their aging parents are both high-priority issues for empty-nest couples.

Dealing with Menopause

Although many jokes have been written about the hot flashes and mood swings of menopause, it isn't a laughing matter. Menopause can be a rough time in a marriage for both spouses. Every husband should figure out ways to be supportive of this aspect of his wife's life. Encourage her to see her physician if menopausal symptoms are evident. It is important that you support her treatment decisions. Make time to exercise with her. Be willing to have a healthier diet that includes more fruits, vegetables, and soy products and less caffeine, alcohol, and white sugar. Learn how to give her a massage. Consider doing relaxation or meditation exercises together. If you know the symptoms and can understand both the physiological and emotional changes she experiences, you can make this transitional time less stressful. Remember to focus on the positive aspects of this stage of life.

When a woman is menopausal she may have hot flashes, gain weight, and have a decreased libido. Due to fluctuating hormone levels, she may become forgetful, moody, hostile, and depressed. Other physical changes that can be alarming to a menopausal woman include thinning hair, vaginal dryness, skin flushing, irregular menstrual periods, a fast heart beat, loss of pleasurable sensations during sex, and osteoporosis concerns.

Don't make fun of her moods, hot flashes, or forgetfulness. She has a lot of feelings of fear and confusion as she faces growing older. This is a time when a woman naturally re-examines her life. Listen to her as she shares her feelings. Nurture your relationship by making time to spend with her.

ALERT!

Every woman will experience menopause in her own unique way. Don't believe all the old wives' tales. It can be a wonderful time of change and personal empowerment for both of you.

The Male Perspective

One of the major complaints a wife may have after retirement is tripping over her husband because he has turned into a couch potato or because he follows her around watching and criticizing her every move. The reality of growing older is that men experience physical, emotional, and hormonal changes as they age such as sweats, hot flashes, irritability, low libido, forgetfulness, weight gain, low self-esteem, sleep problems, depression, moodiness, and fatigue. However, hormonal decline in males is gradual and doesn't happen to all men.

During the second half of life, men may be witnessing the illness or death of their parents and friends. They watch their children leave home, notice their physical strength has decreased, feel unneeded because they aren't earning a paycheck any longer, and their libido is lower. As they look at a calendar, the realization hits that there may not be enough time left in their lives to satisfy all their dreams and hopes. They experience a sense of going downhill.

Men need to let go of worrying about their sexual ability and rejoice in the sense of sexual fulfillment in their marriage. Wives can support their husbands through this difficult adjustment period by helping their husbands recognize the importance of *being* rather than *doing*.

Drifting Apart

With all the activity that goes on and the responsibility that having children places on a marriage, some couples drift apart without realizing it. Once it is just the two of them again, they may wake up one day with a sense of having nothing in common and nothing to talk about. When a couple finds themselves playing the game of blaming the other, or they seem to go out of their way to put one another down or criticize accomplishments, the marriage is in trouble. Significant negativity, withdrawal, alienation, and avoidance are other signs of growing problems in the relationship.

What You Can Do

When you find yourselves alone at last, take advantage of it! Empty nests tend to be refilled with boomerang adult kids or aging parents, visits from children and grandkids, and sometimes, even grandchildren on a full-time basis. Many spouses do put their marriage relationship on a back burner during their parenting years. If this is your situation, it is time to focus your marriage on one another and not on your kids.

FACT

It is a myth that moms react stronger to the empty-nest syndrome than dads. The sense of regret over missing opportunities to spend more time with their kids often hits fathers harder than mothers.

If you have past issues, regrets, or disappointments that you haven't had closure on, seek counseling so you can move forward together. Forgive one another. Work on keeping a deep friendship with your spouse. Share your feelings daily. Accept that you both may experience a sense of grief when your children leave home. Limit the number of times you call your adult children each week. Don't place guilt trips on your kids for decisions they make that may cause them to move to a different locale.

Be aware of how you spend or waste time each day. It is surprising how much time you can both putter away in a day. Even though you're together physically, you can find yourselves not really present for one another. Make time to enjoy just being with your partner. Discuss how you can be flexible in your changing roles with your adult children and your aging parents. Be romantic. Remember that although you may be growing older, you can both still enjoy sex. Don't overlook your sexual relationship. In order to keep your emotional and physical intimacy alive, go out on dates and flirt with each other again.

QUESTION?

How can we approach our new lives as empty nesters?
Take a short trip to celebrate the start of the next stage of your life and use this time to reaffirm your commitment to one another.

When you've retired, take things more slowly. It is important that you don't rush into filling your hours with volunteer roles in your community or church. It's okay to enjoy a slower pace of life for a while. Find ways that the two of you can relax together. Work on just being with one another. You don't have to always be doing something. Give yourselves some time before you make a lot of changes like emptying out a kid's room, or signing up to take a class, or planning a long trip.

Discuss the achievements of your past that you are each proud of. Talk about the new challenges you are facing. Share your expectations as you approach this new phase of life. Make some short-term and long-term plans on how you will spend your money and time. It is important that you can compromise on how you will prioritize the energy and expense you plan on spending on home, travel, career, education, volunteer efforts, family, friends, recreation, and pets. Relish your quiet moments with one another. Keep your life simple and rediscover ways to have fun together.

Downsizing

Couples spend the first half of their lives accumulating stuff, and the second half of their lives getting rid of the same stuff. It's natural to think about downsizing when it is just the two of you again. Downsizing can create less cleaning and less yard work. Moving to a smaller house may result in lower property taxes and, therefore, more freedom to travel or take on other activities.

But you don't have to move to downsize. Look at your involvements in your community and all the things you have around you. Just the simple act of dropping one activity, or donating or selling off some items, can lessen stress and simplify your life. Living simply often results in having more with less. You will have more free time, which will give the two of you more walks together, more books to read, more off-the-beaten-track type of trips, and more time to enjoy one another.

The Sandwich Generation

You are part of the Sandwich Generation if your nest is cluttered and not empty. Many couples are feeling the squeeze of dealing with parenting kids, dreaming about retirement, and facing aging parent issues. You could find yourselves caught in the middle because people are living longer, more kids stay at home to go to college and often postpone getting married, and there is an increase in the number of boomerang kids (kids who move back home as adults) due to loss of employment or a divorce.

Trying to decide who has the highest priority can tear a marriage apart. The major stress comes when a couple realizes that their dreams of a secure retirement, travel, and slowing down are jeopardized by their relationships with their children and parents. It's not practical to assume that your empty nest will stay empty. These assumptions can culminate in unrealized expectations. Feelings of anger, resentment, frustration, disappointment, and fear are common when new and unexpected responsibilities surface.

Boomerang Kids

Most couples have a commitment to be there for their children and other family members in times of crisis or great need. This desire to be a safety net for those they love is a positive sign of their love and compassion. Yet, when kids do return home, usually in the midst of their own crisis and self-doubts, a couple can find themselves reeling from feelings they didn't think they would ever experience.

If boredom is creeping into your relationship with your spouse, create a list together of things that you've never done before but would like to try. Include things both large (perhaps a trip you couldn't find time to take before) and small (learning to canoe or trying a new food you've never eaten, for example), and make an effort to try one or two of the things from your list as a couple.

Don't attempt to control the lives of your boomerang kids. They probably already feel as if their lives are in a tailspin. Don't make their self-image worse by exerting power over their decisions or how they keep their room. Keep your relationship with your adult kids on an adult-to-adult basis. If your adult kids fall back into the child role, mention that you see it happening. When talking with a child, ask what role he or she needs you to play. Sometimes they do want you in the parent role, but more often an adult child needs a friend, a mentor, or someone to just listen. Slipping back into a parenting role on a regular basis isn't healthy for either your marriage or your child.

Coresidency

Intergenerational households were once the norm in many cultures. Today in the United States they are not as common and are the exception, rather than the standard. However, economic factors along with health issues are now making having three or four generations under one roof a necessity for some. Since this isn't something many couples have experienced firsthand in their own lives, they have to learn as they go if they find themselves in this situation. If there is good communication, this type of living arrangement can enhance the well-being of the family, gives young children a sense of belonging and being rooted in family, assists teenagers in their journey toward adulthood, and lessens the amount of chores that need to be done by each individual because of the extra helping hands.

Successful Intergenerational Households

To have good experiences with several generations living under the same roof, make a commitment to not neglect your marriage. Make time for one another and keep the lines of communication open not only between yourselves but between the other members of your family, too. Everyone needs to share his or her expectations of this sort of living arrangement.

Remember how to take care of yourselves and refuse to put your lives on hold. Be practical and don't overextend yourselves financially, physically, or emotionally. Know how to say, "no." Protect your privacy and create time alone both as a couple and as individuals. Share your expectations and request that both your boomerang kids and your aging parents be responsible. All members of an intergenerational household need to feel involved, productive, and needed. Respect the privacy of other members of your family. If some of your hopes and dreams have been delayed or unfulfilled, talk about them and look for alternative ways to achieve your goals.

Let all the members of your family know what you need. It could be solitude now and then, or time to be with friends or pursue hobbies and interests, or help with dishes or laundry. Be extremely specific with your expectations about the household rules. Put everything out on the table such as quiet times, laundry duties, cooking and cleaning tasks, grocery shopping, meal schedules, transportation, and vehicle issues like where to park and accessibility.

Raising Grandkids

You expected grandparenthood to be a joy—visiting your children's children often, watching them grow up, spoiling them from time to time. But what happens when circumstances occur that require you to take on the role of actually raising your grandchildren?

More and more studies and surveys are showing that the number of grandparents who are raising their grandchildren is increasing at an alarming rate. Why? The many reasons include divorce, teen-age pregnancy, deceased parents, neglect, incarceration, abuse, unemployment, alcohol or drug usage, and abandonment. Furthermore, any couple, regardless of their ethnicity, finances, or religion, is potentially at risk for having to cope with this issue. It is a situation that is becoming more and more common in all socioeconomic groups.

Many aspects of a long-term relationship are affected when a couple takes on the parental role once again. It can be especially difficult in a marriage when one spouse is more open to the responsibility than the other. Concerns surface about health, finances, housing, medical care, privacy, and retirement dreams. The social life and circle of grandparents who take on the responsibility of raising their grandkids change considerably. Along with the physical challenges that parenting in retirement years brings, there is an emotional toll. Most will feel a wide range of feelings including anger, resentment, grief, fear, shame, helplessness, thankfulness, and joy.

FACT

The average couple will need about a year to make the adjustment after they accept responsibility for raising their grandchildren. During that time, their marriage can be severely strained.

Survival Needs

It is important that you educate yourselves on the latest trends in parenting. Psychological and medical studies have made a lot of changes in what is recommended in child care and what isn't. Many communities have free classes and support groups to assist grandparents in adjusting to their new role. Acquiring medical care and health insurance for your grandchildren will be difficult. Seek legal and financial advice on your situation so that you can protect yourselves from losing your home due to unexpected medical costs. You may be able to get assistance on health insurance from your state Children's Health Insurance Program (CHIP). If you live in a senior citizen complex, get legal advice as to whether or not your grandchildren can reside with you. Find out and post telephone hotlines that you could need. Look for organizations that provide short-term respite care for your grandkids. You will need to take a break from them now and then.

Keeping Your Marriage Healthy

If you want your marriage to remain successful while parenting a second time, consider these suggestions.

- Although your alone time together will be lessened, keep the lines of communication in your relationship open.
- Discuss and prioritize your needs, wants, and goals.
- Share the workload. It's too big a task for one of you to try to deal with alone.
- Don't do too much. Pace yourselves so you don't damage your own physical or emotional health.
- It isn't necessary to totally change your lives for your grandkids. Don't sacrifice everything you've worked years to achieve.
- Realize you can't do everything the same way you did twenty or thirty years ago. You may find that you need to lower your expectations when it comes to housekeeping and other activities.
- Value your time alone. Making time for yourselves will help you both to regroup and to be re-energized.
- If taking trips with one another was part of your retirement plans, make arrangements so you can still do this. Your trips may be shorter, but you should still follow your dreams.
- Don't be afraid to ask for help. Joining a support group of others dealing with the same issues can be very affirming and helpful.
- If you find yourselves having self-doubts about your ability to take on this role, remember why you said, "yes." Think about all that you've done right.

As difficult a task as raising grandchildren is, many grandparents say that all the sacrifices are worth it. They feel younger and more active and believe they have a greater purpose in their lives.

Traveling in the Golden Years

Take advantage of being just the two of you again and plan some trips together. Planning is the key to having an enjoyable and stress-free experience on the road.

Make sure you discuss your expectations of the trip with one another. Do whatever you can so that at least one of each of your hopes is fulfilled. Spontaneity on a trip is good and can be entertaining, but make sure that you don't pressure your partner into agreeing with you. You're not playing fair if on the trip you suddenly decide you want to do something that you hadn't discussed previously.

Deciding to travel together in a recreational vehicle can be an exciting choice. However, a couple needs to seriously consider the impact that this experience can have on their relationship. Vacations are usually thought of as an escape from the chores of every day life. That doesn't happen when you travel in an RV.

If you do go this route, throw out any thoughts of color-coordinated dishes and sheets. Keep your life simple and go for paper plates and sleeping bags. Prepare yourselves for no privacy. The bathroom isn't big enough as a place to retreat to. On the plus side, you can save money on overnight accommodations and food costs. You don't have to lug suitcases around and pack and unpack them. While on the road, you have immediate access to a bathroom if the need arises. Just don't allow yourselves to become slaves to cooking and cleaning while on your trip.

ALERT!

If one of you is not all that thrilled with recreational vehicle travel, or if along the way you find yourselves becoming hostile to one another, rent a hotel room for a night or so. It's amazing how a hot bath can alleviate stress and lift spirits.

By maintaining good health, the two of you could still have more than one-third of your lives to be together after your children leave home. With a new sense of freedom and adventurous spirit, this can be the most fulfilling and enjoyable stage of your marriage. Keep lines of communication open, work on your sense of humor, and schedule time alone with each other to keep your hopes and dreams from vanishing.

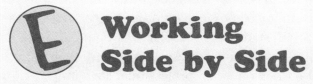

Chapter 17

Working Side by Side

Many couples have a dream of being able to work together as a team to earn their living. Working side by side requires putting aside competitiveness and focusing on one another's strengths. The keys to sharing this aspect of your lives and being together twenty-four hours a day ("24/7") are communication, respect, having common goals, and trust.

Sharing Work Life

There are many scenarios that enable couples to earn a living together. They may be employees in the same department at the same company. One may own an established business but need the expertise and talent of the other. They may find themselves being pulled into one of their families' established business. Or they both recognize that with their combined skills, resources, and ambition, together they could build a business of their own.

Whatever their circumstances or reasons for wanting to work together, it is imperative that husband-wife business teams share their expectations and goals of both their personal and professional life with one another on a regular basis. They also need to truly examine whether or not their relationship can handle living a 24/7 lifestyle.

The 24/7 Lifestyle

Being with your spouse all day, every day can be wonderful or it can be a tremendously frustrating, stifling experience. Creating a lifestyle of togetherness that is both enjoyable and meets one another's emotional needs requires a great deal of communication. Don't assume that this will be a natural transition for the two of you. When you are apart for eight to ten hours each day, you may be able to more easily overlook some annoying behavior because you don't have to be around it that much. Once that buffer zone decreases, irritation can grow as little things bother you.

ALERT!

There are many couples in successful, compatible marriages that find being in business together hurts their marriage. Don't be afraid to admit that working together isn't a right fit for your relationship.

You may discover that some of your own personal habits drive your spouse up the wall when faced every day. Simple acts like leaving plates and cups in the kitchen sink, or not replacing the toilet paper roll, or tossing documents on one another's desks can mushroom into larger problems. The best way to deal with these triggers is to express them.

Remember, you can't change your spouse, but you do have the right to communicate your thoughts and feelings. Don't do this in a criticizing tone, but just share how the behavior or habit is annoying. The key to making a 24/7 marriage work is being in touch with your own wants and needs, communicating well, and respecting and trusting one another.

Autonomy

When working together it is important to recognize that although you are married to one another, you don't have to do everything together all the time. Working together can enhance your marriage relationship if you allow one another space to be alone. Having separate offices is a good idea. It is important not to monitor how your spouse spends his or her time. Don't question every trip out of the office or every phone call.

Being together all the time can create problems if you don't schedule some alone time away from the office for each of you. While couples talk about being together twenty-four hours a day, the reality is they aren't. Their marriage probably wouldn't survive if they didn't have some time away emotionally and physically from one another each day.

That sense of autonomy and physical space can be provided by having time to follow individual interests and being able to go shopping, walk around the block, or visit friends without having to explain who, where, when, how, and why. When your spouse is on the telephone, don't hang around to listen in on the conversation. Respect one another's privacy by not reading mail or e-mail that is not addressed to you. If your partner doesn't want to have lunch with you every day, don't assume that there is a problem. Don't spy on your spouse. If you have concerns about your partner's work performance, talk about it.

When you've made the decision to trust in one another's decisions in business, don't second-guess decisions already made. Trust and respect are vital in any marital relationship but especially when couples work together.

FACT

Autonomy is allowing each other the physical and emotional space you each require, and not discounting one another's feelings or intuitions.

Going into Business Together

When you make the decision to work together, one of the first things you should do is to set the ground rules of your business partnership. Having different opinions will be inevitable, so agree to disagree. You can eliminate power struggles and control issues by dividing up the tasks and knowing who will be responsible for different aspects of the business. Be flexible. Set some long-term and short-term goals together by sharing your visions of your business, family, and marriage.

Keep your expectations realistic. Talk about how you will handle a down turn in clients and sales. Discuss the impact and lifestyle changes that working together will have on your relationship and family. Ask yourselves why you want to be in business together. If it is to have less stress in your lives or a slower lifestyle, then be open to having low expectations of quick financial rewards.

There are many issues you should discuss together before you make the commitment to start your own business together:

- Agree that your marital relationship must come first. Your marriage must be your top priority.
- See if your relationship can handle being together 24/7 by taking a week's vacation and spending it at home doing everyday types of chores together.
- Talk honestly and practically about money. Do the calculations to see if you can truly afford to quit your current jobs and launch your own business. Discuss your concerns about debt and putting your assets at financial risk. Decide how you will handle your business finances and whether or not you will each receive an income.
- Make decisions about your business structure, percentage of ownership, and stock considerations. Consulting an attorney for advice on these decisions is recommended.
- Appraise your realistic chances for success. Compare your business idea to other similar existing businesses. Be honest with each other if you have doubts or concerns.
- Agree to place as high a value on your family time as you place on your business time. Don't let your business overtake your lives.

- Make sure that your goals and values for your business partnership are compatible.
- Clarify each of your roles in the business. Be very specific. If the business will just be the two of you, you'll have to talk about who will take out the trash and vacuum the floor as well as who will handle sales and bookkeeping chores. If you hire other employees, you need to know who will be managing them.
- If you decide that one of you needs to remain in a current job, be fair in setting expectations for housework, yard work, child care, running errands, along with the new business involvement. If you don't, one of you will burn out quickly.
- Determine if one of you will be the "boss" or if you will make business decisions jointly. Otherwise, control and power issues will tear you apart.
- Decide what types of decisions will be shared and which ones you will defer to the expertise of the other. Be clear in defining the types of decisions that you can each make individually.

Communicating as Business Partners

Start your business day together by sharing your expectations of the day with each other. Include which errands need to be run, shipments that need to be sent out, orders that need to be processed, calls that should be returned or made, approaching deadlines, e-mails that need responding to and other correspondence that requires attention, inventory concerns, staffing issues, lunch breaks, and so on. Realize that you will need to make tough decisions together. You also need to be able to communicate well with your employees. They need to know which one of you to turn to for questions or advice and whom they should consider the boss.

Pros and Cons of a Family Business

On the plus side, when you are calling the shots, you may have more time to spend with your spouse and children. Neither of you will have to endure the energy drain of a long commute or from working with difficult, demanding individuals. The two of you will have a sense of accomplishment in working together and effectively handling the stress and success of owning a business.

On the negative side, you may work long hours and lose quality time with your spouse and children. The stress and worry of being able to provide for your family can put a large strain on your marriage. If you can't communicate well about business and financial decisions and household tasks, feelings of frustration and resentment from these work issues can hurt or eventually destroy your marriage.

Ongoing Discussions

Many entrepreneurial couples actually write down specifics on how their business will be managed. The discussions about working together need to be held on an ongoing, regular basis. You should:

- Designate job responsibilities.
- Set up work schedules.
- Decide on how you will share in the profits.
- Have a fall back plan for rough times financially.
- Talk about vacations.
- Determine how you will handle child-care concerns.
- Discuss what equipment, individual health insurance, lack of paid vacations, extra phone lines, etc., will cost you.
- Share on whether or not you will want to expand your business.
- Decide which one of you will handle emergencies at home.
- Reappraise if you want to work out of your home or have your business in a commercial space.

ALERT!

Keep your business relationship on a professional basis. That means that you treat one another as business equals with sensitivity and respect.

Re-evaluation

Making time to re-evaluate your business partnership is vital to maintaining a good business relationship with one another. Aside from looking at whether or not you are making any money from your cooperative work, and looking at the impact being a husband-wife team has on your family life, it is important to assess how you both feel about working together. You may find that working together isn't good for your marriage. If this happens, both of you will have to decide which relationship is more important to you. Hopefully, if your business is interfering with your home life, you will care more about being married than having your own business.

Respecting Expertise

When you made the decision to work together, you did so because you believed you could count on one another's talents and expertise. Continue to have respect and trust for those aspects of your spouse's personality. However, you must acknowledge that you are two different people and will probably work differently.

Being on different body clocks can also affect how you work together. If one of you is a late-night person, don't expect your morning-type spouse to stay up late with you to complete a project. Having your own computers is a plus. You can network them together, and share a printer, but you won't have to wait for your partner to finish a task before beginning something you want to do. You should each have your own desk, and ideally, individual office space.

Divvying up tasks and chores gives a couple opportunities for both mental and physical separation. It also ensures that your business will operate smoothly and efficiently.

Handling Conflict

Working together creates a natural breeding ground for differing opinions and conflict. Be prepared to handle conflicts effectively. Don't argue with each other in front of your employees or clients. Make sure that you two know how to handle disagreements in your marriage and in your business. If you don't, the negativity will severely impact both aspects of your lives. Deal with areas of disagreement right away. Going into denial or playing an avoidance game will not only hurt your marriage, your business could fail. Remember to stick to the subject at hand. Bringing up other areas of contention will only muddy the water, and your problems won't be solved. Keep the conflict between the two of you and by all means don't involve your employees or customers. Don't stoop to calling one another names or pointing out past mistakes.

Differences

When you both have the same vision and attitudes about running a business, the possibility of conflict will be less. However, many entrepreneurial couples often discover while operating their business that one is open to taking risks while the other prefers a more conservative approach. One looks at opportunities in a more optimistic way than their more pessimistic partner. Some partners prefer dealing with behind-the-scenes duties while the other likes to be the spokesperson for the business. If you understand these personality differences, they can become a key to having a successful business. If they are to be beneficial to your business partnership, your differences in personality and perspective must be both respected and appreciated.

Competition

Couples often decide to work together when they discover that their strengths complement one another and offset their individual weaknesses. It is critical that you not compete with one another. Competition between the two of you, both in your marriage and in your business partnership, will end up driving you away from each other. There will be no winners, only losers.

Competition generally allows one spouse to shine brightly, while the other feels likes a burnt out star. You can only work successfully together when you both are willing to let go of the need to compete with each other. You each have your own areas of expertise. Appreciate one another's strengths and talents. Trust that when you each say that something will be done, that it will be accomplished. Divide your responsibilities and business chores according to what you each like to do, have a talent for, or don't want to do.

Flexibility is key when things get stressed or your business is in a time crunch trying to meet a deadline. If your business or home roles are set in stone, you won't be able to help one another complete a task or meet a deadline during an emergency or other stressed time.

A Sense of Humor

One of the best ways to reduce stress when you are working together is to have a good laugh together. It lightens the mood; eases conflict; releases healthy, energizing endorphins in the brain; and is a natural way to add to the quality of your marriage. Humor can even help you be more productive. Some medical experts say that humor needs to be a daily part of a healthy lifestyle. When you have humor in your life, ordinary things become more enjoyable. It's true that humor won't change a difficult situation, but it can change the way you respond to the problems facing the two of you. Laughter can release anger and clear your mind so you can cope more effectively.

Keep humor clean. Off-color jokes are inappropriate in any workplace. Don't make fun of something your spouse said or how your partner looks. While working together, especially when others are around, avoid practical jokes, gag gifts, horseplay, and funny stories that could embarrass your partner. You know your spouse and know which topics in your marriage shouldn't be joked about. Don't sabotage your spouse through humor.

As you go through your day with one another, be aware of the silly things that you notice and share them with your spouse. Make a point of smiling more often at your partner, especially when you first wake up in the morning. Save some of those favorite cartoons that you see in the newspaper or on the Internet to share with your partner. Take yourselves less seriously, watch a funny movie, read something hilarious so you chuckle or giggle a few times each day.

Home Life versus Work Life

When you decide to be your own bosses, the gap between your work lives and your personal lives becomes blurred. You will be juggling your spousal roles and working roles all the time. Some couples can handle the multiple personality aspect of working together, but it can be difficult to separate your personal relationship from your work relationship. One partner may take comments from their spouse at work too personally. Unresolved personal issues can create problems at work. It is important to leave home issues at home.

ALERT!

Talk about what you need to pick up at the grocers or problems with your kids on your lunch or break times. Keep the personal aspects of your lives at home. Your employees aren't interested in your married life.

Work or managerial attitudes can impact home life. Leaving work at the office or continuing a business discussion during dinner may become a point of contention if one of you is more inclined to bring work home than the other. Talking about the business during your off-hours is okay as long as it is something that the two of you previously agreed to. Know when to rely on your voicemail and when to keep the computer turned off. You must have time together that is free from the business portion of your relationship. Set a work schedule and try to stick to it. If one of you has difficulty observing the boundaries you both previously agreed to in your business, issues about control can surface.

Many couples who work together find that they are much more effective as a team than when they try to do things alone as individuals. There are many benefits of working together. Your marriage may even become stronger for it. Ⓔ

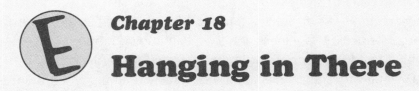

Chapter 18

Hanging in There

Every marriage will face illness, financial concerns, job changes, death, and other tough times. How a couple handles these situations will either bring them closer or pull them apart. As with other aspects of a successful marriage, communication is the key to getting through difficult times while keeping your marriage strong.

Facing Difficult Times

The best-laid plans often get sidetracked or even totally destroyed by forces a couple has absolutely no control over. There is no guarantee that your life together will be free of crisis, trauma, or heartache. Bad things *do* happen to good people. The newspapers and television news reports are full of stories about natural disasters such as hurricanes, floods, earthquakes, tornados, and fires. These tragedies along with automobile accidents, illness, job loss, bankruptcy, random crime, and troubled children can rock solid marriages off their foundation.

Dealing with hard times can be extremely draining when there is no one to blame. The flood of decisions that have to be made after being hit by a disaster can be overwhelming. Dealing with insurance companies and worrying about money in a crisis can be frustrating, scary, and depressing. Some decisions either of you make—like holding on to a wet soggy picture after a flood or a scorched doll after a fire—may seem entirely irrational. Though they may be irrational, they are emotionally necessary.

It is important to remember that each of you will handle the stress and frustration of a difficult situation in different ways. Again, you can't change your spouse's reactions; you can only change your own behavior. This shift in attitude will often improve your marriage even if the difficulty you are facing doesn't improve.

Negative thinking during difficult times can fuel more problems and conflict in a relationship. Try to keep a positive outlook focused on getting through the crisis.

In Sickness and in Health

Chronic illness could enter a marriage in a variety of ways. A parent, a child, a spouse, or you could become chronically ill. Although the feelings that accompany each of these situations may be different, the strategies for coping are the same. The sense of being scared and worried can be overwhelming.

It has been estimated that nearly half of the U.S. population has some form of chronic illness. Eventually, most married couples will have to face this crisis. Many feelings and issues will surface. Anger, denial, isolation, grief, financial concerns, fear, parenting issues, spirituality questions, and sexual worries are just a few.

FACT

Nearly 75 percent of marriages dealing with a chronic illness eventually fail. However, many question which actually came first—the illness or the propensity toward divorce? Other studies have shown a high percentage of couples staying with one another while dealing with chronic illness.

Realities of Illness in a Relationship

When one spouse is very ill, the relationship becomes unbalanced. The healthy spouse necessarily takes on more and more chores and responsibilities in addition to giving care and emotional support to the ill spouse. The healthy spouse may have to work longer hours and could end up trying to do too much. The ill partner may have feelings of frustration at being dependent and self-doubts can increase. Concerns whether pity, guilt, or gratitude is keeping the healthy spouse in the marriage may surface. Worries about holding the healthy spouse back from being fulfilled can fill an ill spouse with feelings of insecurity and guilt.

Coping Strategies

It is vital that both partners feel free to ask for emotional support and keep talking openly with one another. Accept that your lives have changed and are being disrupted, but hold on to the fact that a person with chronic illness can live a very full and meaningful life.

Lower your expectations about sex, but look for ways to still have physical intimacy. If you are unsure as to what you can and can't do sexually, talk to your physician about it. When meeting with your doctor, ask questions so you both have a full understanding of the illness and treatment options. Ask your doctor if you can tape-record your meetings, or take notes. In talking with the physician treating you or your spouse, be honest. Don't hold back information or questions.

Other people you both should be open and honest with include your children. They will sense the disruption in your lives so there's no sense in hiding this from them. Letting them know what is happening will ease their feelings of fear or possible guilt. Although it may be painful to do, take some time together to look at your hopes and dreams for your life together. Decide what is still important and what isn't to the two of you. Discuss what you can still accomplish together. Take each day at a time.

Post-Traumatic Stress Disorder

If you find yourselves experiencing flashbacks, nightmares, extreme anxiety, memories, and painful images you can't get out of your head—as well as and feeling emotionally numb—seek help immediately. These are symptoms of post-traumatic stress disorder (PTSD). PTSD can be the result of being very close to a crisis or the trauma of a loss.

The best thing you can do for yourself is to talk about it. The best thing you can do for your spouse is to listen. Be aware that listening to someone speaking about traumatic experiences can lead to compassion stress. This consequence of caring and loving is usually temporary but can lead to fatigue, avoidance, anxiety, and numbed emotions. Take this seriously and seek the support you need.

Staying Mentally Healthy

If you are the well spouse, it is imperative that you find a way to create balance between your love and concern for your partner and your practical need for independence and stability. It is okay if you have to get away now and then in order to pursue some things that interest and renew you. You must take care of yourself. Although it may sound coldhearted, you must have a life apart from your spouse's illness. Having a strong support network of others who have traveled this road will help you do this. Be open in your communication with your spouse about the diagnosis and feelings of denial or acceptance. Keep your communication honest in dealing with sexual, parenting, and financial matters. Protecting your spouse from these issues and concerns only creates more frustration and distance between the two of you.

Surviving the Loss of a Child

The loss of a child is the ultimate unthinkable grief and every parent's nightmare. Although couples facing this trauma experience tremendous stress, their marriages aren't destined to fall apart. For a marriage to survive the heartache of the death of a child, a couple needs to make sure that both are getting through the grief process okay. One way is to face the reality of their situation and to not stay in the denial or avoidance stage.

New Realities

The death of a child will leave you feeling weak, dazed, and in shock. Along with anger and disbelief, you may find yourselves feeling alone and sullen. Good memories of times past can get you through some rough times. And if you have other children, regardless of their ages, they need you.

Yes, people make dumb statements about how lucky you are to have other healthy kids or how your child is in a better place. Of course, having surviving children doesn't lessen the pain of losing a child. Nothing truly lessens the pain. Yes, time does heal, but the amount of time needed varies from person to person.

The hardest time for a couple is the first six months following the loss of a child. During this period they often encounter communication problems, disagreements on parenting or overprotecting their other children, arguments about having another baby, differences in grief patterns, inability to deal with a child's possessions, financial concerns, increased alcohol or drug use, not wanting to seek counseling, avoidance, and feelings of blame, regret, and guilt. One partner may feel anger sooner than the other, or feel sadness more deeply. One spouse may want to do something to make things right again even though that is impossible. One mate may want revenge, while another wants to do something to honor the life of the child, and to make sense of the senseless loss. All of these feelings and desires must be talked out and not judged.

FACT

It is important for couples to realize that their marriage will never be the same after the death of a child. If problems exist in a marriage prior to a child's death, those problems generally increase later. Most marriages do survive the initial negativity spouses often feel toward one another and return to a fulfilling relationship.

What to Do

Remember that life is precious. Being overprotective of your remaining children only robs all of you of the gift of living each day to the fullest. Accept that you can't always keep your children safe and that you can't be in total control of your lives. It's okay for men to cry. Neither one of you has to be the strong one nor the one to tough it out.

Try to live your lives in the present moment. It is vital that you communicate your feelings with one another. Don't ignore or try to bury your feelings. Share your feelings of helplessness, confusion, anger, depression, pain, guilt, fear, and even hate.

It is important to educate yourselves about the stages of death and dying. Don't allow yourself or your spouse to get stuck in one of the stages. Accept that there are no quick fixes to the heartbreak you are experiencing. Although the first two years are the most difficult, the pain is long-lasting. Holidays and birthdays can be exceptionally hard to endure. Although it is important to not judge or discredit your feelings, it is also important to get on with living your life and to not dwell on your grief. If having a memorial rosebush or a tree or a plaque at a park or church in memory of your child is soothing to you, then do this. Find ways to laugh with one another. Remind yourselves of all that you have to live for and all that you have to offer to one another and your family. With your love for one another, you will weather this storm together.

ALERT!

If you find your spouse becoming distant, or if disharmony begins to get more intense in your relationship, seek counseling. Trying to maneuver alone through this time of confusion and pain is a huge mistake.

Things to Do During a Crisis

When a crisis descends upon your marriage, make a decision that the experience will not destroy your relationship, but will strengthen it. If you take things one day at a time and keep the lines of communication open between you, a crisis or traumatic event does not have to mean the end of your strong marriage. Remember to:

- Take care of yourselves by exercising, eating healthy foods, drinking water, having some fun (if possible), and getting enough sleep.
- Prioritize what absolutely has to be done. Focus on getting those tasks completed.
- Try to not place blame on either yourself or your spouse for the crisis. If it is obvious that you are at fault for the situation, admit it.
- Share your feelings and thoughts with one another. Don't keep them bottled up inside.
- Make time for one another. Hold on to each other. Watch a funny movie together and laugh. Snuggle close to your partner, hug one another, or have sex.
- Focus on your commitment to one another.
- Look for the positive things happening around you. Compliment one another.
- Be patient. Realize that the crisis won't last forever.
- Seek help and emotional support from family, friends, or a support group.
- When dealing with grief, accept that you may each deal with it in your own way and on your own schedule.

Getting Help and Support

Feeling helpless can be a stifling feeling that pushes those you love away from you. Although asking for help is one of the hardest things for anyone to do, it is very important to get help and support when you need it. Libraries usually have lists of support groups and organizations whose primary purpose is helping marriages. Other good resources for marital and family support are churches and synagogues. They can point you toward recommended marriage and family therapists. Local community resources provide practical help and emotional support for the ill spouse, healthy partner, and other family members. Contact Meals on Wheels, groups like St. Vincent De Paul, neighbors, relatives, healthcare providers, and professional caregivers. If a support group is available, consider joining it. This is a journey that the two of you should not attempt to travel alone.

A strong marriage needs good communication, affirmation, ability to listen, trust, respect, fun, willingness to ask for help, and a sense of humor. These needs don't change because a couple is in the midst of difficulties or a crisis. When a crisis hits a marriage, both partners often feel a loss of control. In spite of this sense of helplessness, it is vital that a couple discuss their individual needs and desires. Take an honest look at whose life is being changed the most by the crisis. A marriage is forever changed when confronted by crisis and trauma but the change doesn't have to be negative. If a couple can work through the troubled times together through communication and caring, their marriage can come through the experience stronger and with a deeper understanding of what commitment to one another means. Ⓔ

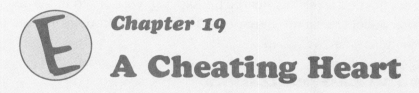

Chapter 19

A Cheating Heart

Statistics don't lie. Infidelity occurs in a large percentage of marriages. However, infidelity doesn't have to mean the end of your marriage. Discovering that your spouse has cheated can be a heart-wrenching time, but you can make changes to your relationship to reconcile and rebuild your marriage to be stronger than it was before. You both must make marriage your top priority.

Why Spouses Cheat

The fact that some spouses cheat on their partners is well known. If you are in the midst of experiencing this betrayal, listen to the advice of family and friends with caution. Although the reasons for your spouse's infidelity could fall into a classic pattern or behavior, each individual relationship that faces this heartache has its own story to tell. The reasons people cheat are numerous. The ways that couples handle this heartache are just as varied.

Reasons and Rationalizations

Although not always the case, an act of unfaithfulness is usually a symptom of other problems in a marriage. Some people enjoy the thrill of the chase and the rush that comes from forbidden fruit. Sexual addiction or seeing unfaithfulness as an act of retaliation can be other reasons people cheat.

When a spouse wants to end a marriage but doesn't feel like she has a solid reason to do so, she may embark on an affair as a way to force her partner to file for divorce. Trying to reason with an unfaithful spouse is usually unsuccessful. Someone in the midst of an affair may seem possessed and is often immune to recognizing the danger of losing children, self-respect, money, home, social status, sometimes even employment.

The high, excited feelings cheaters experience from a forbidden romance seem to cloud all reasoning. Cheating spouses often rationalize their behavior so that they don't have to face being responsible for straying or for the pain that the infidelity creates within their family.

Marriage Dissatisfaction

Affairs begin when one partner is dissatisfied in some way within the marriage. Although infidelity can stem from a sexual need, generally, it is an emotional need that is not being met. For many, the main appeal of an affair is not sex, but a sense of being cared for, acceptance, and being able to talk to someone who understands. Lack of conversation and not being listened to are some of the reasons many give for being unfaithful. It is unfortunate that a spouse who has these needs can't express them to his or her partner. Choosing to have an affair is a cowardly and unfair way to get one's needs met.

QUESTION?

Why do people choose to be unfaithful?
Some of the reasons commonly given for why a spouse is unfaithful include anger, unresolved issues, avoidance of conflict, career difficulties, looking for excitement, fear of growing older, jealousy of a new baby, feeling trapped, financial pressures, sense of remorse after the wedding, desire for a one-night stand, being a chronic cheater, and an involvement with a long-term relationship outside of marriage.

Knowing the type of infidelity sometimes makes dealing with it easier. Was it a one-night stand or a long-term affair? Did it happen just once or has there been a long string of affairs? However, knowing all the details can backfire. If you really must know, then ask the questions. Be prepared, though, for the information to haunt you.

Many unfaithful spouses continue to deny having an affair unless they are confronted by actual evidence proving the infidelity. Many will not apologize for their unfaithfulness, nor will they feel guilty about what they've done. Accept that you may never truly know why your spouse strayed. Many cheaters don't always know the answer to why they strayed themselves. Sometimes it takes the gift of time and the ability to look back with clarity before an unfaithful spouse can truly admit to why they strayed.

Warning Signs of Infidelity

Some chronic cheaters are good at covering up their tracks, and there are spouses who are genuinely surprised when they learn that their spouse has been unfaithful. However, most spouses have a feeling deep inside that tells them that there is something going on. Listen to your inner voices. There are nearly always warning signs that a marriage is in trouble and that a spouse is straying.

Many times an unsuspecting spouse is too busy coping with job, kids, activities, and life in general to recognize the warning signs that are flashing in front of his or her eyes. It is also common for a spouse to not want to notice the signs or to not want to admit that a partner is cheating. The consequences of this knowledge are too great for some spouses to bear. So to avoid having to deal with the possibility of a divorce, they go into denial.

Avoidance will not save a marriage. The distance that will continue to grow between spouses will ultimately bring the relationship to an end.

Some suspicious behaviors to watch out for include the following:

- Sexual intimacy is nearly nonexistent. There may be sexual activity in a marriage, but it isn't intimate.
- Your spouse complains about being bored with life in general and seems to be seeking a way to have thrills in his or her life.
- The two of you have difficulty communicating and defensiveness is the usual response to even simple questions about spending money or time spent away from home.
- Your partner is working longer hours at work, running more unexplained errands, dressing nicer, looking better, and is concerned about weight gain.
- Charges on your credit cards don't make sense, and money has become a big issue between the two of you. Some unfaithful spouses even hide credit card and telephone bills.
- Your spouse seems indifferent to being present at family events and gatherings, and shows a lack of desire to go anywhere or do anything with you.
- You catch your spouse telling lies about a variety of things, and he or she seems more secretive.
- You feel distance from your partner and even an unwillingness to disagree or argue with you.
- Your partner decides to quit attending church.
- Your spouse asks for a separation to "sort things out."

Cyber-Affairs

Some people don't consider cyber-sex an act of infidelity. Others do. Online affairs have the luxury of being pure fantasy. The anonymity of cyber-sex makes it very addictive. Everything about the cyber-relationship is perfect because it doesn't have to cope with the real world. Even though your partner may know that it is all too good to be true and just make-believe, it doesn't make any difference. It makes it very difficult for a real life spouse to compete with a dream lover.

If you suspect that your spouse is having a cyber-affair, ask yourself if there are other problems in your marriage. Some issues that can trigger this type of behavior include sexual dissatisfaction, financial problems, relocation, and lack of communication. If your partner has changed passwords on the computer, spends more time than usual on the computer, resents interference, and is staying up later than usual or getting up earlier in the morning, there could be a cyber-sex problem. Other signs of cyber-sex include a lack of sexual desire or enthusiasm, apathy when it comes to family celebrations, avoidance of household or job-related responsibilities, moodiness, dishonesty, and denial or rationalizations about the amount of time spent at the computer or alone. Additionally, if your spouse is erasing computer history files and cookies, moves the computer to an isolated location, and refuses to talk about the issue, your concerns are probably justified.

Seek counseling before the cyber-affair turns into a physical encounter. To get over this addiction and to recognize that true intimacy can only come from a real relationship, a person will need the help of a therapist.

FACT

Although there is no physical connection in an online affair, the emotional attachment is tremendously strong and seductive.

Pornography Concerns

Married couples often have very different attitudes and opinions about pornography and what it is or isn't. Pornography becomes a problem in a relationship when these thoughts and feelings about the issue are not talked out. If a spouse doesn't realize the depth of a partner's dislike of or attraction to pornography, then there is no understanding of how much viewing it can affect a marriage.

The discovery of a spouse's desire to view pornography on the Internet or on a video or in a magazine can trigger an array of emotions that can range from indifference to curiosity to rage. Men and women often have different attitudes about what is and what isn't sexually explicit material. Some individuals think, "What is the big deal?" while others believe pornography is insulting and degrading to both men and women. While a woman may not object to her husband looking at a pretty woman walking past them on the street, she may question his love for her and consider him unfaithful if he spends time viewing pornography.

Experts even have different views on the impact of pornography on a marriage. Some think that a marital sexual relationship can be enhanced when imagination is allowed to run free by viewing pornographic pictures or reading romance novels. Other experts notice how guilt, mistrust, and anger about pornography can decrease sexual satisfaction within a relationship and eventually tear a marriage apart. Additionally, receiving instant gratification through pornographic fantasies may cause some people to withdraw from their marriage.

Pornography can also make it difficult for individuals to see sex as a loving form of communication. It is impossible to censor your spouse's thoughts. Whether or not pornography will add to or lessen your sexual enjoyment is up to the two of you and depends on your own values. Remember that your role as a spouse is not one of a law enforcement officer or a spy. Try to discuss this issue without heightened emotions and accusations.

Rebuilding Your Marriage

The first thing a couple needs to talk about after an infidelity is whether and why they want to save their marriage. Realities of the work that lies ahead of them in salvaging their marriage must be faced. They also need to acknowledge whether counseling is needed to help them understand why the infidelity occurred in the first place. There are a lot of emotions and heartache to work through. Waving a magic wand and thinking all will be well again is foolish thinking. No one enters into an adulterous relationship without realizing that they could cause a great deal of pain for their family. Yet the decision to be unfaithful is made anyway. This is one of the hardest aspects of unfaithfulness to get over. The resentment of feeling betrayed and unimportant is devastating. Therefore, healing the wounds of an affair takes a great deal of time.

What Was Before Is Gone

Realize that your current marriage has died. Give yourself time to grieve that loss before attempting to rebuild your relationship. Part of the grieving process is to allow yourself to experience the five stages of death and dying: denial, anger, bargaining, depression, and acceptance.

This doesn't mean your marriage can't be renewed and strengthened, because it can. But you must accept that your relationship will be different and hopefully stronger. Your spouse will need to show an understanding of what you have felt and experienced, and needs to prove that he or she is truly sorry, willing to change offending behaviors, and working on earning your trust once again. Your marriage can't be sustained if there is no agreement to build trust once again between the two of you.

ALERT!

Think twice before you tell your family or your spouse's family about the infidelity. You may discover that family members will hold a grudge against your spouse for a long time.

Coping after an Affair

If you just learned that your spouse has been unfaithful, the news has probably hit you like a ton of bricks. You feel sick inside even though you've talked with one another and there is some hope that your marriage can survive. This pit in your stomach is due to increasing doubts if you even want to try to save your relationship. You may have wobbly legs and your heart pounds. This is normal.

Don't make a quick decision about ending your marriage. Take some time to reflect on your marital relationship. Balance is the key to getting through this difficult time. Your sense of uncertainty, shock, fear, pain, confusion, disbelief, disappointment, depression, rage, and agitation are emotions that nearly every betrayed spouse feels.

You may experience some physical reactions such as nausea, diarrhea, sleep problems (too little or too much), not wanting to eat or binge eating, shakiness, and difficulty concentrating. You have a lot of decision making to do and you need to be both physically and emotionally healthy in order to make rational decisions. It is important that you try to take care of yourself by making a commitment to eating healthy foods, staying on a schedule, sleeping regular hours, getting some exercise each day, drinking plenty of water, and, yes, having some fun.

Although it may be unconceivable to you to laugh and have fun, it is essential. Watch some funny movies or TV shows. Remember that tears are healthy, too. If they aren't coming naturally, put on some blues type music or watch a sad movie. Force yourself to get outside and walk around the block or play basketball with your kids. If you are tempted to survive on potato chips and soda, keep these items out of the house and stock your refrigerator and cabinets with healthy foods. Even if your partner insists there was no unprotected sex, it is essential that you both be tested for AIDS/HIVS and sexually transmitted diseases before you resume sexual intimacy without protection.

Your kids will know that there is something wrong so be honest with them, but don't give them details. Make sure that neither of you promise them something that you may not be able to keep. What they need to hear is that each of you will be okay. Some other ways to cope include:

- Write down your thoughts and feelings in a journal.
- As you talk with your spouse about the infidelity, ask all the questions you want.
- Seek counseling.
- Realize that blaming one another or the third party for the affair is just wasted energy and won't change anything.
- If you are jumpy, yell at trivial actions, snap at the kids a lot, feel like

you are walking on eggshells, and continue to have physical reactions when you are reminded of the infidelity, you may be experiencing post-traumatic stress. Set an appointment to consult with a physician as soon as you can.

- Try not to push others away from you because your spouse has betrayed you.
- Be practical. Have a backup plan. Look at your finances, housing situation, transportation, and so forth. If you don't have an individual bank account, consider setting one up for your own peace of mind.
- Take it one day at a time. It is important that you not lose confidence in yourself or in your decisions. Despite what it may seem, remember that life will go on.

Letting Go of the Hurt

Carrying anger and hostility in your heart is as physically and emotionally draining as carrying large, heavy buckets of water on your shoulders all day. You truly hurt yourself more than your spouse when you are not willing to let go of the hurt, or you decide to hold a grudge and not to forgive. But don't expect everything to be back the way it was just because you've decided to forgive your spouse and made a commitment to save your marriage. It takes time for the mixture of feelings, the sense of confusion and limbo, and the mistrust to go away.

FACT

The only way to truly let go of the pain of the past is to make a decision to stop thinking or obsessing about it. Find ways to distract yourself any time you find yourself starting to think about your spouse's infidelity.

You both deserve open and honest answers to your questions about the affair. The wounded partner must be allowed to share his or her pain and believe that the devastating hurt has been acknowledged. To do this, you both must listen completely to one another with both your head and your heart.

Forgiveness

It is important that you can decide to forgive or to be forgiven. Take responsibility for your own actions and decisions without blaming your spouse. If you are the unfaithful spouse, the only way you can show that you can be trusted is to change your behaviors. Set some specific, short-range goals for your marriage and renew your commitment to your relationship. Being open to seeking counseling is a sign of this commitment. Rebuilding trust takes time. Don't place a timetable on this process.

Calling It Quits

If the betrayal was so hurtful, that, after counseling and giving it some time and thought, you've decided to divorce, then it is important that you spend some time reflecting on the situation. Be honest in asking yourself questions about what you could have done or possibly should have done differently. However, don't get into a self-blaming game. No one deserves to be betrayed. No matter what you did or didn't do in your marriage, you are not to blame for the unfaithfulness. Realize that it is necessary to go through the process of grief over the loss of trust and the sense of being betrayed. Mourning these losses will help you bring closure to this painful time in your life.

Affair-Proofing Your Marriage

If you feel tempted to have an affair, ask yourself why you are vulnerable to the temptation. Take time to sit down and write it out. This will be for your eyes only. Then reflect on what you can do in your relationship with your partner to solve the issues that are creating the temptation. If the person you are attracted to is in your social circle or is where you work, consider making changes so you don't see this person on a daily basis.

When you recognize what is missing in your relationship, don't fall into the trap of placing all the blame on your spouse. Accept that you are the one responsible for making yourself happy and for your own feelings.

No marriage is completely affair proof. If you believe this, then you could be taking your spouse for granted. Take time to know yourselves and to understand what you desire from life. Handle troublesome issues and disagreements with healthy conflict. Don't let things build up inside or fester for long periods of time. Seek balance in your lives. Be sure to support one another's dreams and ambitions. Make sure that you communicate with one another on a daily basis and that you discuss not only your thoughts and values, but also your feelings as well. Work at finding ways to rekindle your intimacy with each other by planning dates with one another, spicing up your sex life, and discovering new ways to have fun together. Discuss the pressures in your lives and brainstorms to reduce the stress that you are both feeling. Remember why you fell in love with each other and tell that to each other.

Marriages can and do survive infidelity but only if both partners are willing to work at making the marriage successful. The third party has to be absolutely out of the picture before any attempt at reconciliation can be successful. A couple dealing with adultery will need courage, determination, renewed commitment, and a great deal of love and forgiveness to be able to overcome the devastation that unfaithfulness creates. Being able to face the past with honesty is the only way a couple can successfully move into the future together. There also needs to be the acceptance that the original marriage has ended, and that it will take time for the new marriage to be whole again. Ⓔ

Chapter 20

When Marriage Is No Longer a Safe Place

Whether it be through emotional or physical abuse, domestic violence occurs when a dominating spouse creates an environment of fear at home that prevents a partner from freely choosing how to live his or her own life. Everyone has a right to live free of fear and violence. This chapter covers what you need to know to identify and get out of abusive situations.

Are You Being Abused?

Many abusive spouses aren't sure if they are in an abusive situation or not. They think that their partner's behavior is normal. They believe they are truly loved and that their spouse is honestly sorry when he or she apologizes with gifts for a violent argument or outburst. You must realize that no one has the right to control anyone else, especially through fear and intimidation. Domestic abuse comes in many forms and includes sexual abuse, isolation, emotional abuse, verbal abuse, economic abuse, physical abuse, harassment, name-calling, extreme possessiveness, destruction of property, deprivation of resources and withholding money, and other threatening behaviors. If you have some doubts about whether or not you are being abused, ask yourself these questions.

- Do you find yourself tip-toeing around your spouse to avoid an angry outburst?
- Do you get yelled at and are you told that you are worthless or no good? Are you humiliated or embarrassed in front of other people?
- Do you believe that you can't do anything right?
- Has your spouse threatened to harm or kill you or your children? Has your partner ever pulled your hair or hit, choked, tripped, punched, pushed, or slapped you?
- Does your spouse force you to have sex or to do things sexually that you abhor?
- Do you live in fear?
- Is your time on the phone, or Internet, or visits with friends and family limited by your spouse? Does your spouse prevent you from leaving the house whenever you want? Is your access to bank accounts, credit cards, your car, or receiving mail nonexistent? Are you forced to account for every cent you spend?
- Are you forced to do things you don't want to do?
- Have others expressed any concern about your marital relationship?
- Do you think you deserve to be treated the way you are?

Along with violence, threatening, and anger, some other tactics that abusers use include trivializing, name-calling, denial, accusing, blaming, discounting, joking, diverting, withholding, ordering, countering, undermining, forgetting, blocking, judging, and criticizing.

Are You an Abusive Spouse?

Depending on the type of home you were raised in, you may believe that the way you treat or talk to your spouse is normal when in fact it is abusive behavior. You are an abusive spouse if your spouse is afraid of you because you have hit, pushed, slapped, or choked your partner or you have threatened to kill your spouse. You may have abusive tendencies if you are the jealous type or if you believe that your way is the only way. If you think of yourself as in charge and think you have the right to know what your spouse is doing or where your spouse is all the time, you are controlling and abusive. You have an abusive personality if you rationalize that your partner deserves to be yelled at or hit and believe that your spouse "asked for it."

ALERT!

If family or friends have told you that you have an anger problem, but you don't see it, you may be abusive without even realizing it. Seek help from a therapist to avoid destroying your marriage.

Destroying any of your spouse's belongings and enjoying seeing your partner cry, hurt, or in pain are all abusive behaviors. Limiting the social activities of your spouse or keeping all the financial information a secret reflect abusive behaviors. Many abusers don't seek help because they are fearful of losing everything. They think that saying they are sorry will be enough. But this type of apology *isn't* enough. You must take responsibility for your abusive behavior and seek counseling. Expecting your spouse to forgive and to forget right away is unrealistic.

Reasons for Abusive Behavior

There are many opinions as to why some people abuse those they say they love. Some motivations include being raised in a dysfunctional family, poor communication skills, stress, economic hardship, perceived provocation, wanting control over another person, low self-esteem, sense of ineffectiveness or inadequacy, lack of respect for women, and chemical addiction. Most abusers are very good at appearing to be charming and caring individuals to outsiders. The abusive behavior continues when there is a lack of economic or social consequence. Abusers come from all socioeconomic groups and backgrounds but one may display extreme jealousy, has a quick or bad temper, acts cruelly toward animals, is very possessive and keeps tabs on family members, has extreme highs and lows, likes to act tough, has a tendency to overreact to small problems, keeps tight control of finances, punches walls or throws things when frustrated, exhibits unpredictable behavior, and is prone to verbal abusiveness.

If sex is nonconsensual or a spouse uses force, intimidation, or other threats to get a partner to submit to sexual acts, it is considered to be marital rape, which is illegal in all fifty states in the United States. The sexual acts include any sexual activity that is unwanted, painful, or humiliating. Marital rape can be motivated by anger, or a need for power over the victim, or by a desire to have perverted sex.

Impact of Marital Abuse on Children

A controversial issue, both psychologically and legally, concerns the impact of marital abuse on children. If children live in a home where one parent is being abused, the kids are considered to be victims of abuse even if they haven't been physically hurt. Additionally, studies have revealed that when children witness violence in their home they can be psychologically damaged and feel emotionally deprived.

Statistically, these kids are also at a high risk for eventually being physically abused themselves. These children often display delinquent behavior when they reach adolescence. When these children reach adulthood, they are at a higher risk for being an abusive husband, an abused wife, or an abusive parent. Children living in an abusive home are susceptible to:

- Poor health, frequent illness, and poor sleeping habits
- Rebellion against authority, and angry, hostile behavior such as hitting, biting, being argumentative, and fighting
- Difficulties at school, not wanting to go to classes, poor grades, and difficulty concentrating
- Withdrawn or passive personality, severe shyness or clinging, and social isolation from peers
- Feelings of sadness, depression, and anxiety
- Low self-image, tending to blame self for negative situations
- Excessive screaming in infants

Protecting Yourself

Although you can't control your abuser's actions, you can increase your own safety and protect yourself by choosing to let family and friends know that you've been abused and by developing a plan so you can leave quickly. It is vital that you have some plans in place. If you are considering leaving an abusive marriage, don't make this decision alone.

QUESTION?

Where can I turn if I'm being abused?
A local domestic abuse shelter can help you determine your options and they will assist you in finding a safe place to stay while you sort things out and make decisions about your future.

Get advice from either an attorney, domestic violence advocate, or a counselor to make sure that you and your children will be safe. They will be able to help you contact the many resources that are now available to protect victims of domestic violence. These resources provide temporary shelter, free counseling, financial aid, and protection from losing your job.

Problems in Leaving an Abusive Relationship

The main reason a victim doesn't leave an abusive situation is because it is often dangerous to do so. Many abused spouses worry about losing custody of their children, have no financial resources, and fear for the safety of themselves and their children.

Once a person has been abused, feelings of embarrassment, shame, and confusion become prevalent. If an abuser has isolated and limited a victim's contacts with friends and family, leaving can be even more difficult. Some victims are concerned about being charged with desertion, and facing a decline in living standards and the impact on the children. Lack of knowledge and access to help and resources also keeps victims trapped.

A person's attitudes toward marriage and divorce can also create a barrier to escaping from an abusive relationship, especially if he or she views the failure of a marriage as a personal failure. Some victims have been made to believe that they have nowhere to turn, that they are lucky to have a partner at all, or that they are the cause of the abuse. They may rationalize that their abusive spouse is a good person in spite of the abuse. They certainly don't stay because they enjoy the way they are being treated.

ALERT!

Call 911 if you are in immediate danger. Another source of help is the National Domestic Violence Hotline at ☎ (800) 799-7233.

Safety Planning

Do not tolerate abusive behavior from your spouse. Denying it won't make it go away. In fact, if you don't do something about it, the situation will only grow worse. Look for a safe room to go to if your spouse becomes abusive. Don't choose a room with no exits, or a room on a second floor or higher. Avoid retreating to the kitchen as there are too many items there that could be used as weapons.

Look around your dwelling to see how to get out of it in a hurry. Plan on what door, window, stairwell, or elevator (if you live in an apartment building) would be the quickest exit. Devise a code word so that your family, friends, and coworkers know to call for help. Make an emergency kit that is easy to grab. It should contain change and extra money, a checkbook, credit cards, health and vaccination records, school information, birth and marriage certificates, your driver's license, social security numbers, a list of people you trust to contact, deeds and leases, proof of income, insurance policies, and your house and car keys. Memorize all the important numbers just in case you can't reach your emergency kit. Make sure that your children know how and when to use the telephone to dial 911.

Your emergency kit should be kept in a place where your partner can't find it. You may want to consider having a duplicate kit in the trunk of your car or at a neighbor's home.

Consider your options for temporary shelter if you have to leave quickly. Talk with friends or family members or your local domestic violence shelter to see what would be available to you and your children.

Evasion and Change of Identity

If you've left your spouse, you still need to be cautious. Vary your schedule and routine. Shop at different stores at different times. Drive to work or school using various routes. If you have to meet with your partner, always have the meeting in a public location. Change your phone number and screen all calls. Document all meetings, messages, or other contact with your spouse. Stay in touch with a shelter for battered women and let your children's school and your employer know of your situation.

If the situation is so dangerous that the only way you can be safe is to flee, seek guidance before making this move. Evading your abuser can be very difficult even when you change your name, move to a different area of the country, have an unlisted telephone number, enter a different profession, or change your Social Security number. It is very important to keep copies of all records documenting domestic abuse with yourself and your children. Keep originals in a safe, secure place.

Although the Social Security Administration allows a victim of domestic violence to obtain a new Social Security number and assume a new identity, there are many consequences to this procedure:

- Don't assume that your identity and whereabouts will be secure. Your old number may be cross-referenced with your new one. The SSA does require an in-person interview to obtain information about a SSN that was changed due to abuse, harassment, or life endangerment.
- You won't be able to get a passport or other federal identification because you won't have a birth certificate. This lack of documentation may make it more difficult for you to travel, may delay benefits from the state or federal government, and could create problems for your children regarding school records requirements.
- A new identity will mean losing previous work history and references along with past medical records and court records that are in a different name.
- The SSA will not assign new numbers for children if the other parent has court-ordered visitation rights.

Getting Help

If you are in an abusive marriage, it is imperative that you seek help and support immediately. Living with an abusive spouse is not recommended unless the abusive partner receives treatment and has shown ability to control anger and aggression. Get help for your children so that they understand and believe that they are not responsible for the violence at home.

Many victims worry that if they call the police they may end up being the one arrested or their children will be put in foster care because they fought back or threw something at their spouse in self-defense. Try to put these thoughts aside if you have been physically attacked or your children are threatened or harmed. Don't hesitate in calling the police.

Once called, they must investigate. They will look for evidence of injury to you or your children, or damage to your home like broken windows, smashed furniture, and so forth. If your spouse left a threatening note on your voicemail or wrote you an intimidating note, show these to the police. The police need evidence to show probable cause in order to make an arrest. What you say to the police will also be considered evidence. Don't sign any statement that doesn't reflect exactly what you said.

You should receive a form that informs you of your legal rights. It usually includes information on domestic violence resources in your locale. If your spouse isn't arrested, request the reasons for this in writing. Realize that even if your spouse isn't arrested when you call the police, that the incident is still on record. The documentation could prove helpful if you need to call the police again or decide to ask for a protection order.

Legal Concerns

Child protective investigators generally consider domestic violence as child maltreatment. In some cases, they may consider allegations of failure to protect on the victim's part if he or she is not protecting their children by getting out of the abusive situation. Many believe that the justice system is heaping further abuse on victims by holding them legally responsible for protecting their children from domestic abuse. The actual perpetrator of the abuse needs to be held accountable for his or her actions. Conviction of domestic violence abusers generally only results in probation, a fine, or nonjail or short jail sentences.

Many abuse victims don't realize that they are in legal jeopardy themselves if they don't assume their moral and legal responsibility to protect their children from the long-term effects of domestic violence.

Orders of Protection

An Order of Protection won't guarantee your safety, but your abusive spouse could be more easily arrested if such an order is violated. Orders of Protection usually direct an abuser to stop the abusive behavior, and to stay away from you, your home, your job, your family, and your children's school or daycare facility. This also includes preventing contact with you through phone calls, letters, or messages through other people. If you have questions concerning how to get an Order of Protection or how to have one enforced, your local domestic violence center can help you.

Hiring an Attorney

Before you hire an attorney, have a meeting so that you can ask questions and have a clear understanding of their bias, experience in handling domestic violence cases, fees, and payment schedules. Don't be afraid to ask how many domestic violence cases the firm had represented and who their clients generally are (victims, children, or abusers). Ask about their attitude toward joint custody awards in domestic violence cases especially in cases where children have been abused. Make sure there is no conflict of interest in handling your case or that the firm has not ever represented your partner.

Ask specific questions regarding attorney fees. You need to know if a retainer is required, if any part of an unused retainer is refunded, what work the fees cover, if you are being charged an hourly fee or a flat fee for the case, if there are any additional charges for court appearances, and if there are other expenses you could be required to pay. Find out who would be working on your case and if you will be charged for speaking with their secretary or receptionist. If you are concerned about finances, ask if the firm has payment plans available. If so, make sure the payment arrangements are in writing. If you give your attorney any important documents, make sure you have copies of all the paperwork, including papers filed with the court, stored in a safe place.

Victims need to get help to get themselves and their children out of an abusive situation. Remember that you are not to blame for the abuse nor do you deserve to be treated in this way. This is not a simple issue. Please don't try to walk this journey alone. (E)

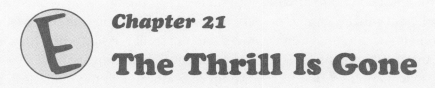

Chapter 21

The Thrill Is Gone

If you have reached a point in your marriage where you are having serious problems, you must recognize that and admit your marriage may be in trouble. This is a first step in rebuilding a hurt relationship. The fact that both of you are able to recognize that you need help is a positive sign that there is still hope for your marriage.

The Decision to Seek Help

When the thrill is gone in a marriage, people wonder what happened to the passion, excitement, joy, and tingle of loving one another. It seems improbable that the hope, dreams, and commitment to one another have been lost. For some couples, the thrill slowly fades away due to being in a rut and taking one another for granted. The passion may fade so slowly and quietly that a couple doesn't realize it until they find themselves strangers with one another. Others find the thrill missing when they are in the midst of a crisis. Some couples realize that things aren't quite right in their marriage when they wake up one morning to the realization that there is a tremendous distance between them. Continuous fussing with one another over unimportant issues also wears away at a relationship.

When things are difficult in your marriage, a healthy sign is that both of you are recognizing that the two of you have problems. Many couples do desire to save their marriages. The couples who come back from the brink of disaster are the ones who know they truly want their relationship to be successful, but they just aren't sure how to keep it together. They know they love one another but they don't know how to live together in harmony and joy. They need better communication skills so they can more easily express their thoughts and feelings to one another, and be able to handle conflict in a healthy way. They recognize that seeking professional help can be a solution and a means to acquiring the skills and communication tools they need.

The next step is getting that help. If you settle for living a life of "peace" (or nonconfrontation) at any price, you will ultimately be throwing away your marriage. Getting help will enable the both of you identify your roles in the problems you have. Don't wait until too much damage has been done to your marriage and it is too late to save it.

Taking Classes Together

One way to deal with a troublesome topic or area in your marriage is to take a course together so that you are both on the same playing field in dealing with the issue that is causing problems. For instance, if finances are a touchy subject and one that causes a lot of conflict between the two of you, attending a course at a local community college will provide the opportunity and environment to talk about the issue in a nonconfrontational way.

Other courses you could take together include family planning classes, communication workshops, conflict management sessions, household management classes, landscaping courses, or other marriage education programs. Even taking classes together for recreational activities such as bowling, golf, tennis, sailing, or dancing can be good for your relationship.

Giving Up

Separating or calling it quits isn't the easy way out. Getting a divorce won't necessarily solve your problems and will surely complicate your life in many ways. If you don't figure out why your marriage is struggling, and bring some closure to those issues, you are likely to have to cope with the same problems in a different relationship. The problems will just follow you around. Additionally, if you have children, you will still need to be able to cope with your ex-spouse in dealing with parenting issues, holidays, custody situations, and important family events.

FACT

Over 40 percent of divorced people not only regretted getting a divorce, but they believed the demise of their marriage was preventable.

Does Counseling Work?

Marriage counseling can't save every marriage. After many years of discord and heartache, some relationships have been so severely damaged that reconciliation is very improbable. If a couple is attending therapy sessions just so they can say they tried everything, the marriage is probably over before the therapy even begins. However, if a couple is open to identifying their problems, reaching compromise, and working on improving their communication skills, they will have a better success rate in saving their troubled marriage.

Therapists often use a variety of techniques to help their clients. Determining whether marriage therapy has been a success or a failure is not easy as success or failure depends a great deal on the expectations of the couple. If you hope that counseling will help you save your marriage and you end up divorced, does that mean the therapy wasn't effective? Not necessarily, especially if your spouse was dead set against salvaging your marriage in the first place. If either of you are in therapy because you're willing to agree to almost anything to keep your marriage together, don't make the mistake of making promises you won't keep, and thinking that things will settle down after the therapy ends. Going back to your own bad or inappropriate habits can bring about the termination of your marriage very quickly. It is important that you both understand the root of your problems and seek to make the individual changes that are called for.

ALERT!

Your chances of receiving positive assistance for your marriage from therapy are lessened if you wait too long before asking for help.

An Exercise in Reflection

Before you actually see a counselor, each of you needs to sit down and write out some reasons why you want help for your marriage. Express your expectations of being in counseling. Reflect on how willing you are to make changes in your own behavior to save your marriage. At this point in time, only share this with the counselor and not with your spouse. This exercise will help you each focus on your feelings and openness toward counseling before you have that first appointment with a therapist.

Cinematherapy

Cinematherapy is often used in marriage counseling. Prescribing movies for what ails you is a proven, legitimate clinical tool of therapists. It has evolved from bibliotherapy, which started in the 1930s. Bibliotherapy uses books to explore relationship issues. In cinematherapy, couples are assigned to watch a movie or perhaps several scenes from a movie. Cinematherapy helps spouses face issues such as change, love, self-discovery, sexuality, grief and loss, family relationships, divorce, adultery, values, conflict, parenting styles, dealing with in-laws, and more. By watching specific prescribed movies, couples can often see their own problems more clearly, understand that they aren't alone in their situation, and realize that they can triumph over difficult times, opening the door for more communication about their problems.

Counselors usually ask clients to discern what message the movie may have for them personally. Post-viewing questions are often offered to help couples dig deeper into their own reactions and feelings about the movie. Viewing the consequences for the characters in the movie and seeing alternative responses to problems can often help individuals explore and reflect on their own life experiences. This will ultimately lead to an understanding of their feelings and reactions in their own life situations.

Watching certain movies can help couples remember their own days of courtship and why they fell in love with one another in the first place. Couples are already used to watching movies together and discussing them, so cinematherapy is a nonthreatening tool.

An example of a movie that can teach a husband about his wife's need for intimacy is *The Bridges of Madison County*, introduced in 1995. Clint Eastwood's character demonstrates how little things can be intimate moments when he helps Meryl Streep's character chop carrots. Movies have the power to make people cry, laugh, think, question, and to heal.

Finding a Counselor or Therapist

In seeking out a counselor, it is important to realize that this will be an intimate relationship and you need to find someone who will not only help you but whom you will also be able to trust. This also needs to be a decision made by the two of you jointly. Confidence in whom you choose is also very important. Don't pick someone just because you think he or she will say what you want to hear. Find a therapist who will teach you communication skills. You want to choose someone who will help you make your relationship work.

Before you make a final decision on using a therapist, ask him or her to describe their training in marital therapy. Inquire about attitudes toward salvaging a troubled marriage versus working toward a good divorce. Find out what percentage of the practice is devoted to marital therapy. Some individuals are uncomfortable dealing with a therapist of the opposite sex. If this is an issue, talk about it with one another and be sensitive to it when you choose a therapist.

FACT

There are many marital therapists and experts who believe that the divorce rate can be reduced significantly without increasing the number of truly unhappy marriages. This goal can be achieved by providing couples with direction, structure, communication skills, and guidelines.

Look for a marriage counselor who is encouraging, motivating, calming, and a good problem solver. At this point in your relationship, you need encouragement and motivation as you work on restoring your marriage. You also need help in dealing with your marital and emotional problems, learning communication and conflict resolution techniques, and learning how to effectively come up with your own solutions.

When you call for your first appointment, don't be afraid to ask some questions so you have an idea of the education, experience, and philosophy of the counselor, and a time frame as to how soon you can have an appointment. If you have to wait more than a week or two, call another provider. Ask if the counselor will meet with each of you separately for a few minutes before seeing the two of you together. Some will do this, some won't. Ask why or why not.

Don't expect overnight miracles from your sessions with the counselor. However, if you don't believe that the counselor is right for you, or you don't see any improvement in your marriage within thirty days, then it may be time to look for another counselor. You will experience some good weeks and some bad weeks while in therapy, but if things are just dragging along, terminate treatment. Don't just go through the motions. If you are determined to get a divorce, save yourselves and your children the pain and terminate your relationship quickly.

FACT

Although solution-focused treatments have a high rate of effectiveness, it is against the code of ethics of the American Association for Marriage and Family Therapy for therapists to directly tell people what they should or should not do, or whether they should stay married or get divorced. It is best for a couple to come up with their own solutions.

Forgiveness and Reconciliation

There is a difference between asking for forgiveness and saying, "I'm sorry." When you just say you are sorry, you are keeping control of the situation. But asking for forgiveness is putting the ball in the other court. You are giving control to your spouse and making a decision to be vulnerable. This vulnerability is because your spouse may say, "no."

Making the decision to forgive someone doesn't mean you are condoning the offending behavior. When you've forgiven, you will feel differently. You won't necessarily be reconciled with the person you've forgiven, but you will no longer feel the anger and hurt from your past. You can still remember everything that happened, but it is as if there is a white picket fence in your mind that keeps you from feeling the negative feelings and pain. There is an internal peace that will let you move on with your life. Being able to forgive is like lifting heavy water buckets from your shoulders.

However, when you decide to not forgive someone, you are letting that person live rent-free in your head. Holding on to resentment, grudges, and hurts also drains you emotionally and lowers your energy level.

Rebuilding Trust

Infidelity, lies, or broken promises will deeply damage the trust between husband and wife. To rebuild the trust you have in your spouse, you will have to make a decision to love by trying to let go of the past. It is important that you stop obsessing about the experiences that severed your feelings of trust. You must also choose to forgive or to be forgiven.

If your behavior is what damaged the trust, then you must be willing to change that behavior. It is critical that you both take responsibility for your individual actions and decisions. The hurt partner must be allowed to share the pain and heartache that is felt, and to have these feelings acknowledged. Additionally, all questions need to receive open and honest answers. You must honestly communicate what is both in your head and in your heart. Try not to use blaming statements or words like *always*, *must*, *never*, or *should*.

QUESTION?

Will I ever be able to forgive my spouse?
Even though you may remember incidents concerning the betrayal or infidelity, the pain will eventually go away. Rebuilding trust takes time. It won't happen overnight.

As you work on setting new and specific goals for your marriage together, you must also renew your commitment to one another. Although it takes a long time to rebuild trust, celebrate the joys and new discoveries in your relationship one day at a time. Let go of the past and don't dwell in the hurt and pain. You will find in the midst of that journey together that the trust between the two of you will deepen.

Improving Your Marriage

Every marriage can be improved since no marriage is absolutely perfect. Be honest with one another. Laugh together daily but make sure that you are laughing with one another and not at each other. Humor can hurt. Know how to fight fairly. Be open to forgiving and asking for forgiveness. Share goals and expectations together every day. Support and praise the goals and achievements of each other. Show respect for your partner. Work on continuing to improve your communication skills. Decide to daily dialogue with each other. Pick a question, write about it, and share your responses with one another. On a daily basis, tell one another which endearing quality you noticed that day. Make decisions together regarding the larger issues in your life, such as disciplining your children, taking vacations, spending or saving money, coping with chores, and so on. Make time to be alone with one another by scheduling regular romantic getaways or dates. On a daily basis, make a decision to trust, make a decision to listen, and make a decision to love.

Showing Respect

We often place a high value on practicing civility with strangers, but less so with those we love. It is simple to show love and respect for your spouse. Look at your spouse when spoken to. Say please and thank you. Listen to what your partner has to say. Don't put your spouse down or belittle your partner's accomplishments. Be willing to apologize and ask for forgiveness when you've been wrong. Do your share of the household chores, hang up your clothes, and pick up after yourself. Let your spouse know when you are proud of his or her achievements. Don't interrupt. Refrain from embarrassing your mate in public or in private. If someone were watching you two interacting with one another would they say to someone else that they noticed a couple that honored one another?

Connecting Through Expressions of Love

It is important that you can express your love to your spouse in a way that he or she can understand. Although you may not realize it, you may be talking in a different language. Ask yourself how you express love to others. Do you give gifts to show your love or do you give hugs and massages? Are you the type to express your love in the things you do around the house, or by the amount of time you spend with your partner, or do you think you are being loving when you compliment your spouse on how well the dinner tasted, or how clean the house looks?

The way you express love is probably the way you primarily prefer to receive love. Usually, couples don't speak the same love language. He gets upset when she doesn't seem to appreciate the fact that he fixed the dishwasher, and she is upset because he didn't "ooh" and "ah" over the new tool she bought him. They are both expressing love, but not feeling loved in return. Notice how your spouse expresses love to you, and make an effort to return that love in the same way.

An example of this type of decision to love is the way Pete and Gloria express their love for one another. Pete is very generous and buys many unexpected presents for Gloria. He loves receiving gifts himself. The best way Gloria can express her love for Pete is by giving him a gift. On the other hand, Gloria is very helpful. She looks for ways to make life easier for Pete. Pete can show his love for Gloria by surprising her by doing the laundry or dishes now and then. Stretch yourselves to reach out to one another in this way. It will take a conscious decision to love because it will not be your natural way of expressing love.

ALERT!

When your marriage is having problems and you sense that the two of you are heading toward a divorce, seek help right away. Don't put this off. Marriage courses or Marriage Encounter and Retrouvaille-type weekends are other sources of help.

Simple Activities to Deepen Your Relationship

Don't try to do too much all at once, but try one or two of these activities as a way to reconnect with one another:

- Tape record yourselves for about an hour during a typical evening or morning at home with one another. Listen to it together a few days later and talk about your thoughts and feelings in response to what you heard on the tape.
- If you have a habit of continually asking your spouse to get you a cup of coffee, or help you find your glasses or keys, or run an errand for you, refrain from all these for one weekend. Instead, do these things for your partner.
- Pay attention to the number of times you interrupt your partner. Pick an evening or an afternoon and don't state your opinion on a topic until your spouse has completely finished talking.
- Choose a book you are both interested in and read it together.

- Reflect back on the past ten years. Select some periods of time when you each felt very happy or when things seemed to be going well. Talk with one another about those times and why you think they were positive times in your marriage.
- When a song or movie touches your heart or reminds you of something or someone, share that information with your spouse.
- If possible, together visit your childhood towns. Walk down the street where you lived, look for the house you lived in, find the schools and church you attended, and play on the playgrounds you enjoyed in your youth. Talk about your memories with each other.
- Talk about how and where you would like to live if you two had all the money you could possibly ever need. How different is this dream lifestyle from the way you live now?

Saving Your Marriage

If you want to save your marriage even though you know it is in trouble, make time to sort things out. Recommit to one another. Admit to your mistakes. Make sure you fight fairly and that you listen to one another. Don't allow yourselves to get caught up in repetitive arguments over trivial issues. In the midst of your work to reconnect, take time to do something enjoyable with each other. The result can be a relationship even stronger than what you'd imagined. (E)

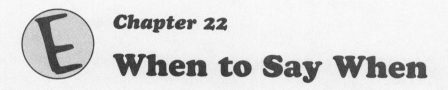

Chapter 22

When to Say When

When all is said and done, sometimes it is better to end a marriage. Only you will know when you've had enough and it is time to say that your marriage is over. Here's help in knowing when a marriage is truly over and how to confront the issues divorce will bring.

The Divorce Decision

Many people stay married in an unhealthy relationship because they have firm beliefs in the vows they said at their wedding. Other people remain in a dead marriage because they are concerned about the impact of the divorce on their children. Some remain out of a sense of security, or out of fear of physical consequences if they leave, or a fear of being on their own, or because they don't want to give up the lifestyle they are accustomed to. Although staying in an unhealthy, dysfunctional marriage works out for some people who can handle a marriage of convenience and just being roommates, this sort of relationship usually continues to disintegrate. The inevitable is just being postponed.

Throwing in the Towel

The decision to end a marriage is an agonizing one. Many trying to make this decision find they have problems with moodiness or lack of concentration, escape into sleep, try to survive on junk food, and generally let their appearance go. Living in limbo creates frustration, anger, impatience, and fear. Knowing whether or not a marriage is worth saving is a tough call. The amount of time already invested in a relationship has considerable influence on whether to stay or go. If you are making this life-changing decision because you are unhappy, think twice. Being single won't guarantee that you will be happier.

Questions to Ask Yourself

Have you or your children been physically or emotionally abused by your spouse? Has your partner been unfaithful? Are you arguing with one another over the same issues over and over again? Do you feel as if you are being constantly criticized or put-down? Are you irritated by just about everything your spouse says or does? Do you find yourselves fussing a lot over really trivial matters? Can you communicate with one another at all? Do you have any respect for one another? Do you two fight fairly? Are you still sexually intimate? Can you remember the last time you had fun together? Do you have any compatible goals or values? When was the last time you were able to compromise? Do you have anything left to give to your marriage?

Are you having dreams that your spouse died? Do you think you are strong enough to deal with the emotional and financial consequences of divorce?

ALERT!

Some relationships are not healthy, probably should not have happened at all, and need to be ended. Reasons to end a marriage include physical abuse, sexual abuse, verbal abuse, emotional abuse, child abuse, serial adultery, lack of forgiveness, alcohol or drug addiction, and abandonment.

Point of No Return

You will know when you've hit bottom and all hope of saving your marriage is gone. Your dreams will include what it would be like if your spouse passed away. All sense of forgiveness, hope, and patience has evaporated. You no longer want to forgive for the stuff you've dealt with and your view of your future with your spouse has no sense of hope. Patience is gone—you are snapping at everyone and everything. You honestly believe that you have nothing left to give to your marriage.

One of the best things you can do is to get away from the shambles of your life and spend some time alone. Getting away physically isn't always possible, but you need to get yourself into an emotional place where you have calmed down and you aren't making decisions in anger. You need to be in a good place mentally to handle all that needs to be dealt with. You can't do that when you are in the midst of what is tearing your life apart. Although it sounds impossible, before making any major decisions, attempt to reduce the stress in your life. Being on stable ground will enable you to handle all the additional decisions that will come your way. Remember that the failure of a marriage doesn't mean you are a failure as a person.

Should You Get an Annulment?

Although many people think annulments are easier to obtain than a divorce, that's not necessarily true. Annulments are much more narrowly defined, legally speaking, than divorces, which means that they can be more difficult to receive. Additionally, an annulment is a legal document granted only by a judge who states that a marriage never existed. If you have received a canonical annulment from the Catholic Church, you are still legally married in the eyes of the government and you will need to get a divorce in order to marry anyone else.

Being married only a short time is usually not enough grounds for an annulment. The grounds for an annulment are varied depending on your locale, and maintenance or alimony payments are generally not offered in an annulment. An annulment action usually does have to be filed within two years of the date of the marriage. If you have children, they would be considered legitimate.

Some grounds for receiving an annulment include bigamy, fraud, insanity, incest, mental incompetence, impotence, being under age, a misunderstanding, concealment, incapacity due to drugs or alcohol, marriage not consummated, and duress. Since annulments are such a complex issue, consult an attorney for help in making this decision.

Financial Impact of Divorce

If you are sure your marriage is over, it is time to move into a practical mode. One of the first things you need to do is to work on getting your financial records in order. Cancel any joint bank accounts and open an individual account with your private mail address. This will ensure that you have some funds available. Cancel all credit cards and close all unused credit accounts at department stores. Apply for a credit card in your own name.

You must make time to gather information so you can have an understanding of the status of your finances. Educate yourself on your rights and obligations under the law. Decide where and how you want to live your new life.

If you don't know the details of your family finances, learn all you can about family income, debts, investments, and so on. Look for past tax returns to give you a better understanding of your financial status. Ask for written verification of your spouse's salary, benefits, stock options, and bonuses. Don't fool yourself into thinking that your spouse will be fair in the division of property and funds. Protect yourself financially and educate yourself.

There's no getting around it. Divorce severely affects a family's finances in a negative way. If you can be civil toward one another, you can cut down on the costs of your divorce. One of the primary concerns of both partners should be the emotional and fiscal health of the children. Write up a budget showing how much you think you will need for child support. Paying child support is both a legal and a moral obligation that should not be abandoned. If you feel that the amount the court ordered is too much or too little, deal with these disagreements through your attorneys.

FACT

Marital assets include more than your house, cars, and bank accounts. Other marital assets include boats, stocks, stock options, bonds, mutual funds, artwork, antiques, retirement plans, tax refunds, loans to others, cash value life insurance policies, vacation pay, bonus payments, tools, frequent flier miles, and collectibles.

Do some research on the value of your assets. If you have considerable assets, consider consulting a financial planner who will help you look at tax consequences and long-term planning when considering a divorce. The division of your marital assets will depend on where you live. Nine states (Arizona, California, Idaho, Louisiana, Nevada, New Mexico, Texas, Washington, and Wisconsin) consider all assets acquired during the marriage as community property to be divided equally. The other states have various laws based on an equitable distribution of property.

If you are thinking about not fighting for what you deserve financially, think twice. Your divorce settlement can have a negative impact on your finances for years to come and you may not be able to buy a house or car down the road. Don't be so anxious to get your divorce over with or so fearful of alienating your spouse that you sign everything away.

Effects on Children

Children who live with parents who have had multiple failed marriages are more likely to divorce as adults. This may be because kids learn from their parents that the only way to deal with relationship problems is to bail out. Some other experts argue though that kids who grew up in successful stepfamily relationships have long-lasting marriages as adults.

Not all children are negatively affected by their parents' divorce. It's true that there are a high percentage of kids who will suffer emotional problems over the long-term, and who will have school problems. However, there are lots of kids who bounce back from the emotional turmoil of divorce. Realize that the negative impact of a divorce on children results from the unsolved problems that their parents had in the first place. This often includes poor communication and conflict skills, and an unwillingness to make time for the family.

The negative effects on kids are part of the same problem that the parents had that led to their divorce. The way a divorced couple treats one another after their divorce plays a huge role in how well the children adjust to the turmoil in their lives. Kids need to know that they are still loved by their parents and that they weren't the reason for the divorce.

The Stress of Breaking Up

Divorce is one of the most stressful situations a person will ever have to face in life. The stress of dealing with your ex-spouse, your attorney, the courts, your children, your in-laws, and your own family may have you feeling as if you are being pulled in ten thousand different directions. Believe that you can get through this and remain a whole individual and you will.

FACT

On most stress scales, divorce rates number two, just behind the death of a spouse, as a cause of stress in one's life.

Negativity

It is inevitable that you will experience stress and heartache as you deal with your divorce. One of the worst things you can do is to focus on the negative aspects of your life. Negativity drains you of positive energy and you will be unable to get out of the trap you built for yourself.

Refrain from calling your ex-spouse names. It serves no purpose and only reinforces in your mind the negative personality traits of your former mate. Let go of the blame game. Whether you are blaming your ex-spouse or yourself, it really doesn't make any difference once you've filed for divorce. Try to not use terms like *never*, *totally*, *every*, and *always* when discussing your relationship. These are generally not true. Sure, you will be angry, depressed, frustrated, stifled, scared, confused, and moody. However, staying immersed in these feelings will limit both your present and your future.

What to Expect

The first year after your divorce or separation is generally considered to be the hardest. It is the first time that you will have to deal alone with milestone dates such as your wedding anniversary and holidays. Your feelings of loss and sense of being alone may be heightened. You may find yourself alone if your children are spending the holidays with your ex-spouse.

ALERT!

The dangerous aspects of this stage are the tendency to drown your sorrows in alcohol, drugs, overeating, or sex to relieve the deep pain you feel. If you sense yourself feeling out of control, talk to a friend, family member, or therapist about it.

You can better handle these painful times if you are realistic in what you can afford to do, not only financially, but from a time perspective, too. If you are uncomfortable with sending out holiday cards, then don't. You don't have to send your in-laws an anniversary gift or birthday gift, but you do need to remember that they are still a big part of your children's lives. Be open and share what you are feeling and thinking with your family and friends. If you are invited to spend time with friends, accept the invitation.

FACT

Expect to go through some universal patterns as you journey through the divorce process.

For the first year after your divorce, you are at a high risk of getting sick or having an accident. A frightening and numbing phase is that of shock and denial. You may feel as if you are on the edge with all sorts of emotions ranging from rage to optimism overwhelming you. You may have problems sleeping and experience an inability to remember what you are doing or where you put things. Eating may become either a source of comfort or something to avoid.

Make sure you don't allow yourself to remain stuck in your heartache. Feeling as if you are on a roller-coaster ride is very normal. One day you will be looking forward to your life alone and making plans. The next day a song on the radio or the smell of something cooking, or a flash of a memory from your past can set off feelings of depression, anger, hopelessness, or grief.

The final lap of the journey is one of acceptance. Making plans, discovering who you are again, and dealing with present realities can re-energize you and your self-esteem.

What to Do

It is critical that you face your fears. You will probably have a lot of issues that seem scary to confront. Denying that you are fearful of being on your own and taking care of yourself and your kids, denying your fear of the future or of your ex-spouse, or avoiding confronting your fear of being hurt will only intensify your worries and fears. Face these fears one at a time.

In order to let go of the past, you need to be patient with yourself and to not judge your feelings. You also need to take care of yourself both physically and emotionally because no one else will. Make sure that you get exercise, sleep regular hours, have moments of quiet, eat healthy foods, drink plenty of water, and laugh. Find ways to pamper yourself. Keep your life simple and free from complications. Consider writing your thoughts and feelings in a journal.

If you are having problems controlling your anger, take an anger management class. Otherwise, your anger may have devastating consequences on both you and your children. Angry people tend to drive others away from them and end up lonely and depressed. Your anger toward your ex-spouse will turn self-destructive and will get in the way of effectively dealing with problems facing you. Quit viewing yourself as a victim as this only reinforces your dependency and perceived personal weaknesses. If you think you need support, then find a divorce support group or a counselor to help you through this difficult time.

Dealing with Ex-Spouses

Just as you are going through stages of recovery and dealing with issues of self-esteem, loneliness and despair, financial concerns, worries about the kids, and dealing with decisions that have to be made, so is your ex-spouse. Breaking the bonds of intimacy that held the two of you together for many years is not easy for either of you regardless of who filed for divorce or why. If you don't have children, it is possible, with time, to completely sever the emotional and practical ties between you. However, if you have children, you are joined together for life by the creations of the love you once held for one another. The best thing you can do for yourselves and your children is to let go of the animosity and hostility between you.

Co-Parenting

When you are co-parenting your children with your ex-spouse it is vital that you don't play mind games. Don't subtly try to deny the existence of your ex-spouse by not allowing your kids to have photos, ignoring the other parent at school meetings or important family gatherings, and making visitation difficult. Although communication may have been one of your problems while married, it is imperative that you keep the lines of communication open between you as co-parents. Keep your ex-partner informed when it comes to important school or extra-curricular events. Don't criticize, make jokes, or talk negatively about your ex-spouse or in-laws in front of your children. Don't place your kids in the middle of your relationship by asking them to act as spies or messengers.

Your children need to know that it's okay for them to love both their parents and that it has no impact on how much you love them. If you have more than one child, make arrangements to spend time with each child individually. Use this time to answer questions, and to reassure your child of your never-ending love and support. Your children will need to have an understanding that they are not to blame, that your divorce is final, and that they have no responsibility in trying to get you back together with your ex-spouse.

Don't turn your child into your confidant or place adult responsibilities on your kids. Let them be kids. Don't ask your children to choose between you and your ex-partner. Don't try to buy your children's love or loyalty with expensive gifts or trips. Don't use the children as pawns in your post-divorce battles by threatening to withhold visitation rights or payments. The ones who truly lose are the kids. You will be co-parenting your children with your ex-spouse for the rest of your life. Don't let your antagonism for one another ruin your children's special moments like graduations and weddings.

Moving On

Though you may find it hard to feel stable after a divorce, there are many things you can do to help yourself move on. You will find that having a job, be it paid or volunteer, will force you to get up in the morning and stick to a schedule, which can help give stability to your life as you try to get back on your feet. The sense of accomplishment that comes from working will also help you believe in yourself and your capabilities. Continue to be open to learning about yourself and growing as an individual.

Legalities

After your divorce, you will still have legal matters to take care of. Update your will. Ask to see a new credit report in your own name to make sure it is correct. Change beneficiaries if necessary on life insurance policies, retirement plans, and so forth. Check to see if the documentation on your house deed, car title, and stocks and bonds has been changed to reflect current ownership.

Dating Again

Even though you may feel as if you are strong and ready for a new intimate relationship, don't rush it. Wait at least one year before dating. You really do need this time to deal with all the emotional, practical, and legal issues of your divorce. It takes time to achieve a sense of balance in your life once again. Use this time to reflect on your marriage and the reasons it didn't work out. This year will also give you a chance to see that you can make it on your own and will be a chance to know yourself more fully.

There are some unhealthy relationships that are not meant to succeed. Trying to make sense out of a relationship or solve unsolvable problems is a form of self-destruction. Life is too short to live for a long time in a relationship filled with unhappiness, resentment, anger, and pain especially if only one spouse is willing to work on saving it. Ⓔ

Chapter 23

The Second Time Around

More second marriages end in divorce than first marriages. It is important that individuals learn from their mistakes before they make a commitment to a new relationship. Couples in second marriages often face issues that are more complicated and potentially hurtful than issues in a first marriage.

Embarking on a Second Marriage

Most couples entering a second marriage are aware that two out of three second marriages break up. Both partners need to realize that old issues don't just evaporate. Unresolved problems from past relationships will ultimately surface again in a second marriage. The issues created by blending families and being stepparents are additional challenges for couples in second marriages. If you don't take the time to honestly appraise what went wrong in your first marriage, you are doomed to repeat the mistakes of your past.

It is never easy to look back at painful times. Whether it was divorce or death of a spouse that has ended your first marriage, you may find that old memories can create problems in the present. If you want to change the statistics and make a second marriage successful, you will have to make the decision to spend time reflecting on the role that you played in the breakup of your previous relationship or letting go of the belief that because you once had a great marriage, you have all the answers and know all there is to know about marital relationships.

No one has had a perfect marriage without its ups and downs and moments of disillusionment. Attitudes generally don't change, only behaviors. Can you honestly say you are not living out in your current relationship some of the old, harmful attitudes that you had in your previous relationship? Attitudes like "my way or the highway," or behaviors such as not sharing thoughts and feelings, will be just as devastating to your current marriage as they were to your first marriage. It isn't easy to change behaviors that are deeply rooted in the core of your personalities.

You should not play the blame game or take on guilt for the death of your first marriage. That serves no purpose. But you do need to objectively reflect back and honestly appraise what went wrong and what mistakes you and your previous spouse made.

Changing these behaviors, and making sure you don't continue to respond to some of your harmful attitudes, will take a decision to love and a decision to trust your spouse. Spend time talking with one another about your families of origin, too. It doesn't make any difference how old you are, or how long you were previously married, or why your marriage ended. You need to approach your new marriage as if it were your first. Your second marriage deserves being free of the behaviors that contributed to the failure of your first marriage.

Avoiding the Same Mistakes

It is so easy to try to erase from your minds the painful memories of failed relationships. Yet these past relationships are a great source of knowledge if you take the time to glean informative lessons of what to do and what not to do in a marriage. It is very important that before you marry a second time, whether it is with your ex-spouse or a new partner, you honestly appraise what caused your divorce.

Facing the Past

Financial difficulties from the past and child-support or maintenance payments of the present have a way of haunting subsequent relationships. Disagreements about parenting styles or discipline methods are made more complicated by the presence of stepchildren. If your previous marriage ended due to unfaithfulness, carefully examine your ability and willingness to trust. Take a marriage communications seminar together. Don't assume that you know all about marriage because you've been through it before. Be willing to take a premarital education course and share your expectations, hopes, and dreams with one another.

The two of you need to be open and honest with one another about your previous marriages. Eventually, the truth will come to the surface anyway, and it is better to have your cards on the table early in your relationship. Talk about problems from your past that you think might create problems in the future. Don't ignore your previous mistakes or classify them as a onetime occurrence.

Common Mistakes

The most common mistakes made in failed first marriages are a varied bunch. A lack of respect for one's spouse could have roots in a person's childhood. An inability to listen and communicate effectively isn't going to disappear without learning new communication skills. Low libido is another situation from a past relationship that will require either therapy or medical help to get beyond. The attitude of having to be right all the time, or of not being able to apologize, is another deeply rooted aspect of a person's personality. Simply saying you won't act this way anymore isn't enough. Knowing why you have this need to be superior is necessary to overcome it.

Professing belief in living a certain way, then acting differently, is not walking the talk. This type of behavior negatively affects and disrupts the entire family. Hurtful teasing of either a spouse or children can be considered emotional abuse. It is damaging to the emotional health and stability of the victims. If you were lied to in your first relationship, chances are you will use this strategy to protect yourself in your current marriage. Dishonesty will surface and the consequences could be the end of your second marriage.

FACT

The higher statistical divorce rate of second marriages is largely due to people who don't change the bad habits they had in their first marriages.

If your previous spouse complained about some of your behaviors such as hogging the remote, not picking up after yourself, always being late, not helping around the house, yelling, withdrawing, working late hours, leaving towels on the floor, viewing pornography, controlling the finances, being obsessed with a hobby, and so on, take some time to honestly appraise just how annoying your behaviors may seem. No one is perfect, but ask yourself if you do need to make some changes in the way you respond to situations and people. Being selfish and not willing to share money, things, or yourself with your spouse or children is detrimental to any relationship. If your nature is to be controlling, seek some counseling. Trying to control the lives of your spouse and your children will only drive them away from you.

If you shy away or avoid conflict, or refuse to fight, or try to yell the loudest or fight about trivial issues a great deal, your marriage is doomed. You must have the ability to handle conflict in a healthy way in your marriage because every relationship will have disagreements. It is imperative that couples in second marriages take all of these mistakes seriously. If any of these mistakes are showing up again in your marriage, it is a very bright red flag. Make sure that the two of you are open to discussing these attitudes and behaviors so they don't become problem areas in your relationship.

Your Spouse's Ex

You don't need to be best friends with your spouse's ex-partner to have a working relationship for the sake of the kids. However, you do need to face some realities. The first reality is that the ex-spouse will be around for a very long time. Some do disappear into the hills, but not very many. Feelings of bitterness and jealousy toward this individual you hardly know will only hurt your current marriage so try to remain on speaking terms. The second reality is that your role is not that of peacekeeper between your partner and his or her children, ex-spouse, or ex–in-laws.

The important question that you need to have answered concerning your spouse's relationship with his or her ex-partner is whether or not they are *emotionally* divorced from one another. Just because the papers have been signed and a divorce is finalized doesn't mean a couple are truly disengaged from each other emotionally. This can be a tremendous roadblock in creating marital harmony in a second marriage.

QUESTION?

How can I deal with my new partner's children?
Your new marriage won't last if you don't show respect for your partner's children. Even if the kids are hostile, uncooperative, and infuriating, they deserve respect. You may not like them, you may not ever love them, but do respect them.

Emotional involvement with children from a previous relationship is to be expected. However, when an ex-spouse has continued reliance on your partner and calls about trivial matters, you have reason to be concerned. Feelings of resentment and frustration can be the result when a previous relationship hasn't experienced closure.

Creating Blended Families

No one enters a second marriage planning to turn into the wicked stepmother or overbearing stepdad. But it can happen if either of you have poor communication and even poorer conflict management skills. Becoming a stepparent requires persistence, a sense of humor, compromise, and agreement on the consequences of the children's unacceptable behavior.

It is important that you clearly define what you each consider to be inappropriate or unacceptable behaviors. You must both agree to not give in to manipulation or to not change the rules in midstream for one kid and not for another. Inconsistency will divide a household quickly. If you can't agree with one another to respect one another's children and parenting styles, then your marriage will be a rocky journey. Establishing a successful blended family takes patience, understanding, work, love, and time. Sitting back and hoping for things to work out will only lead to disaster.

Age Matters

A key factor determining the success or failure of a blended family is the age of the children at the time of the second marriage. The chances of success are much greater when children are less than five or six years old because they are still in a formative stage in their personalities. Couples will have more difficulties as stepparents when they try to meld families with children over nine or ten years of age. These kids have well-established personalities and are not as open to change. You may need to be satisfied with the roles of friend and confidant rather than "mom" or "dad." Keep the lines of communication open between the two of you so that you each have a clear understanding of the dynamics of the sibling interaction in your family.

Noncustodial Parent Issues

There can be a tremendously large mix of emotions if one or both of you are noncustodial parents with weekend visitation rights. You will find yourselves wanting time for just the two of you on weekends now and then, yet you don't want to lose the only time you can spend with your kids. Additionally, merging your two families on an irregular basis is much more difficult than trying to create a blended family that lives together all the time.

Continue communicating with each other about both the difficulties and joys that the role of being stepparents brings into your lives. Don't fall into the trap of believing that you need to entertain your children while they are visiting you. Yes, providing them with fun activities and educational experiences while they are in your care is a good thing to do now and then. However, it shouldn't be the norm. Plan on having some family projects that all the kids can help with. Make sure that each of you has some time alone with your own children.

Don't treat your children like guests in your home. Provide your noncustody kids with a bed of their own and closets, drawers, and places to permanently keep their clothing and other belongings. Having responsibilities and chores and taking part in family decisions and plans will make your kids feel more like true members of the family.

Post some of your child's artwork and pictures on the family refrigerator. Assure your children that your new spouse is not trying to take the place of their other parent. Consider saying, "yes" to a child's request to bring a close friend with them now and then when they visit. Allow your kids to express their own feelings and thoughts about being a member of your new family. Listen to their concerns and problems and try to ensure that none of your children will feel as if they are second-class citizens or as if they are being pushed aside. If you love one another, and keep the lines of communication open, the two of you will be able to keep your expectations realistic and your family intact.

Blended Holidays

Holidays could be one of the first and most difficult hurdles to approach together. The best way for stepfamilies to survive the holiday seasons and special family events is to do a lot of planning. Don't allow the hostility that either of you feels toward an ex-spouse ruin a birthday party, graduation, wedding, or other memorable family event. It's not fair to your kids to mar these special times in their lives.

Make sure you cover all the classic requirements of who, what, where, why, when, and how. This will require meaningful communication between the two of you, your ex-spouses, and other extended family members. Make sure that you keep your relationship a priority when making decisions about which children will be home, which ones will be spending time with their other parent, who will be invited to your home, or if you will be escaping to Tahiti by yourselves. You will also need to be sensitive to family traditions that each of your children value. Don't attempt to have a picture-perfect celebration, but do schedule time for the entire family to do things together like baking cookies, popping popcorn, and taking walks together. Plan on having a short time alone with any child who is coming home for the special time, and then use this time to have both you and your offspring share expectations of the visit and to reconnect. As you review your holiday plans, consider choosing alternate dates to celebrate special times with your own new traditions. Realize that compromise is the only way the two of you can cope through these stressful days. It's also important to discuss the financial implications of gift giving to one another's children. Impress on grandparents the importance of not playing favorites when remembering the grandkids. And don't make any decisions about these important times without talking it over with one another first. Willingness to be flexible is the key to planning a successful blended holiday.

ALERT!

It is critical for your children's sake that you both be civil with your ex-spouses by showing respect and watching what you say.

The Stages of a Blended Family

Just as a married couple goes through stages on their journey through life together, a blended family evolves through stages, too. Don't assume that all families will experience these five stages or that the stages will occur in the order presented here, each family is unique.

1. **The Honeymoon Phase.** Typically, the first phase is the honeymoon phase. Everyone is on his or her best behavior, and no one wants to rock the boat of family unit. This stage doesn't usually last very long.

2. **The Questioning Stage.** The next stage is the questioning stage when differences start showing up. Children start voicing their disapproval of the changes in the family dynamics and stepparents may have nagging doubts about their new roles. It is common for couples to deny that things aren't still great in spite of the feelings of fear and confusion that are entering their lives.

3. **The Confrontational Stage.** The third stage is the confrontational stage. The newness of the relationships has worn off, irritation with behaviors has surfaced, resentment and anger may grow more intense. Power struggles between kids and parents may erupt.

4. **The Reconciliation Stage.** If a couple doesn't bail out during the third stage, the fourth stage of reconciliation will occur as individuals learn how to resolve their problems with one another.

5. **The Bonding Stage.** The final stage is one of bonding and growing. Families who reach this point have fine-tuned their conflict management and communication skills. They have learned how to be themselves and be in relationship with one another at the same time.

If You Have to Make a Choice

Some children can become troubled and exhibit disturbing behavior patterns. During the adolescent years, the tension between a stepparent and child can develop into a huge communication gap over unmet and unrealistic expectations that can result in a total break in their relationship. Hopefully, you won't ever find yourselves in the position of having to choose between your spouse and your children.

But if your spouse makes the huge mistake of spouting off ultimatums that result in the teen leaving your home or refusing to allow you to have contact with your child, you may be faced with a tough decision. No matter how committed you may be to your relationship, being placed in this type of situation could lead to the breakup of your marriage. Counseling may be the only way the two of you can work through such a disruptive issue.

ALERT!

Don't underestimate the importance of communicating effectively with one another about your children. Issues related to children are the cause of divorce in over 50 percent of second and third marriages.

Setting Boundaries

Couples who are setting up a second marriage household that includes children must be very specific in sharing their expectations. This type of home requires explicit guidelines and boundaries or chaos will rule in the midst of kids' schedules and visitation demands.

Don't try to gain the trust and love of your stepchildren too quickly. Give them time to make adjustments to the new lifestyle that your remarriage has called them to live. You will probably feel their distance and uncertainty at times. If you do feel hostility from them, don't disengage and retreat from the family. Hang in there so that you can gradually build a genuine relationship with the kids. It will take time for the children to trust you. Loving and being supportive of their parent is a positive sign of your commitment to being in relationship with them.

A stepparent should not be involved in the discipline of stepchildren at the beginning of a second marriage. Your spouse's kids generally won't accept your role as a disciplinarian in their lives. Discuss parenting concerns in private, and then let the birth parent be the one who administers the discipline. As the years go by, even though your relationship with your stepchildren deepens, be prepared at special family events to take a back seat to their birth mom or dad.

FACT

It may take up to seven years for a stepfamily to adjust and adapt to each other before they feel like a real family.

Common Mistakes

All couples dealing with the mixed feelings of building a blended family will make mistakes. The more prepared you are for what lies ahead, the more easily you can deal with the consequence of an error in judgment. Some couples enter their second marriage with unrealistic expectations that the new marriage will solve all of their parenting and financial problems. They assume that love will be enough to get them through the tough times. This is a sure way to set yourselves up for failure a second time around.

Spouses may also have unrealistic expectations about what having stepchildren will entail. They think there will be instant respect and love from the children and that they can build a "Brady Bunch" style of family immediately. The reality is that you can't rush the process of creating a functional and supportive family unit. It may take years for all the children and adults to adjust to one another.

FACT

Remember that children dealing with two households are forced to live with two different parenting styles, two types of family rules, and two different sets of expectations. This dual lifestyle creates tremendous stress and a sense of loss in a child. Don't discard their feelings and thoughts.

Another mistake is to turn over the care of your children to the stepparent. Children will often rebel both outwardly and subtly to this type of transference of responsibility. Another difficult situation is when children perceive, whether it's true or not, that they are being treated unequally in the family. Small moments of inconsistencies can lead to major problems.

A common mistake some stepparents make is to avoid meeting with the children's other parent. Like it or not, this individual is a part of your lives and will be for many, many years. A deceased parent, whom children idealize in their minds, can also create conflict in a family. If a child wants to visit a cemetery or talk about their loss, don't dismiss these desires as trivial or unnecessary.

Try to not judge your relationship with your children against the relationship they have with their other parent. The love a child has for a parent should not be a source of jealousy or resentment. If, as a stepparent, you find that you can't warm up to your partner's children, don't be too hard on yourself. Your feelings toward these children may be difficult to admit to and to deal with, but your responsibility is to not allow your feelings to dictate the way you treat your new stepchildren.

Making Remarriage Work

One of the most important things you can do when you are in a second marriage is to not make mountains out of molehills. Pictures saved from the past are an example. A person can have closure and still have boxes of old photos, letters, and so forth from their ex-spouse. Some spouses don't like the fact that their partner still has pictures of their former spouse. Asking your spouse to toss out photos and mementoes of a previous relationship is not fair. Everyone has a right to keep such pictures and mementoes if they want. It is fair for you to ask that they not hang on your living room walls. However, if your spouse is keeping them in an album or stored away in a box, you shouldn't be overly concerned.

- Make sure you learn from your past. If there is any unfinished business from your previous relationships, get them resolved and bring closure to that aspect of your lives.
- Don't be in a hurry to get married again. It is important that you take your time and truly look before you leap the second time.
- Discuss all aspects of your financial situations with one another before you marry. Make provisions in your wills for how your prior assets will be passed on to your children in the event of your death.
- Realize that you can't always have things your way and be willing to compromise.
- Don't criticize your ex-spouse in front of your children. Set some ground rules that the two of you can live with regarding the care and discipline of the kids. Don't try to be a super-stepparent.

- Be honest with one another about your thoughts and feelings. Share your expectations with one another daily.
- Fight fairly. If you don't have good conflict management skills, attend a class together so this aspect of your communication is focused.
- Make room on your busy family schedule to have private time alone together.
- Don't allow your marriage to fall into a rut of taking one another for granted. Treat one another with kindness and respect.
- Keep your sense of humor.

Couples entering a second marriage often need even more premarital education and counseling than couples marrying for the first time. Trying to create an instant happy family is an unrealistic expectation that will only breed stress and depression. The only chance a blended family has of success is when the husband and wife put their relationship first. A blended family needs the strong love and support that only a committed couple can bring to the family unit.

Chapter 24

Celebrating Your Coupleness

Keeping your marriage strong takes work, and you should take time to celebrate yourselves as a couple. Make time for fun together, celebrate important dates, and show your love for one another on a daily basis. There is tremendous joy in having your spouse as your best friend. This chapter gives you lots of ideas for fun ways to celebrate each other.

Simple Ways to Be Romantic

There are many ways to reintroduce romance into your life. Find ways to pleasantly surprise one another. Consider the following:

- Play card games or board games with one another.
- Go for walks in the moonlight.
- Hold hands when you are shopping.
- Plan monthly dates minimally. Weekly dates are better.
- Watch romantic movies together.
- Plan a candlelight dinner.
- Take a drive out in the country.
- Perform small acts of kindness for each other every day.
- Leave little love notes around the house or in your car.
- Work on a project together.
- Plan little surprises for each other.
- Laugh together.
- Listen to romantic music with one another.
- Compliment each other often.
- Leave unexpected notes of praise.
- Send loving e-mails to one another.
- Prepare a special meal.
- Develop code words or signals that mean, "I love you."
- Remember birthdays and anniversaries.

Romantic Gifts

Gift giving is a way of expressing care, appreciation, and love in all cultures. Historically, people have been giving gifts to one another throughout the ages. Most spouses expect to receive a gift on anniversaries, birthdays, Valentine's Day, Christmas, and other special occasions. Presents do not need to be expensive or elaborate to send a message of love. People often have great memories of simple, spontaneous, unexpected gifts.

The Gift of Your Talents

Reflect on your own creative talents to find ways that you can give something from your heart, mind, and hands. You could make a card, cook a favorite dish or dessert, grow an exotic flowering plant, draw or paint a picture, design a collage, write a love letter, compose a song, or create a special CD or video. The list of what you can create with your talents is unlimited.

The Gift of Your Time and Energy

Making time to be with your spouse is a wonderful gift of love. You can create coupons that are redeemable for a back rub or a sensual massage, a weekend away together, a walk together in the rain, a day free of responsibilities of child care and housework, attending a class together to learn how to sail a boat or some activity that your spouse would like to try, going shopping with your partner, having a picnic in a park, going to the movies, or cooking a meal with one another.

The Gift of a Promise

Everyone has made promises to finish a project, replace a lightbulb, pull some weeds, or clean the garage. Think of the things that you know your spouse has wanted you to do, but you've procrastinated in accomplishing.

The Gift of Listening

Keep a small notebook with you and when you are shopping with your partner and he or she lingers over a particular item, make a note about it to yourself. Pay attention to items your spouse has mentioned particularly liking. You will have a list of gift ideas that are sure to please.

ALERT!

If your spouse has mentioned wanting something fun and unnecessary (like a new CD or a piece of jewelry), don't buy something practical instead. It's no fun to receive a toaster or a set of bookshelves when you were hoping for a "treat."

The Gift of Thinking Twice

Before putting down your cash and paying for a present that you've selected, think twice. If the gift will create more work for your spouse, don't buy it. Even if it is something cute and cuddly like a pet, anything requiring care and maintenance can foster resentment. When you are buying clothing, make sure you know your partner's correct size and preferred colors. If you are considering buying something for the kitchen or an appliance, don't make this purchase unless you are absolutely, positively, 100 percent sure that your spouse wants it as a gift.

Buying Books

Buying a book on marriage or sex can be considered a romantic gift. It could also be considered an insult, so be cautious. This type of book shouldn't be a surprise. Talk with your spouse and make the decision together to buy any instructional books about sexual relationships or marriage. Some books on sex have illustrations that you or your spouse may consider too offensive or explicit. You are safer choosing books for your spouse if you know his or her favorite author, style of fiction, or you look for the coffee table books or ones related to your spouse's hobbies or interests.

Giving Pets

Although the gift of a cute, cuddly kitty or puppy may seem romantic, it could be just the opposite. Don't make the mistake of giving your mate a cute, cuddly kitten or puppy without being very, very, sure that your partner really wants a pet. Owning a pet should be a mutual decision as it requires constant care and commitment.

Remember that true romance is showing respect and care for one another in the everyday pattern of your lives.

Be practical about the type of pet that your home and lifestyle can handle, both space-wise and time-wise. Additionally, a couple needs to set boundaries as to where the pet will sleep, what areas of the home may be off limits to it, who will care for it and feed it, and how much money can be spent on the animal. If you don't think you will be able to agree on these issues, think twice about giving a pet as a gift.

Having Fun Together

Don't forget to have fun together. So often, the busyness of everyday life takes a priority over enjoying one another. It's okay to actually schedule fun time together so that it doesn't get pushed aside:

- Consider going out on a date and pretend that you've just met.
- Go to a park and swing on the swings.
- Make plans for an overnight trip without any destination in mind.
- Spend a weekend in bed just sleeping, watching television, having sex, and eating junk food.
- Have a quick-nic (an unplanned picnic).
- Dance with one another in your living room or in your backyard.
- Make some S'mores together over a campfire in your backyard.
- Plan an afternoon with nothing scheduled to do when the kids are away enjoying other activities.
- Take a penny hike. Once you are out the door, flip a penny at every corner. If it is heads, turn right. If it comes up tails, turn left.

Whatever you choose, don't lose the spirit of play in your marriage.

FACT

A major factor in the happiness of a marriage is the amount of fun time spouses have with each other.

Humor and Teasing

Humor and laughter release endorphins in the brain that are energizing and healthy. The more satisfied a couple is with their marriage, the more playful they can be with one another. Humor is a natural part of any relationship and adds to the quality of a marriage. However, as discussed previously, humor needs to be balanced. Too much horseplay, too many gag gifts or practical jokes, and too much teasing can create hostility and hurt feelings in a marriage. Make sure that your humor and teasing are a fun way of interacting with one another, and not a smoke screen for hostility or control issues.

FACT

Never make fun of any of your spouse's imperfections or mistakes. It won't be funny to either those who hear your remarks or to your partner.

New Beginnings

New Year's Eve is a natural time of celebration and new beginnings. Make this evening a way to renew your love for one another and to make at least one resolution that will benefit your marriage. When deciding on a resolution, make sure it is achievable and doesn't depend on winning the lottery. Reward yourselves when you are successful.

Here are some suggestions to get your own creative juices flowing:

- Work on your photograph albums together.
- Exercise together.
- Share a positive thought about each other every night before going to bed.
- De-clutter one room.
- Volunteer together for a cause you both believe in.

Romantic Getaways

At some point, every couple needs to be able to get away from home, kids, business, yard, cats, dog, volunteer obligations, neighbors, chores, relatives, telephone, computer, and television. Time away alone can give you spontaneous intimate moments, uninterrupted conversations, freedom from distractions and chores, and time to just relax with one another. Plan a spontaneous trip by going to the airport and getting tickets on the first flight out you can find. You should have a budget in mind, but other than that, just enjoy and explore the surprise locale.

Planning a Trip

Make arrangements with friends or family members to take care of your children or household pets. Try to find unique, intimate hotels or quaint bed and breakfast inns. Don't schedule too many activities. Keep it an experience that is free of stress. Leave the laptop computer at home. It's okay to want to check on the kids now and then, but just don't make the calls too often.

One-Night Stands

If your budget doesn't allow for a trip out of town, consider having an occasional "one-night stand" at the motel around the block. You will still have to make arrangements for your kids and critters, but you can have a relaxed, fun-filled, intimate evening together free of distractions. Plan on having dinner at a nice restaurant, seeing a movie, then escaping to the motel together. It is a great way to re-energize your marriage and to celebrate your love for one another.

You don't have to wait until a wedding anniversary or other special occasion to have a one-night stand. You could even pitch a tent in the backyard and look at the stars together!

Celebrating Your Marriage

Although most couples make time to celebrate their wedding anniversary, that isn't enough. It is important throughout the year to have celebrations of your love that are not anniversary-related. This type of celebrating doesn't have to involve a lot of money or even going out on a date together. In fact, the simpler and less expensive you keep your celebration, the more often you will celebrate.

Mini-Celebrations

The anticipation of the experience will heighten the impact and joy you receive from it. The result will be an enhanced and deeper relationship. Don't let finding ways to celebrate your marriage turn into a competition to see who can be the most creative. The idea is to find ways to feel stronger and closer as a couple. Continue creating special rituals and meaningful experiences together throughout your years together. Your sense of celebration of your love for one another will grow and deepen.

Some suggestions for mini-celebrations include:

- Find an old movie that you watched many years ago and watch it again. Reminisce with one another about that time in your marriage journey.
- Tell stories about your courting days to your kids or grandkids.
- Brag about one another's accomplishments.
- Listen to songs and music that bring back happy memories for the two of you.
- Renew your wedding vows in the presence of friends or at your church.
- Once a year, write letters of recommitment to one another. Keep these in an album so you can read them again in later years.
- Look at old photo albums together.
- Toast one another at meal times.
- Get together for lunch now and then. Meet in a park on nice days.
- Dialogue with one another daily (see Appendix A). It's only twenty minutes out of each day to celebrate your love for one another.

Volunteering Together

There is an old phrase that says that love isn't love until you give it away. This is so true for a married couple. Sharing your coupleness from a marital relationship helps keep the fire of love glowing brightly. Look for ways that you can share your gifts and talents together for the same cause. A very rewarding volunteer opportunity is with organizations that promote and support marriages, such as Worldwide Marriage Encounter,

Engaged Encounter, and Retrouvaille. They are always looking for couples to share about their relationships on the weekends they sponsor, along with couples that will do behind-the-scenes type work.

Realize that when you say, "yes" to volunteer roles, you both also have to know how to say, "no." Overscheduling your time and giving too much of yourselves to others can lead to conflict in a marriage. It is important for the two of you to accept that life will be chaotic at times. During such times, accept that some things probably won't get done. When you are considering helping another group or giving your time to another cause, make sure that it won't have a negative impact on your relationship. One of the benefits of giving your time to a marriage-centered organization is that your marriage is enhanced by the experience, too.

Finding Quality Time for Each Other

Being married doesn't guarantee that you will have quality time with one another. Even couples who work together need to plan for some quality time together. Get your calendar out and schedule some time for the two of you. Teach your children that when your bedroom door is closed it means that the two of you are not to be disturbed unless it is an emergency. Doing chores together can be quality time well spent. Develop shared interests such as gardening, gourmet cooking, hiking, walking, bicycle riding, and so on. Hire a babysitter to watch your kids for a couple hours even though you are home. When you are out running errands together, turn off the CD player or radio and use that time to talk. Attend a Marriage Encounter weekend or a marriage enrichment seminar.

When you are spending time on others, you need to make sure that you both put your relationship with one another first. If you don't do this, through time and neglect, your marriage will weaken and eventually fall apart. Support one another and don't take your marriage for granted. If the two of you don't schedule time for one another, and stick to it, you won't have any quality time together. How you spend time together isn't as important as just making the time for each other.

ALERT!

More couples state that lack of time together is a bigger problem in their marriage than lack of money.

Successfully juggling time commitments and activities so as to have time to celebrate your union will require the two of you to brainstorm solutions, make choices, and set priorities that have your relationship as the top priority. You will find that organization, delegation, toleration, and flexibility will help you both keep balance in your lives. When you make time for one another to celebrate and rejoice your love for one another, you are not only having fun and being romantic, you are also letting others see how a marriage can be a fulfilling and wonderful experience. ⒠

Appendices

Appendix A

Daily Dialogue Sample Questions and Hints

Appendix B

Additional Resources

Daily Dialogue Sample Questions and Hints

Dialogue Hints

1. Make a commitment to write to one another every day. Ten minutes is usually enough writing time. Then schedule ten minutes alone together to share and discuss what you wrote.

2. When your relationship is going through a difficult time, keep the questions positive and try not to deal with tough subjects. Use questions that center on what attracted you to one another, the best date you ever had, your idea of a dream vacation, or endearing qualities you see in one another. They will help you focus on the positive aspects of your marriage.

3. Remember that the purpose of daily dialogue is to help you know and understand one another's feelings. It is not a tool to manipulate or change each other. Don't worry about thoughts. Concentrate on feelings.

4. When the two of you are apart due to business travel, you can still have daily dialogue. Use the same question for each day you are apart. A question like "How do I feel today?" or "What were my feelings today?" works well. Once you are back together, read all the letters from your time apart, and then dialogue on the feelings you have while reading all the letters. You could also dialogue through e-mail or private chatrooms.

5. Keep a couple of favorite questions handy to fall back on when finding the right one is difficult.

Sample Dialogue Questions

❧ *Why do I think you chose me to be your lifetime partner? How does my answer make me feel?*

❧ *What do I think are your priorities? How does my answer make me feel?*

❧ *What are my priorities? How does my answer make me feel?*

❧ *What do I want our priorities as a couple to be? How does my answer make me feel?*

❧ *What do I think is important for your happiness? How does my answer make me feel?*

❧ *What do I think is important for my happiness? How does my answer make me feel?*

❧ *What do I think is important for our happiness as a couple? How does my answer make me feel?*

❧ *How would I describe our sexual relationship? How does my answer make me feel?*

❧ *What role does faith play in our relationship? How does my answer make me feel?*

❧ *What do I think is fun for you? How does my answer make me feel?*

❧ *What is fun for us as a couple? How does my answer make me feel?*

❧ *How do I feel about my attitudes?*

❧ *What are my feelings when you are sick?*

❧ *What are my feelings about chores around our house?*

💗 *How do I feel when you smile?*

💗 *How do I feel about our goals as a couple?*

💗 *What are my feelings when I see you cry?*

💗 *What are my needs? How does my answer make me feel?*

💗 *How do I feel when you hug me for no special reason?*

💗 *What special moment do I remember? How does my answer make me feel?*

💗 *What is my favorite romantic song? How does my answer make me feel?*

💗 *How do I feel about the last time I did something romantic for you?*

💗 *How do I feel about the ways you show me that I am special?*

💗 *Have I affirmed my love for you today? How does my answer make me feel?*

💗 *When was the last time we held hands in public? How does my answer make me feel?*

💗 *How do I feel about marriage being a lifetime commitment?*

💗 *What do I think is "our" song? How does my answer make me feel?*

💗 *How do I feel about the ways I try to show you that you are special?*

💗 *Has my love for you changed since we were first married? How does my answer make me feel?*

💗 *What does Valentine's Day mean to me? How does my answer make me feel?*

❤ *What is romance? How does my answer make me feel?*

❤ *Are we in romance or disillusionment or joy now? How does my answer make me feel?*

❤ *How can I show you more love? How does my answer make me feel?*

❤ *What do I think you love most about me? How does my answer make me feel?*

❤ *How do I feel about the way you affirmed your love for me today?*

❤ *What do I love most about you? How does my answer make me feel?*

❤ *How do I feel when we plan a romantic evening together?*

❤ *What do I like best about our relationship? How does my answer make me feel?*

❤ *When was our last moonlight walk? How does that make me feel?*

❤ *What romantic memories do I have from our dating days? How does that make me feel?*

❤ *How do I feel when I feel the most romantic?*

❤ *How do I feel when I feel the least romantic?*

❤ *When did I feel closest to you this week? How does my answer make me feel?*

❤ *Are we romantic enough? How does that make me feel?*

Additional Resources

Books

Anderson, Katherine, Don Browning, and Brian Boyer. *Marriage—Just a Piece of Paper?* (Grand Rapids, MI: Wm. B. Eerdmans Pub. Co., 2002)

Arp, David and Claudia. *10 Great Dates to Revitalize Your Marriage.* (Grand Rapids, MI: Zondervan, 1997)

Barbeau, Clayton C. *Delivering the Male: Out of the Tough-Guy Trap into a Better Marriage.* (Gainesville, FL: Ikon Press, 1992)

Barbeau, Clayton C. *Joy of Marriage.* (Gainesville, FL: Ikon Press, 1992)

Bialosky, Jill and Helen Schulman, et al. *Wanting a Child.* (New York: Farrar Straus & Giroux, 1999)

Boteach, Rabbi Shmuley. *Kosher Adultery: Seduce and Sin with Your Spouse.* (Avon, MA: Adams Media Corporation, 2002)

Boteach, Rabbi Shmuley. *Kosher Sex: A Recipe for Passion and Intimacy.* (New York: Doubleday, 1999)

Chapman, Gary. *The Five Love Languages: How to Express Heartfelt Commitment to Your Mate.* (Chicago: Northfield Pub, 1992)

Crohn, Joel, Howard Markman, and Susan Blumberg. *Fighting for your Jewish Marriage.* (San Francisco: Jossey-Bass, 2000)

Doherty, William J. *Take Back Your Marriage.* (New York: Guilford Press, 2001)

Dowric, Stephanie. *Intimacy and Solitude: Balancing Closeness and Independence.* (New York: W.W. Norton & Company, 1996)

Evans, Patricia. *The Verbally Abusive Relationship: How to Recognize It and How to Respond.* (Avon, MA: Adams Media Corporation, 1996)

Fowers, Blaine J. *Beyond the Myth of Marital Happiness: How Embracing the Virtues of Loyalty, Generosity, Justice, and Courage Can Strengthen Your Relationship.* (San Francisco: Jossey-Bass, 2000)

Gordon, Lori. *If You Really Loved Me.* (Palo Alto, CA: Science & Behavior Books, 1996)

Gottman, John. *Why Marriages Succeed or Fail: What You Can Learn from the Breakthrough Research to Make Your Marriage Last.* (New York: Simon & Schuster, 1994)

Gottman, John and Nan Silver. *The Seven Principles for Making Marriage Work.* (New York: Crown Publishers Inc., 1999)

Harley, Willard F. Jr. *His Needs, Her Needs: Building an Affair-Proof Marriage.* (Tarrytown, NY: Fleming H. Revell Company, 2001)

Jaffe, Azriela L. and John Gray. *Honey, I Want to Start My Own Business: A Planning Guide for Couples.* (Collingdale, PA: DIANE Publishing Co., 1996)

Jordan, Pam, Scott Stanley, and Howard Markman. *Becoming Parents: How to Strengthen Your Marriage as Your Family Grows.* (San Francisco: Jossey-Bass, 1999)

Keirsey, David. *Please Understand Me II: Temperament, Character, Intelligence.* (Del Mar, CA: Prometheus Nemesis Book Co., 1998)

Kelley, Susan and Dale Burg. *The Second Time Around: Everything You Need to Know to Make Your Remarriage Happy.* (New York: William Morrow, 2000)

Kippley, John and Sheila Kippley. *The Art of Natural Family Planning.* (Cincinnati, OH: Couple to Couple League International, 1997)

Krasnow, Iris. *Surrendering to Marriage: Husbands, Wives, and Other Imperfections.* (New York: Miramax, 2001)

Larson, Jeffry. *Should We Stay Together: A Scientifically Proven Method for Evaluating Your Relationship and Improving its Chances for Long-Term Success.* (San Francisco: Jossey-Bass, 2000)

Lusterman, Don-David. *Infidelity: A Survival Guide.* (Oakland, CA: New Harbinger Publications, 1998)

McGonigle, Chris. *Surviving Your Spouse's Chronic Illness.* (New York: Henry Holt, 1999)

McGraw, Phillip C. *Relationship Rescue: A Seven-Step Strategy for Reconnecting with Your Partner.* (New York: Hyperion, 2000)

McKay, Matthew, Patrick Fanning, and Kim Paleg. *Couple Skills.* (Oakland, CA: New Harbinger Publications, 1994)

Markman, Howard and Susan Blumberg. *Fighting for Your Marriage: Positive Steps for Preventing Divorce and Preserving a Lasting Love.* (San Francisco: Jossey-Bass, 2001)

Miles, Linda and Robert Miles, M.D. *The New Marriage: Transcending the Happily-Ever-After Myth.* (Fort Bragg, CA: Cypress House, 2000)

Moir, Anne and David Jessel. *Brain Sex: The Real Difference Between Men and Women.* (New York: Dell Books, 1993)

Parrott, Leslie and Les Parrott III. *Becoming Soul Mates.* (Grand Rapids, MI: Zondervan, 1997)

Peck, M. Scott, M.D. *The Road Less Traveled: A New Psychology of Love, Traditional Values and Spiritual Growth, 25th Anniversary Edition.* (New York: Touchstone Books, 2003)

Stoddard, Alexandra. *Alexandra Stoddard's Living Beautifully Together.* (New York: Avon Books, 1991)

Tieger, Paul D. and Barbara Barron-Tieger. *Just Your Type: Creating the Relationship You've Always Wanted Using the Secrets of Personality Type.* (New York: Little Brown & Co., 2000)

Wallerstein, Judith S. *The Good Marriage: How & Why Love Lasts.* (New York: Warner Books, 1996)

Weiner-Davis, Michele. *Divorce Remedy: The Proven 7-Step Program for Saving Your Marriage.* (New York: Simon & Schuster, 2001)

Organizations and Web Sites

Coalition for Marriage, Family and Couples Education
www.smartmarriages.com

This site is a clearinghouse for marriage information and has an archive of press releases related to marriage and marriage education.

Marriage at About
http://marriage.about.com

Guided by Sheri and Bob Stritof, this site covers all aspects of marriage along with thousands of links to other worthy sites that focus on marriage.

Engaged Encounter

✐ *www.engagedencounter.org*

This site has information about this Catholic premarital education program with additional links to where encounters are held and whom to contact to register for a weekend.

National Domestic Abuse Hotline Website

✐ *www.ndvh.org*

Don't try to handle domestic violence alone. This Web site has numbers for you to call and other helpful information.

The National Marriage Project

✐ *http://marriage.rutgers.edu/publicat.htm*

This site lists the top ten myths about marriage.

Retrouvaille

✐ *www.retrouvaille.org*

If your marriage is in jeopardy, this weekend experience may help the two of you recognize what you need to do in order to keep your marriage alive. The site has location and contact information and explains the philosophy behind the weekend process.

World Wide Marriage Encounter

✐ *www.wwme.org*

After you've been married three to four years, contact these folks for a weekend to give your marriage a boost. Contact and location information is on the Web site along with an explanation of the weekend and its benefits.

Index

THE EVERYTHING ROMANCE BOOK

By Donald and Pamela Baack

Enhance the intimacy, passion, and energy in your relationship now! *The Everything® Romance Book* is filled with suggestions that will help you charm and delight your partner—from simple displays of affection to elaborate celebrations for holiday or relationship milestones. From the first date to a fiftieth wedding anniversary, you'll learn there is no wrong time for romance. *The Everything® Romance Book* is packed with recommendations for exciting seasonal treats and adventures, tips on creating just the right ambience, ideas for romantic weekend getaways, and more!

Trade paperback
$12.95 ($19.95 CAN)
1-58062-566-5, 304 pages

HISTORY

Everything® **American History Book**
Everything® **Civil War Book**
Everything® **Irish History & Heritage Book**
Everything® **Mafia Book**
Everything® **World War II Book**

HOBBIES & GAMES

Everything® **Bridge Book**
Everything® **Candlemaking Book**
Everything® **Casino Gambling Book**
Everything® **Chess Basics Book**
Everything® **Collectibles Book**
Everything® **Crossword and Puzzle Book**
Everything® **Digital Photography Book**
Everything® **Family Tree Book**
Everything® **Games Book**
Everything® **Knitting Book**
Everything® **Magic Book**
Everything® **Motorcycle Book**
Everything® **Online Genealogy Book**
Everything® **Photography Book**
Everything® **Pool & Billiards Book**
Everything® **Quilting Book**
Everything® **Scrapbooking Book**
Everything® **Soapmaking Book**

HOME IMPROVEMENT

Everything® **Feng Shui Book**
Everything® **Gardening Book**
Everything® **Home Decorating Book**
Everything® **Landscaping Book**
Everything® **Lawn Care Book**
Everything® **Organize Your Home Book**

KIDS' STORY BOOKS

Everything® **Bedtime Story Book**
Everything® **Bible Stories Book**
Everything® **Fairy Tales Book**
Everything® **Mother Goose Book**

EVERYTHING® KIDS' BOOKS

All titles are $6.95
Everything® **Kids' Baseball Book, 2nd Ed.** ($10.95 CAN)
Everything® **Kids' Bugs Book** ($10.95 CAN)
Everything® **Kids' Christmas Puzzle & Activity Book** ($10.95 CAN)
Everything® **Kids' Cookbook** ($10.95 CAN)
Everything® **Kids' Halloween Puzzle & Activity Book** ($10.95 CAN)
Everything® **Kids' Joke Book** ($10.95 CAN)
Everything® **Kids' Math Puzzles Book** ($10.95 CAN)
Everything® **Kids' Mazes Book** ($10.95 CAN)
Everything® **Kids' Money Book** ($11.95 CAN)
Everything® **Kids' Monsters Book** ($10.95 CAN)
Everything® **Kids' Nature Book** ($11.95 CAN)
Everything® **Kids' Puzzle Book** ($10.95 CAN)
Everything® **Kids' Science Experiments Book** ($10.95 CAN)
Everything® **Kids' Soccer Book** ($10.95 CAN)
Everything® **Kids' Travel Activity Book** ($10.95 CAN)

LANGUAGE

Everything® **Learning French Book**
Everything® **Learning German Book**
Everything® **Learning Italian Book**
Everything® **Learning Latin Book**
Everything® **Learning Spanish Book**
Everything® **Sign Language Book**

MUSIC

Everything® **Drums Book (with CD),** $19.95 ($31.95 CAN)
Everything® **Guitar Book**
Everything® **Playing Piano and Keyboards Book**

Everything® **Rock & Blues Guitar Book (with CD),** $19.95 ($31.95 CAN)
Everything® **Songwriting Book**

NEW AGE

Everything® **Astrology Book**
Everything® **Divining the Future Book**
Everything® **Dreams Book**
Everything® **Ghost Book**
Everything® **Meditation Book**
Everything® **Numerology Book**
Everything® **Palmistry Book**
Everything® **Psychic Book**
Everything® **Spells & Charms Book**
Everything® **Tarot Book**
Everything® **Wicca and Witchcraft Book**

PARENTING

Everything® **Baby Names Book**
Everything® **Baby Shower Book**
Everything® **Baby's First Food Book**
Everything® **Baby's First Year Book**
Everything® **Breastfeeding Book**
Everything® **Father-to-Be Book**
Everything® **Get Ready for Baby Book**
Everything® **Homeschooling Book**
Everything® **Parent's Guide to Positive Discipline**
Everything® **Potty Training Book,** $9.95 ($15.95 CAN)
Everything® **Pregnancy Book, 2nd Ed.**
Everything® **Pregnancy Fitness Book**
Everything® **Pregnancy Organizer,** $15.00 ($22.95 CAN)
Everything® **Toddler Book**
Everything® **Tween Book**

PERSONAL FINANCE

Everything® **Budgeting Book**
Everything® **Get Out of Debt Book**
Everything® **Get Rich Book**
Everything® **Homebuying Book, 2nd Ed.**
Everything® **Homeselling Book**

Everything® **Investing Book**
Everything® **Money Book**
Everything® **Mutual Funds Book**
Everything® **Online Investing Book**
Everything® **Personal Finance Book**
Everything® **Personal Finance in Your 20s & 30s Book**
Everything® **Wills & Estate Planning Book**

PETS

Everything® **Cat Book**
Everything® **Dog Book**
Everything® **Dog Training and Tricks Book**
Everything® **Horse Book**
Everything® **Puppy Book**
Everything® **Tropical Fish Book**

REFERENCE

Everything® **Astronomy Book**
Everything® **Car Care Book**
Everything® **Christmas Book, $15.00 ($21.95 CAN)**
Everything® **Classical Mythology Book**
Everything® **Einstein Book**
Everything® **Etiquette Book**
Everything® **Great Thinkers Book**
Everything® **Philosophy Book**
Everything® **Shakespeare Book**
Everything® **Tall Tales, Legends, & Other Outrageous Lies Book**
Everything® **Toasts Book**
Everything® **Trivia Book**
Everything® **Weather Book**

RELIGION

Everything® **Angels Book**
Everything® **Buddhism Book**
Everything® **Catholicism Book**
Everything® **Jewish History & Heritage Book**
Everything® **Judaism Book**

Everything® **Prayer Book**
Everything® **Saints Book**
Everything® **Understanding Islam Book**
Everything® **World's Religions Book**
Everything® **Zen Book**

SCHOOL & CAREERS

Everything® **After College Book**
Everything® **College Survival Book**
Everything® **Cover Letter Book**
Everything® **Get-a-Job Book**
Everything® **Hot Careers Book**
Everything® **Job Interview Book**
Everything® **Online Job Search Book**
Everything® **Resume Book, 2nd Ed.**
Everything® **Study Book**

SELF-HELP

Everything® **Dating Book**
Everything® **Divorce Book**
Everything® **Great Marriage Book**
Everything® **Great Sex Book**
Everything® **Romance Book**
Everything® **Self-Esteem Book**
Everything® **Success Book**

SPORTS & FITNESS

Everything® **Bicycle Book**
Everything® **Body Shaping Book**
Everything® **Fishing Book**
Everything® **Fly-Fishing Book**
Everything® **Golf Book**
Everything® **Golf Instruction Book**
Everything® **Pilates Book**
Everything® **Running Book**
Everything® **Sailing Book, 2nd Ed.**
Everything® **T'ai Chi and QiGong Book**
Everything® **Total Fitness Book**
Everything® **Weight Training Book**
Everything® **Yoga Book**

TRAVEL

Everything® **Guide to Las Vegas**

Everything® **Guide to New England**
Everything® **Guide to New York City**
Everything® **Guide to Washington D.C.**
Everything® **Travel Guide to The Disneyland Resort®, California Adventure®, Universal Studios®, and the Anaheim Area**
Everything® **Travel Guide to the Walt Disney World Resort®, Universal Studios®, and Greater Orlando, 3rd Ed.**

WEDDINGS

Everything® **Bachelorette Party Book**
Everything® **Bridesmaid Book**
Everything® **Creative Wedding Ideas Book**
Everything® **Jewish Wedding Book**
Everything® **Wedding Book, 2nd Ed.**
Everything® **Wedding Checklist, $7.95 ($11.95 CAN)**
Everything® **Wedding Etiquette Book, $7.95 ($11.95 CAN)**
Everything® **Wedding Organizer, $15.00 ($22.95 CAN)**
Everything® **Wedding Shower Book, $7.95 ($12.95 CAN)**
Everything® **Wedding Vows Book, $7.95 ($11.95 CAN)**
Everything® **Weddings on a Budget Book, $9.95 ($15.95 CAN)**

WRITING

Everything® **Creative Writing Book**
Everything® **Get Published Book**
Everything® **Grammar and Style Book**
Everything® **Grant Writing Book**
Everything® **Guide to Writing Children's Books**
Everything® **Screenwriting Book**
Everything® **Writing Well Book**

Available wherever books are sold!
To order, call 800-872-5627, or visit us at everything.com

Everything® and everything.com® are registered trademarks of Adams Media Corporation.